Collapse of an Industry

Cornell Studies in Political Economy

EDITED BY PETER J. KATZENSTEIN

Collapse of an Industry

NUCLEAR POWER AND THE
CONTRADICTIONS OF U.S. POLICY

JOHN L. CAMPBELL

CORNELL UNIVERSITY PRESS

Ithaca and London

First published in 1988 by Cornell University Press.

International Standard Book Number (cloth) 0-8014-2111-X
International Standard Book Number (paper) 0-8014-9500-8
Library of Congress Catalog Card Number 87-47856
Printed in the United States of America
Librarians: Library of Congress cataloging information
appears on the last page of the book.

The paper in this book is acid-free and meets the guidelines for
permanence and durability of the Committee on Production Guidelines
for Book Longevity of the Council on Library Resources.

To Kathy

Contents

Preface

This is a story about one of the most controversial of technologies, commercial nuclear power, and its collapse as an industrial enterprise in the United States. It is also a story about capitalism and democracy, their often contradictory institutional arrangements, and the effects those arrangements have on political and economic planning. A variety of scholars have argued that capitalism and democracy may, at least occasionally, be incompatible and that this incompatibility may undermine their smooth functioning. In this book I explore that proposition in detail, using the nuclear energy sector as a case in point.

The institutional forms of capitalism and democracy in the nuclear power sector, and typical throughout much of the U.S. economy, I shall argue, establish contradictory decision-making logics that have prevented makers of both public and private policy from devising the plans necessary to sustain the commercial viability of a complex, expensive, and potentially very dangerous technology. Had other institutional arrangements been present, as they were in some West European countries, the possibilities for planning and for the sector's future would have been different. The argument presented here contributes to debates about the relative merits of the free market, industrial planning, and the state's appropriate role in managing economic activity—debates that stretch back at least to the writings of Karl Marx and Adam Smith but that continue to command the attention of scholars, policy makers, activists, and members of the business community concerned with a wide array of current political and economic problems.

This book addresses questions about the nature of the state and political power in advanced capitalist democracies, questions that have preoccupied many social scientists, particularly since the advent of neo-Marxist political theory during the 1960s and 1970s. Is the state merely a set of institutions at the service of powerful elites, classes, and interest groups in society? Is it an autonomous and independent force in its own right? Or is it something in between, something only relatively autonomous from external political, economic, and other constraints? My thinking on such questions differs from much of the conventional wisdom of mainstream political sociology and political science. I advocate a synthesis of important elements from both institutionalist (some might call it neo-Weberian) and neo-Marxist theories of political economy and the state, theories represented by Peter Evans, Dietrich Rueschemeyer, and Theda Skocpol's *Bringing the State Back In* and Robert Alford and Roger Friedland's *Powers of Theory*, respectively.

Not only does this book confront a controversial empirical subject, in short, it also addresses controversial theoretical issues that carry implications far beyond the specifics of commercial nuclear power. As a result, some readers may accuse me of siding with the nuclear corporations throughout the analysis, whereas others will complain that I have bent over backward to favor the antinuclear viewpoint. Some may interpret this book as advocacy for a technocratic, antidemocratic form of political planning, others will see a concern for preserving democracy in the policy process. I stress, however, that I have tried to present an objective analysis, one that avoids the sensationalism characteristic of many other books about nuclear power. This book does not present horror stories about the technology's dangers or visions of endless supplies of energy that will spur the nation to new heights of economic greatness. I have refrained from making recommendations about whether or not we should try to revive the nuclear sector and, if we should, how best to proceed. I have tried only to point out the advantages and disadvantages of various forms of industrial planning for this sector, rather than advocate one form as being in some sense the best. These are issues readers must ultimately resolve for themselves.

Many people have discussed this project with me or read portions of the manuscript at various stages during its development, offering extremely helpful suggestions and criticisms. In particular I thank the following for their consideration: Steve Baker, Jack Barkenbus, Charles Bonjean, Richard Braungart, Michael Burawoy, Warren

Hagstrom, Charles Halaby, Mark Hertsgaard, J. Rogers Hollingsworth, Greg Hooks, James Jasper, Robert Jenkins, Otto Keck, Herbert Kitschelt, Richard Krannich, Claes Linde, Cora Marrett, Thomas Moore, James Orcutt, Ronald Pavalko, Charles Perrow, Andrew Szasz, Nicholas Watts, and Maurice Zeitlin. I owe very special thanks to four others. Leon Lindberg and Ivan Szelenyi took an early and lasting interest in this project, particularly as they challenged me to enter the hazardous yet fascinating territory of interdisciplinary research. Michael Patrick Allen provided a detailed, insightful reading of the original manuscript and offered friendship, support, and very practical advice that sustained me at several critical moments when I was completing the book. Peter Katzenstein's editorial suggestions and encouragement were invaluable.

Lloyd Velices and John Peters at the State Historical Society of Wisconsin in Madison, Jean Gilbertson at the University of Wisconsin Engineering Library in Madison, and Jeanne Hopkins at the Public Documents Room of the U.S. Nuclear Regulatory Commission in Washington, D.C., provided tremendous assistance in locating the necessary government documents and other data. I also benefited from a brief stay at the International Institute for Environment and Society in Berlin, where I was given an opportunity to present and clarify what eventually became one of the central arguments in the book. I am indebted to the people I met there who shared their work with me and helped me put the U.S. case into comparative perspective. Throughout the course of this study I was fortunate to be able to interview people from the U.S. Nuclear Regulatory Commission, the U.S. Office of Technology Assessment, the Edison Electric Institute, the American Nuclear Energy Council, the Atomic Industrial Forum, the Union of Concerned Scientists, the Critical Mass Energy Project, and the U.S. Committee for Energy Awareness. I thank them all for their cooperation. The Graduate School and the Department of Sociology at the University of Wisconsin–Madison provided financial and other support, as did the University of Wisconsin–Parkside.

In many ways Roger Haydon at Cornell University Press was instrumental in bringing the manuscript to press. Richard Rose helped make my prose more readable. Ann Kremers, Robert Jenkins, and Robert Maleske helped me overcome several technical problems during preparation of the manuscript.

Earlier versions of parts of this book have appeared elsewhere: part of chapter 6 as "The State, Capital Formation, and Industrial Planning: Financing Nuclear Energy in the United States and France," *Social Science Quarterly* 67 (December 1986):707–21, adapted by permission of the University of Texas Press; part of chapter 4 as "Legit-imation Meltdown: Weberian and Neo-Marxist Interpretations of Legitimation Crisis in Advanced Capitalist Society," pp. 133–58 in Maurice Zeitlin, ed., *Political Power and Social Theory*, vol. 6 (1987), adapted by permission of JAI Press Inc., Greenwich, Connecticut; and part of chapter 7 as "The State and the Nuclear Waste Crisis: An Institutional Analysis of Policy Constraints," *Social Problems* 34 (February 1987): 18–33, adapted by permission of The Society for the Study of Social Problems, Inc.

Finally, I thank my parents, John and June Campbell, who provided tremendous emotional support throughout the project, Jessie Sherrieb, who helped me keep it all in perspective, and most of all my wife and friend, Kathy Sherrieb, to whom I dedicate this book.

JOHN L. CAMPBELL

Racine, Wisconsin

Abbreviations

AEC	U.S. Atomic Energy Commission
AEG	Allgemeine Elektrizitäts-Gesellschaft
CBO	U.S. Congressional Budget Office
CDL	Centrala Driftsledningen/Swedish Central Operating Management
CEA	Commissariat à l'Energie Atomique/French Atomic Energy Commission
CFDT	Confédération Française Démocratique du Travail
COGEMA	Compagnie Générale des Matières Nucléaires
DOE	U.S. Department of Energy
DWK	Deutsche Gesellschaft für Wiederaufarbeitung von Kernbrennstoffen/German Society for the Processing of Spent Fuel
EDF	Electricité de France
ERDA	U.S. Energy Research and Development Administration
FAA	U.S. Federal Aviation Administration
FDA	U.S. Food and Drug Administration
FEA	U.S. Federal Energy Administration
FPC	U.S. Federal Power Commission
GAO	U.S. General Accounting Office
GPO	U.S. Government Printing Office
JCAE	U.S. Joint Committee on Atomic Energy
NACA	National Advisory Committee on Aeronautics
NASA	National Aeronautics and Space Administration
NRC	U.S. Nuclear Regulatory Commission
OTA	U.S. Office of Technology Assessment
PEON	Commission Consultative pour la Production d'Electricité d'Origine Nucléaire
RWE	Rheinisch-Westphälische Elektrizitätswerke

Part I

THE PROBLEM OF POLICY CONSTRAINTS

CHAPTER ONE

Symptoms and Diagnoses of Collapse

The U.S. commercial nuclear energy sector burst into the 1970s with apparently unlimited vitality and strength. The nation's electric utilities bought unprecedented numbers of nuclear plants in 1972 and again in 1973, their second ordering spree in ten years. In fact, the market for nuclear power was so bullish that during the first half of the decade nuclear reactor manufacturers sold more electricity-generating capacity than the makers of oil-fired and coal-fired plants combined.[1]

This was not surprising. After all, the United States had pioneered the development of commercial nuclear power in the late 1940s. Advocates felt it was imperative that the country pursue the technology because the benefits in international prestige and economic growth promised to be tremendous. Many of those early supporters such as Lewis Strauss, chairman of the U.S. Atomic Energy Commission (AEC) during the Eisenhower administration, believed that the nation's ultimate reward for adopting nuclear power would be an endless source of electricity so inexpensive that it would be virtually too cheap to meter (Milius, 1975:A4). As a result, the federal government spent billions of dollars helping the private sector develop, demonstrate, and finally commercialize the light water nuclear reactor (Battelle, 1978:103), a technology that became the cornerstone for nuclear energy systems at home and in many foreign countries.

Despite such high hopes, the nuclear sector collapsed by the end of the 1970s. Utilities ordered 231 nuclear plants through 1974, but only 15 after that—none after 1978. Furthermore, they cancelled orders

[1] These data are discussed in detail in chapter 6.

for more than one hundred nuclear plants between 1974 and 1982 even though several were already well under construction. The cost of abandoning these plants totalled nearly $10 billion (Itteilag and Pavle, 1985:36). More recently these costs have run even higher. For example, the Public Service Company of Indiana spent $2.7 billion on its two-unit Marble Hill nuclear project but cancelled it in 1984 before finishing construction (Phillips, 1986:21). As the trend continued, experts estimated that utilities would suffer another $25 billion in abandonment costs by 1990 (Itteilag and Pavle, 1985).

The public often bears a heavy burden for all of this. The Indiana Public Service Commission allowed Marble Hill's owners to recover two-thirds of their investment, $1.79 billion, by approving an 8 percent increase in the utility's electricity rates (Phillips, 1986:21). Even for projects that *will* be finished, customers will hardly enjoy electricity that is too cheap to meter. Some projects will add only a few percentage points to current electricity rates in their service areas, whereas others will produce increases anywhere from 20 to over 60 percent. Customers of the Public Service Company of New Hampshire, principal owner of the $4.5 billion Seabrook nuclear power plant, anticipate a 63 percent jump in their rates when the plant finally comes into service (Cook, 1985:85–87). Several studies have concluded that the average price of electricity will rise from 22 to 35 percent as the costs of both completed and abandoned nuclear plants are charged to rate payers (Itteilag and Pavle, 1985:39). These figures reflect several interrelated trends that have plagued the nuclear sector for more than a decade.

Costs for building nuclear plants have skyrocketed. The U.S. Office of Technology Assessment (OTA) (1984:58–60) found that nuclear plants completed in 1971 cost an average of $430 per kilowatt of generating capacity and those expected to be finished in 1987 would cost $1,880 per kilowatt, more than a fourfold increase. In other words, the cost of a common 1,300 megawatt plant would jump from about $560 million to $2.4 billion. Some cases were much worse. The OTA expected that seven nuclear plants almost complete in 1983 would cost between 550 and 900 percent more than comparable plants finished in the early 1970s. Inflation accounted for only a small fraction of the difference. The relatively low cost for coal-fired generating plants underscored nuclear power's problem. Production costs for coal and nuclear plants were comparable during the late 1960s. However, the costs of building nuclear plants increased faster than those for coal so that nuclear plants were about 50 percent more expensive to build by 1978 (Komanoff, 1981). Coal's advantage will become even greater as new nuclear units enter service. For example,

4

the New York State Electric and Gas Corporation's newest coal-fired plant at Somerset began producing electricity in 1984 for 7.5 cents per kilowatt hour. One hundred miles away, Niagara Mohawk's $5.1 billion Nine Mile Point nuclear facility was expected to generate power by 1987 for more than 15 cents per kilowatt hour (Cook, 1985:82).

A variety of problems leading to delays in construction and licensing increased project lead times, the period between receipt of the construction permit and commercial operation. Lead times grew steadily from about six years for plants receiving their permits in the late 1960s to an average of ten years for those with permits issued between 1971 and 1974 (OTA, 1984:62). One of the most notorious cases was the Long Island Lighting Company's Shoreham station, still not in service as of 1987 despite having received a permit fourteen years earlier. This trend is important because longer lead times make plants more vulnerable to the pressures of inflation, new and more expensive regulatory requirements, higher interest payments, and other factors that contribute to the escalation of project costs. Owners claimed that a five-month delay in starting the Seabrook station in 1986 would add another $250 million to $300 million to the cost of the plant (Wald, 1986b).

Finally, the movement against nuclear power in the United States blossomed in the early 1970s. National organizations formed either to stop the expansion of nuclear power, as in the case of Ralph Nader's Critical Mass group, or at least to improve the technology's management, as in the case of the Union of Concerned Scientists. A host of regional and local organizations such as the Clamshell, Abalone, Catfish, Crabshell, Cactus, and Safe Energy Alliances proliferated with similar goals. Public support for nuclear power declined in other ways too. Opinion polls indicated that although the public generally supported the idea of building nuclear power plants during the first half of the 1970s, they became much less supportive of having plants built near their own communities (Rankin et al., 1984:44). After the well-publicized reactor accident in Pennsylvania at the Three Mile Island nuclear plant in 1979, public support declined and opposition increased even in general terms. The percentage of people who objected to building plants nearby grew to a point where they outnumbered those who did not object by a two-to-one margin, a dramatic reversal of the attitudes found just before the accident (Rankin et al., 1984:62). Alvin Weinberg, one of the scientific pioneers of commercial nuclear power, once wrote that the nuclear sector had struck a Faustian bargain with society, promising an endless source of energy for future generations but at the risk of developing a technology with potentially disastrous side effects in the radioactive and toxic materials it produced (Weinberg, 1972:33). The shift in public opinion indicated that more people were beginning to recognize the dark side of the bargain.

Indeed, nuclear power suffered one of the most dramatic declines of any industrial sector in the United States in recent memory. By 1981 the United States had lost its international lead in the development and production of commercial nuclear technology (U.S. Senate, 1981a:2). The problems of escalating costs, delays, and public opposition were only the symptoms of an extremely complex set of political and economic forces that crippled the sector. What happened?

THE CONVENTIONAL WISDOM

The experts have offered several explanations for the sector's collapse. Ironically, one of the most prevalent blames those directly involved in promoting nuclear power. For example, the OTA (1984:124–27) concluded that utility and construction project managers, inexperienced and inept in dealing with the complexities of nuclear technology, caused many of the problems that led to rising costs. The OTA provided graphic examples of nuclear projects that started with inadequate design plans, technically inexperienced personnel, poorly coordinated systems of authority and decision-making responsibility, and insufficient commitments to quality assurance. Massive cost overruns ensued. Perhaps the single most notorious case of managerial ineptitude occurred at Southern California Edison's San Onofre nuclear project, where one reactor was inadvertently installed backward. In an earlier version of this mismanagement theme, Irvin Bupp and Jean-Claude Derian (1978) suggested that both the federal government and reactor manufacturers were so eager to commercialize nuclear technology in the 1950s and 1960s that they failed to estimate reactor costs objectively and accurately. Manufacturers rapidly increased the size of their plants, hoping to achieve economies of scale, but in the process exceeded the technical limits of the reactor systems themselves, and created various political, economic, and technical problems that proved to be the sector's undoing. In short, the nuclear sector was its own worst enemy.

Others have argued that although corporate managers were at fault, there were more insidious causes. In his scathing attack on the so-called atomic brotherhood, Mark Hertsgaard (1983:249–63) maintained that corporate executives saw nuclear energy as a source of unprecedented riches. High-ranking government officials in Congress and the AEC, often subject to corporate influence, saw commercialization as a means to greater political power. He argued that their

6

self-serving interests led to much of the mismanagement and haste that ultimately caused the sector's demise. Others have made similiar points linking the sector's problems to the blindly optimistic behavior of elite policy makers in business, government, and the scientific community (e.g., Gyorgy et al., 1979; Nader and Abbotts, 1979).

Charles Komanoff, a noted expert on nuclear energy economics, has posed a more explicitly political account of the sector's troubles. He has argued that conscientious, not inept, government regulators recognized the need for new safety precautions, imposed them on the sector, and, as a result, contributed heavily to the cost increases on nuclear projects (Komanoff, 1981). Others, supporting Komanoff's view, have claimed that the continuous imposition of new and tougher regulatory standards to plants completed, planned, or under construction increased costs to a point where the nuclear option was no longer competitive with more traditional forms of energy (Hogerton, 1979; Naymark, 1978). Some have even suggested that just the threat of new regulations may have been enough to undermine investment in nuclear power simply because the cost uncertainties were too great for the utilities and other institutional actors to bear (Sawhill, 1977).[2]

Others have suggested that political forces *outside* these intimate policy-making circles may have struck the critical blow against nuclear power. Bupp and Derian (1978:11) recognized that the public worried about the dangerous nature of the technology and distrusted those responsible for its development. They argued that these suspicions fueled both the controversy over nuclear plant safety and the development of an active antinuclear movement, another important cause for the sector's downfall. Several sophisticated quantitative stud-

---

[2] By focusing on the decision making of government and business insiders this explanation shares certain characteristics with a political sociology literature on how political and economic elites wield power (e.g., Bachrach and Baratz, 1962; Lindblom, 1977; Hunter, 1953; Mills, 1956). For critical reviews of that literature see Alford (1975), Alford and Friedland (1985), Domhoff (1978b), Domhoff and Ballard (1968), Lukes (1974), and Whitt (1982). However, two points require emphasis. First, despite its insights, by emphasizing the significance of elite policy making, this literature tends to understate the effects of political struggle between policy makers and other political actors outside policy-making arenas. More often the discussion of struggle is confined to those conflicts developing within the policy-making organization, not between these organizations and external political groups (cf. Allison, 1971:chap. 1; Welborn, 1977:135). Second, as Steven Lukes (1974) eloquently argued, this perspective tends to neglect the institutional constraints stemming from the broader political and economic context that elites face that limit their range of policy options. These problems are also found in accounts of the nuclear sector's decline that dwell on mismanagement and bureaucratic ineptitude. For example, Bupp (1981) argued that the problem with Komanoff's (1981) otherwise outstanding quantitative study of escalating nuclear plant costs was that it failed to recognize how the important and sometimes subtle political pressures generated by antinuclear groups caused government regulators to impose more stringent and expensive safety regulations on nuclear projects.

ies have supported this political-opposition thesis, showing that antinuclear groups delayed reactor construction by intervening in the
licensing process and increased plant costs as a result (Bupp et al.,
1975; Cohen, 1979a; 1979b; Montgomery and Quirk, 1978). In partial support of Komanoff's position, many have argued that political
pressure contributed to the promulgation of new and more stringent
safety and environmental regulations, which added to plant complex-
ity and increased planning and construction costs at the sector's expense (e.g., Corrigan, 1979; Deddens, 1981; Dellaire, 1981;
Lanouette, 1979; DOE, 1978; Weaver, 1980; Weingast, 1980).[3]

A final explanation for the sector's collapse revolves more around
the economics of supply and demand than around the political and
managerial obstacles to a more efficient and inexpensive technology.
Many believe that perhaps the most important factor undercutting
nuclear energy's viability in the United States was the unprecedented
drop in the demand for electricity following the OPEC oil embargo in
1973–74. Before then demand for electricity grew at annual rates of
nearly 7 percent. Afterward, rates declined dramatically to about 2
percent, leaving utilities with too much reserve generating capacity.
Several government studies reported that many utilities cancelled
nuclear plants because they were suddenly faced with excess capacity
(S. M. Stoller Corporation, 1980; DOE, 1983a:7; GAO, 1980c).[4]

[3] This analysis is reminiscent of the so-called crisis of democracy literature in political
science, which suggests that when the public uses democratic channels to force excessive
demands upon government policy makers, policy failure often results (e.g., Brittan,
1975; Crozier et al., 1975; Mitchell, 1978; Rose and Peters, 1978; Tufte, 1978; Weidenbaum, 1984). In keeping with that tradition, observers of the nuclear situation argued
that public demands for expensive licensing delays and regulatory changes undermined the nuclear sector. As with most theories of interest-group pluralism, this one
adds to our understanding of policy failure. However, it tends to overlook how political
demands are filtered through institutional channels in state apparatuses that systematically afford certain groups privileged access to key policy-making arenas while prohibit-
ing comparable access to others (e.g., Domhoff, 1978a; Friedland et al., 1977;
Lindblom, 1977). Several critics of nuclear power in the United States have suggested
much the same thing with respect to those accounts of the sector's decline infused,
perhaps inadvertently, with pluralist assumptions. They cite a long history of government policy making where a few politicians, political bureaucrats, business representatives, and government scientists, but not the public or antinuclear groups, controlled
most of the critical policy decisions (e.g., Hertsgaard, 1983; Metzger, 1972; Nader and
Abbotts, 1979).

[4] There is a critical institutional context involved here that is generally overlooked in
this sort of analysis. For years the federal government stimulated growth by subsidizing
the production of reactor fuel, research and development, radioactive waste management, accident insurance, and a host of other infrastructure programs that helped
create demand *artificially* (i.e., by means of nonmarket forces) among utilities for
nuclear power. Explanations that equate the nuclear sector's decline with reduced
electricity demand tend to forget how institutional forces have compensated for fluctuations in the otherwise natural ebb and flow of supply and demand—a point political

A RECONSIDERATION

All of these arguments are insightful, well documented, and help-ful in understanding what happened to undermine the nuclear sector's viability in the United States. However, they present a frag-mented picture without a unifying theme to help tie the different parts together. As a result, it is easy to assume that to develop a comprehensive explanation of the sector's decline, all we have to do is to add up the pieces and argue that nuclear power was undermined in the United States by a combination of interest-group pressures, inept policy makers in both the state and the private sectors, and a sharp decline in the overall demand for electricity.[5] Strictly speaking, such an analysis is not wrong so far as it goes. The problem is that most of the conventional wisdom fails to consider the institutional constraints within which these apparently isolated factors existed, constraints that systematically undermined policy-making efforts to provide the com-prehensive planning that would have eased and perhaps solved many of the problems that plagued the sector. Three constraints were particularly important. First, intensely competitive markets for nu-clear plants and support services created incentives favoring short-term profitability at the expense of long-term sectoral planning. Sec-ond, a fragmented and partially decentralized state apparatus, accessi-ble to antinuclear groups especially during policy implementation, facilitated the development and expression of political conflict in ways that disrupted the policy process. Finally, there were few policy tools, such as control over finance capital, powerful enough for government officials to use to counteract these other tendencies and to coordinate planning throughout the sector. My thesis is not that these political and economic constraints either created all of the sector's problems or were the only causes for its decline. These institutional factors were, however, at the very core of the nuclear sector's collapse. Further-more, they helped generate much of the interest-group pressure and policy-making mismanagement that has drawn so much attention in previous explanations.

There have been attempts to grapple with some of the institutional factors that undermined the U.S. nuclear energy sector. Some have argued that several points of access to the policy process, such as

---

economists (e.g., Shonfield, 1965; Solo, 1967; Zysman, 1983) and critics of neoclassical economics (e.g., Hollis and Nell, 1975; Lindberg, 1982a; O'Connor, 1972; Solo, 1982) have made in a more general context.

[5] Recent examples of this additive approach include Cook (1985) and the OTA (1984).

licensing hearings and the courts, provided opportunities for anti-nuclear groups to undermine planning (e.g., Golay, 1981; Kemeny, 1980; Lester, 1978; Nelkin and Pollak, 1981a). This political struggle created what Bupp (1980b; 1979) has called the "nuclear stalemate," a standoff between opposing factions in the nuclear policy debates, which crippled the sector. I will extend and refine this argument. However, I will also complement it with institutional analyses of the economy and the institutional links between the economy and the state that constrained and undermined nuclear policy making.[6] The effects of interest groups and policy-making elites will not be ignored. Instead I will argue that these institutional structures contributed to, and mediated, the important conflicts and struggles among government policy makers, scientists, environmentalists, and industry representatives, that influenced the content of policy and contributed to the sector's decline.

What follows in chapter 2 is an analysis of the important institutional features of the political economy of the U.S. nuclear sector, the structural characteristics that contributed so heavily to the sector's deterioration. This analysis is couched in a broader discussion of the rich political sociology and political science literatures suggesting that we must be aware of the institutional constraints to policy making stemming from the economy, the state, and the relationship between them if we are to understand fully how interest groups or policy-making elites influence policy. The second part of the book shows how these institutional features contributed to policy failures in four planning areas: reactor standardization, safety, finance, and the management of high-level radioactive waste. A series of case studies demonstrates systematic institutional effects. Observers, both for and against the further development of commercial nuclear power, generally agree that the sector's viability hinged in large part on decisions made, or not made, in these four policy areas. Similar issues determined much of the history of the nuclear sectors in France, Sweden, and West Germany, three cases briefly examined in chapter 8 to help put the U.S. experience into comparative perspective. The third part of the book offers a general set of observations about the political economy of advanced capitalism.

---

[6] To the best of my knowledge there has been only one attempt to account for the U.S. nuclear sector's performance in terms of both its unique political *and* economic structures, an excellent study by Måns Lönnroth and William Walker (1979). The strengths and weaknesses of their work are discussed in chapter 8.

CHAPTER TWO

The Political Economy of Industrial Policy Failure

Two major schools of political economy provide the kind of structurally oriented analysis that might help explain the decline of the nuclear energy sector in the United States: neo-Marxism and institutionalism. Neo-Marxists try to link declines in advanced capitalist economies to the contradictory nature of capitalism itself. For example, Paul Baran and Paul Sweezy (1966) argued that capitalists must constantly increase production to survive market competition and accumulate more capital, a process that eventually produces economic stagnation because the economy tends to generate more commodities than it can consume.[1] Neo-Marxists have made admirable contributions to our understanding of capitalism's political and economic problems with such analyses. Yet because they are intent on identifying the contradictory tendencies of capitalism *in general*, most pay relatively little attention theoretically to the structural and performance differences among *particular* capitalist economies. The abstract level of their theory reflects that emphasis.

Some have recognized that the state tries to facilitate the continued growth of capitalism by intervening in different ways into the economy (e.g., Baran and Sweezy, 1966; Habermas, 1973; Offe, 1974; O'Connor, 1973). They often argue that various kinds of state intervention depend on the degree to which policy makers are relatively

[1] For other diverse examples see O'Connor (1973;1984), Habermas (1973), and Mandel (1975). Wright (1978) provides a good review of this literature. See Sweezy (1942) for an excellent statement of the classical origins of these arguments.

autonomous from various political and economic policy constraints.[2] Variation in relative autonomy determines how effectively the state manages capitalism and, presumably, how well the economy performs. However, it is not clear exactly what constitutes more or less relative autonomy because the theorists tend not to specify the institutional mechanisms that prohibit and facilitate successful state intervention.[3] Similarly, the institutional variation among specific capitalist economies is often underemphasized.[4] Again this is not so much a theoretical error as it is simply a concern with studying a different, more general set of issues. As a result, this literature does provide some important clues to help explain why capitalist economies may slide into decline, particularly insofar as the contradictory structure of capitalist democracy itself is concerned, but the question why some capitalist economies perform better than others remains largely unexplored.

Institutionalists focus clearly on the variation in political and economic institutions across capitalist countries and recognize that institutional differences have important effects on economic planning and performance. They also recognize that potential tensions or contradictions within these institutions may undermine capitalism, although they are less convinced than neo-Marxists that these will *inevitably* lead to capitalism's decline (Offe, 1975b:248; Shonfield, 1965:387–88). The point is that they offer the possibility of precisely

[2] For a sampling of the debate among neo-Marxists over the nature of constraints contributing to the state's so-called relative autonomy, see Block (1977; 1980), Carnoy (1984), Miliband (1977:chap. 4; 1983), Offe and Ronge (1975), and the specific exchange between Laclau (1977), Miliband (1973a; 1973b), and Poulantzas (1973b; 1976).

[3] This is why the concept of the state's relative autonomy has been so unsatisfactory even for those sympathetic to its use (e.g., Jessop, 1982:226; Szelenyi, 1981:583). Much of the problem derives from state theories comparing different modes of production (feudalism, capitalism, socialism), rather than differences within a single mode of production. As a result, the concept is not specified concretely enough to account for systematic institutional variations among state planning capacities in capitalism. For elaborations and variations on this argument, see Cohen and Rogers (1983:48–49), Crouch (1979:26), Jessop (1978:11), Skocpol (1985:33, n. 16), and Strinati (1979:196).

[4] Neo-Marxists have distinguished among different types of capitalism, such as competitive and monopoly capitalism (e.g., Baran and Sweezy, 1966; O'Connor, 1973) and early and late capitalism (Mandel, 1975). Even though these analyses provide a variety of important insights, they tend to overlook the important institutional variations among different national economic systems falling within a particular type of capitalism. When they do note the differences, they treat them as relatively unimportant because the search is for similarities, not differences, among national capitalist economies (e.g., Warren, 1972:12). Recently, a few neo-Marxists have tried to explain some of the performance variations among capitalist economies (e.g., Bluestone and Harrison, 1982; Bowles et al., 1983; Cohen and Rogers, 1983). However useful, their focus has been on the important differences in national historical experiences rather than on institutional differences per se.

specifying the important institutional differences among capitalist political economies while remaining sensitive to the possibility that the institutional arrangements involved may subvert economic planning. Many of the institutional features they discuss are relevant to the nuclear energy sector in the United States.

INSTITUTIONAL DIMENSIONS OF THE POLITICAL ECONOMY

Three institutional dimensions are important in planning within industrial sectors: the structures of the economy, the state, and the intersection between the state and civil society. To a large extent an industry or sector's structure, as specified by these dimensions, determines its capacities for planning at the industry or sectoral level.

Structure of the Economy

Any economy includes different economic sectors, each one composed of several industries. The commercial nuclear energy sector includes industries that mine, refine, and fabricate uranium into fuel for nuclear reactors, industries that build those reactors and the rest of the nuclear plant, and industries that manage the radioactive waste the sector produces. Political economists have found that centralized decision making, rather than unbridled competition, often helps coordinate interorganizational economic activity and increase the possibilities for sectoral or industrywide planning (e.g., Hage and Clignet, 1982; Hollingsworth, 1982; Katzenstein, 1978b; Mizruchi and Koenig, 1986). Perhaps the most common indicator of economic centralization is the number of firms competing in an industry. Other things being equal, it appears that fewer firms and, therefore, more centralization tend to facilitate planning for several reasons. First, as centralization increases, the chances for individual firms to survive and profit in the marketplace becomes greater (although not guaranteed) because the threat of being eliminated through competition declines. As a result, firms become relatively less intent on maximizing their individual *short-term* profits and more concerned with striving for their industry's or sector's long-term objectives, such as expanding the overall size of the market or stabilizing prices at some mutually acceptable level (e.g., Baran and Sweezy, 1966:58–62; Solo, 1982:104).[5] Second, greater centralization tends to increase the or-

[5] This is not to say that firms ever completely ignore their long-term interests in survival and expansion, just that the emphasis may shift (e.g., Eichner, 1983:213).

ganizational possibilities for coordination simply because there are fewer firms to coordinate (Solo, 1967:chap. 4). The extreme example is an industry with a single firm capable of coordinating sectoral activity through powers of monopoly or monopsony. Third, centralization tends to reduce market uncertainty and increase the opportunities for industrial planning by stabilizing the supply and demand of production factors *across* industries within a sector through large, long-term, interfirm contracts (Galbraith, 1971:47–50). This also occurs *within* industries. The organizational literature on the structure and strategy of corporations has found that the development of vertical and horizontal integration throughout a sector helps overcome short-term market uncertainties by facilitating the administrative coordination of supply, demand, and production at the level of the firm (e.g., Chandler, 1977; Chandler and Daems, 1980; Ouchi, 1977; Williamson, 1975; Williamson and Ouchi, 1981). Of course to the extent that integration through merger reduces the number of independent firms and, therefore, competition, centralized decision making and the potential for interorganizational coordination and planning are enhanced.[6]

Centralized decision making also counteracts short-sighted competition in other ways that do not necessarily involve either a reduction in the number of firms operating in an industry or their absorbtion into a larger organization through vertical and horizontal integration. For example, industrial trade associations often provide an organizational center for coordinating the activities of firms and industries within a sector. Industry members create associations specifically to

---

[6] For an excellent overview of this organizational literature on the firm, see Caves (1980). For a review of the debates involved, see Van de Ven and Joyce (1981). This is *not* to say that integration always leads to industrial planning or that centralized planning is inevitably good for an industry. For example, Piore and Sabel (1984) argue that vertically integrated corporate heirarchies may not be flexible enough to adjust to rapidly changing economic conditions. Too much rigid vertical integration may cause economic stagnation in some cases. Lawrence and Dyer (1983) argue that too little competition may be as bad for sectoral performance as too much. They show that economic decline may occur in the absence of sufficient competition because there is little incentive for planning innovation under those conditions. The point is that centralization through a reduction in the number of firms in an industry increases the *possibility*, not the inevitability, of planning.

One further clarification is in order. The organizational literature examines planning as it occurs *within* the corporation. The focus of this study is on industrywide and sectoral planning, the coordination among *different* organizational actors within industries and sectors. Although integration increases the potential for intraorganizational planning over a wider area of an industry, as long as different corporations compete against each other there are still limits on the amount of interorganizational planning that may occur.

14

overcome the problems of excessive competition that they perceive as being detrimental to the industry's collective, long-term interests (Foth, 1930:chap. 6; Naylor, 1921:38; Streeck and Schmitter, 1985b; Whitney, 1934:38–40). Stronger and more inclusive associations tend to increase the possibilities for industrywide planning (e.g., Schmitter, 1984; Streeck and Schmitter, 1985a).[7] The important point here is that there are various institutional arrangements that may be available to the private sector to provide opportunities for planning through centralized decision making.[8] All share a common element: a tendency to dampen competition in an industry or sector—competition that could undermine industrial or sectoral coordination.

Structure of the State

The structure of the state also affects planning and policy making. Three institutional dimensions characterize its structure. First, greater vertical centralization within the state apparatus tends to facilitate successful policy formation and implementation (Katzenstein, 1978b; Zysman, 1978:265). For example, the intergovernmental relations literature argues that conflicting policy demands, generated either within or outside the government, undermine coherent policy making where different levels of government share policy formation and implementation responsibilities. Uncoordinated, contradictory policy prescriptions often result (e.g., Advisory Commission on Intergovernmental Relations, 1980; Pressman and Wildavsky, 1979; Walker, 1981:16). Second, the degree to which the state apparatus is horizontally fragmented, providing various agencies and branches of government with overlapping jurisdictions in the policy process, has

[7] Examples of the long-term planning possibilities of associations, cartels, and other forms of industrial centralization in Western Europe, Japan, and the United States are prevalent. For specific illustrations, see the empirical essays in Dyson and Wilks (1983), Goldthorpe (1984), Katzenstein (1978a), Lindberg and Maier (1985), Richardson (1982), Shonfield (1965), and Streeck and Schmitter (1985b). For excellent overviews of the advanced capitalist political economies that make a similar point, see the essays by Katzenstein (1978b) and Dyson (1983).

[8] Much less research is available on the relatively *informal* institutional arrangements among organizations in economic sectors that mediate the atomizing tendencies of competition. For important exceptions, see Hollingsworth and Lindberg's (1985) discussion of clans, Piore and Sabel's (1984:263–68) descriptions of producer federations and other communitylike arrangements, and Streeck and Schmitter's (1985a) analysis of industrial communities. Of course there are rich literatures on the informal interlocking networks among strategic elites in both public and private sectors (e.g., Domhoff, 1983; Useem, 1984). However, this is a different kind of analysis in that it tends to focus on individuals rather than on organizational actors and on national rather than industrywide or sectoral-level policy making.

similar effects. Spreading policy formation and implementation over a relatively wide range of administrative, legislative, and judicial arenas increases the possibility that contradictory demands will subvert policy making (Kitschelt, 1986; Shonfield, 1965:319). In short, more fragmented and decentralized political institutions tend to create the opportunities for political stalemate and obstructionism that can undermine successful government planning. Many observers argue that the impressive planning capacities of both the French and Japanese governments stem partially from the high level of vertical and horizontal centralization in their state apparatuses (e.g., Cohen, 1977; Green, 1983; Katzenstein, 1978b; Shonfield, 1965; Thurow, 1984; Trezise and Suzuki, 1976).

However, decentralization and fragmentation does not necessarily imply an egalitarian and pluralist policy process. Although there may be many access points to policy making, some groups may have greater access to more important arenas than others. In this sense Roger Friedland, Frances Fox Piven, and Robert Alford (1977) identified a third important characteristic of the state apparatus. They argued that there are functionally different decision-making arenas within the government. Some, such as courts and formal hearings, facilitate the democratic expression of demands by various political groups outside the state. Others more insulated from the political demands of the public, such as the Federal Reserve System, the Council of Economic Advisors, and other top-level presidential advisory groups in the United States, facilitate more substantive and often economic policy making. Several theorists have found that the most insulated policy arenas also tend to be those where most policy formation occurs and where only political and corporate elites usually have access (e.g., Domhoff, 1978a; 1978b; Lindblom, 1977; Mills, 1956). Decisions about policy implementation tend to occur in arenas more accessible to the general public, arenas where policy makers interpret and apply substantive policies developed elsewhere. Friedland and his colleagues suggest that the more governments organizationally separate the two types of political arenas, the more effectively they cope with the vital yet potentially antagonistic capitalist requirements of economic growth and political integration.[9] Their implication is that where the public's external demands intrude

[9]Drawing on Habermas (1973), O'Connor (1973), Offe (1974), Poulantzas (1978), and other neo-Martxists, they argue that the more insulated arenas are responsible for promoting capital accumulation, and the more accessible ones help legitimize the state's probusiness interventions to the public.

consistently into economic policy formation, the interests of business in capitalist growth are not served as well as they may be otherwise. This sort of access undermines the state's ability to help plan capitalist economic development.

The State-Civil Society Intersection

Even policy makers housed in a comparatively centralized and unified state apparatus may not be able to accomplish their goals effectively if they lack the means necessary for getting the job done (Hollingsworth, 1982; Skocpol, 1985:16–18). To an extent the structures of the state and economy determine the means. However, the institutional relationships *between* the state and two important aspects of civil society, the economy and polity, also play an important role.

The institutional nature of these policy tools, the mechanisms state policy makers possess for intervening into economic activity, determines the degree to which they are able to exercise control over an industry or sector. Two of the most powerful policy tools are state ownership and state control over the allocation of investment capital. Direct ownership of some portion of the means of production is the most straightforward control mechanism for the government. Institutionalists suggest that in otherwise comparable situations industries with relatively little or no state ownership have a more difficult time planning for the achievement of long-range, industrywide goals than industries with more state ownership. In privately owned firms, little if any financial risk is socialized. Therefore, firm-centered, short-term profitability considerations tend to dominate decision making within privatized industries. Conversely, as state ownership increases within an industry, more risk is socialized, and, therefore, the relative significance of short-term profitability declines as the key determinant of decision making (e.g., Dyson and Wilks, 1983:260–62; Shonfield, 1965:chap. 5). At the sectoral level both total and partial government ownership has been an especially important planning device for many Western European governments concerned with orchestrating the long-term development of critical industries, including utilities such as rail transport in Britain and electricity in France.

In addition to ownership, if state policy makers can manage to control the investment process, they have what many consider to be an extremely dynamic planning tool (Dyson and Wilks, 1983:262–64; Katzenstein, 1978b; Krasner, 1978:61; Skocpol, 1985:17; Solo, 1982:112–13; Thurow, 1984; Zysman, 1983). This control derives from their ability to manipulate either the allocation of investment capital or the rate of profit within an industry. The more policy makers can control investment, the more they will be able to force an industry to follow their plans. For example, a government that is able to manipulate the flow of capital directly to particular industries and firms through the allocation of credit has greater precision and autonomy in the economic planning of those industries than one whose control is limited to the use of aggregate monetary, fiscal, and tax policies, more indirect and less precise forms of intervention.[10] Similarly, policy makers who can directly manipulate profit rates through mandatory price controls, for example, have greater autonomy in their interventions than those with less direct profitability controls. In short, governments possessing more direct and precise financial policy levers are able to act as strong economic players and effectively target their interventions, whereas governments with indirect and aggregate tools are less effective, weak, and distant referees of economic activity (Zysman, 1983:75).

Two models of the state-economy intersection derive from this approach. The first is a market control model in which industrial decision making does not rest with state policy makers but with individual, privately owned firms responding primarily to immediate market stimuli. Especially in situations where business raises investment capital primarily through competitive capital markets, that is, through the sale of stocks and bonds as is common in the United States, a firm-centered, relatively short-term, profit-maximizing calculus tends to inform decision making. Similar decision making on the part of investors determines the allocation of investment capital in such markets. As a result, individual firms have trouble transcending their own particularistic goals, and industrywide or sectoral planning is very difficult to achieve (Dyson, 1983:52–55; Solo, 1967:chap. 3; The Business Week Team, 1982:48–52; Zysman, 1983). The second model is more statist in character. The government exercises strong control over industrial activity through either ownership or the direct manipulation of investment capital through mandatory price controls, selective credit arrangements, or subsidization. Direct and influential state control tends to increase the likelihood of farsighted industrial planning because state policy makers are more likely than individual firms to act with an eye toward broader goals transcending the individual firm's particularistic concern with immediate profit

---

[10] For an interesting qualification of this argument emphasizing the mediating role of historical and contextual circumstances, see Ikenberry (1986).

maximization (e.g., Shonfield, 1965; Solo, 1982; 1967; Szelenyi, 1981; Zysman, 1983; 1978). The government is more likely to be concerned with the overall condition of the industry or sector, especially in terms of its role in the national economy. A graphic example is the French government's ability to coordinate the restructuring of the steel and textile industries in the 1970s and 1980s through the selective allocation of capital (Green, 1983).

This is not to say that statist systems are the only ones capable of long-range planning. For example, private institutions, such as central banks, may assume pivotal coordinating roles and facilitate planning. This arrangement, common in West Germany, is like the market-based model insofar as private actors control the flow of investment capital and are primarily concerned with profitability. On the other hand, it is also similar to the statist model in that banks are not subject to the same short-term whims of investors as capital markets are and, therefore, have the luxury of being able to take a longer-term perspective on profit (Dyson, 1983:52–53; 1982:37; Shonfield, 1965:chaps 11–12; Thurow, 1984). Furthermore, under this system banks may act as policy allies with the state on terms negotiated between the two (Zysman, 1983:72). The government may help coordinate industrial planning by manipulating the flow of investment capital more effectively than under the market model but less than in a statist system.

The degree to which state policy makers have the institutional means of controlling economic activity cuts straight to the heart of their ability to implement industrial policy. However, it also has an important effect on policy formation. Policy makers with great control over the investment process have a wider, more powerful range of policy tools with which to impose their will on an industry. In turn, they have a wider range of policies from which to choose initially because industrial actors are less capable of successfully resisting government policy, especially when those actors disagree with the proposed policy agenda. The possibilities for planning increase accordingly.

The degree to which policy makers are institutionally accessible and susceptible to a variety of political pressures and demands directly affects policy implementation. A policy apparatus that is open and accessible at the point of implementation provides opportunities for obstructionist politics that can subvert the implementation process and, therefore, overall planning. The same is generally true with respect to policy formation (e.g., Dyson and Wilks, 1983:265; Krasner, 1978:66; Shonfield, 1965; Zysman, 1978:262). As Theda

Skocpol (1985:11–14) has argued, state agencies that are relatively insulated have a greater capacity for autonomously planned intervention than those that are not. However, she also noted that the institutional capacities of state policy makers vary within a single government and across time. This is also true for the other dimensions discussed here. The presence of such uneven institutional development across economic sectors underscores the importance of performing detailed historical analyses of particular sectors and being careful not to make sweeping generalizations about national political economies.

SENSITIVITY TO INSTITUTIONAL CONTRADICTIONS

Whether certain institutional arrangements aid industrial or sectoral planning better than others is ultimately an empirical question. However, there are further theoretical reasons to suspect that some general combinations tend to contradict or subvert long-range economic planning more than others in capitalist democracies. Neo-Marxists and some institutionalists have argued that there are two structural conditions that are particularly troublesome for such planning. First is the potential contradiction between the short-term profitability requirements of business and the planning that may be beneficial for the maintenance and sustained growth of the economy (e.g., Block, 1977:15–16; Habermas, 1973; Marx, 1967; Roweis, 1981:172). For example, both neo-Marxists (O'Connor, 1973:101) and institutionalists (Thurow, 1984) agree that the continued growth of any capitalist system depends heavily on the development of an elaborate infrastructure of research and development networks for developing new products and production processes. However, private corporations often balk at funding these projects because the short-term costs and financial risks involved are too large. To overcome this obstacle the government usually absorbs much of these costs either through subsidization or by providing the necessary infrastructure directly. Where it does not, long-term economic growth may suffer.

A second contradiction may develop between democratic political processes and the political stability and predictability necessary for traditional forms of industrial planning (e.g., Cohen and Rogers, 1983; Jessop, 1978; Offe and Ronge, 1975; Shonfield, 1965:387; Solo, 1982:104; 1967; Wolfe, 1977:329). Because the interests of the majority tend to differ from those of the wealthy minority, the former may mobilize against the activities and interests of the latter, particularly when they have the democratic opportunity to do so. Workers may organize for higher wages, or communities may pass strict environmental laws that cut into a firm's profits. The manifestation of this tension between democracy and capitalism may result in a political climate that does not permit business to make the kinds of decisions it wants in order to maximize its profitability and growth (Dolbeare, 1984). In fact, business may feel so threatened by democratic attempts to plan its activities that it moves to other less politicized geographic areas (e.g., Bluestone and Harrison, 1982; Goodman, 1979). Conflict may also focus on the government. If citizens feel that public policy systematically favors the interests of business over their own, the government's legitimacy may suffer, undermining the ability of state officials to make policy and plan (Habermas, 1973; O'Connor, 1973). The point is not that democracy tends to undermine planning per se but that it may conflict with those kinds of planning that systematically neglect the preferences of the majority.[11]

However, the general contradictions at work in advanced capitalist democracies that tend to undermine economic planning may assume a variety of particular institutional forms. In other words, the specific institutional arrangement of the political economy mediates or modifies the degree to which these general tendencies actually materialize and affect policy and planning. Judging from the institutionalist literature, it would seem that these contradictions are more likely to emerge with significant effects where firms are competitively arranged in both industrial structure and capital market financing, and where planning involves state apparatuses with few strong policy tools, and with decentralized, fragmented, and accessible policy arenas. In short, when conducting a sectoral analysis like the one proposed here, we must remain sensitive to both levels of analysis and the interplay between them as each may have pertinent effects on policy outcomes.

Until now I have tried not to suggest that successful industrial performance *necessarily* requires planning. To do so would require engaging a timeworn debate about the virtues of free markets versus planning as the best path to prosperity in capitalist democracies.[12]

[11] For elaborations on this point, see Bowles and Gintis (1986), Bluestone and Harrison (1982), and Dolbeare (1984). They argue that although democratic participation may contradict the requirements of *capitalist* planning, there are other ways to plan more democratically. On a related note Cohen and Rogers (1983:chap. 3) offer an interesting analysis about how the short-term interests among different social groups often coincide and, therefore, inhibit the development of conflict around contradictory long-term goals.

[12] For reviews of that debate in its contemporary form, see, for example, Bowles et al.

However, in the nuclear energy sector planning *is* necessary to sustain the technology commercially. Activity in this sector involves long lead times not only for developing and demonstrating the technology initially but also for building plants once the technology is commercialized. Furthermore, commercial nuclear plants require massive capital investments capable of waiting many years before realizing a return (Lönnroth and Walker, 1979:10). Finally, and perhaps most important, the technology involved is both extremely complex and potentially very dangerous. Given the unique materials and physical processes involved, a major reactor accident could contaminate a large area with radioactivity, causing sickness and death for present and future generations. The Chernobyl reactor accident in 1986 killed dozens of people and contaminated not only the immediate vicinity of Kiev in the Soviet Union but also portions of Scandinavia and Europe. The technology's organization exacerbates these dangers. A nuclear plant involves many extremely complex safety and other technical systems so tightly integrated that when something goes wrong, even something initially quite small and innocuous, serious accidents are more likely to result than in most other types of technology systems (Perrow, 1984). The potential safety hazards in the event of an accident are so high, the time horizons so long, and the capital requirements so great that planning is imperative for this sector's continued political and economic viability.

THE INSTITUTIONAL STRUCTURE OF THE U.S. NUCLEAR SECTOR

Institutionalists have argued that industrial planning is particularly difficult in the United States for several reasons. First, because of its federated structure, government policy making is generally decentralized, fragmented, and, therefore, democratically accessible to a wide range of interest groups. Second, state policy makers lack the

---

(1983:part 2) and Dolbeare (1984). Much of the institutionalist literature suggests that there is a positive correlation between long-range planning and sustained economic growth (Zysman, 1983), less inflation and economic stagnation (Lindberg and Maier, 1985), and an easing of the problems stemming from cutthroat competition (Streeck and Schmitter, 1985b). Of course, other explanations exist as to why industries or sectors rise and fall. For example, some suggest that the so-called natural changes in product cycles are responsible for fluctuations in economic performance within industries across countries. However, that literature also suggests that the political and economic institutions involved mediate the relationship between product cycle and economic performance. Hence, the interesting explanatory variables are again institutional. A good illustration is Kurth (1979).

direct and powerful financial policy tools that would facilitate the government's strong intervention into the economy. Third, given the long-standing ideological commitment in the United States to the free market, as embodied in antitrust legislation, competition has characterized much of the nation's economy. In most sectors there is not a small handful of huge corporations or banks capable of providing leadership privately (e.g., Edmonds, 1983; Krasner, 1978; Shonfield, 1965; Solo, 1967:144; Thurow, 1984; 1980; Zysman, 1983). These institutional arrangements characterize the commercial nuclear energy sector.

Structure of the Economy

In the United States most nuclear industries are decentralized. Several hundred investor-owned utilities generate nearly 80 percent of the nation's electricity and dominate the electric utility industry (Council of State Governments, 1977). Of those, fifty-three were involved in nuclear generating projects by 1982 (NRC, 1982b). Nine produced nearly half of the electricity generated by nuclear power (Nader and Abbotts, 1979:263). Although each enjoyed a monopoly in its own service area, the large number of utilities prevented the development of a national monopsony or monopoly.

The reactor industry was a competitive oligopoly. Four U.S. manufacturers dominated the domestic reactor market. A fifth, Gulf General Atomic Corporation, abandoned the market in the mid-1970s after playing a very minor role, selling only about 3 percent of all the reactors purchased in the country. It appears as of this writing that the reactor accident at Three Mile Island in 1979 will probably force Babcock and Wilcox, the firm that supplied the reactor system, from the industry, leaving only Westinghouse, General Electric, and Combustion Engineering to scramble for what is left of the shrinking domestic market (Walker and Lönnroth, 1983:74).

Twelve architect-engineering firms have been involved in nuclear construction projects, not counting those utilities like the Tennessee Valley Authority and Duke Power Company that have done their own work (OTA, 1981a:28). With the exception of turbine generators, produced primarily by General Electric and Westinghouse, an even larger number of electrical component suppliers participated. The fuel cycle industry was also relatively decentralized, with several large mining and oil companies dominating mining, milling, fuel fabrication, and, until the late 1970s, reactor fuel reprocessing (Hertsgaard, 1983:286–87; Nader and Abbotts, 1979:264–68). The federal gov-

23

ernment has sole responsibility for managing the disposal of high-level radioactive waste.

Structure of the State

The state apparatus responsible for commercial nuclear energy policy was generally decentralized, fragmented, and permeable to a wide variety of interest groups during policy implementation in the 1970s and 1980s (e.g., Barkenbus, 1984; Bupp, 1979; Ebbin and Kasper, 1974; Kitschelt, 1986; Lester, 1978). Regulatory policy, especially with respect to nuclear plant licensing, was subject to public inquiry at several levels of government. Local safety and licensing boards operated by the AEC, courts, utility commissions, and generic rule-making hearings at the national level all provided institutional points of access for citizens trying to influence nuclear policy. For example, a patchwork of state-level public utility commissions, where public interventions were commonplace, regulated electricity rates, thereby influencing both utility profitability and, to an extent, utility investment decisions.

Policy formation was initially very insulated and centralized within the AEC and the Joint Committee on Atomic Energy in Congress. However, this situation changed somewhat after 1975 as policy making was fractured into dozens of arenas at the federal level. Several administrative agencies exercised control over nuclear policy including the Nuclear Regulatory Commission, the Environmental Protection Agency, and the departments of energy, justice, transportation, and defense, among others. A variety of congressional committees contributed to regulatory policy not only by promulgating new legislation but also by controlling agency budgets after Congress abolished the joint committee in 1977 (Barkenbus, 1984; Bupp, 1979). The electoral system also presented possibilities for engaging the nuclear policy process through referenda campaigns at the state and local levels (Mitchell, 1981). More vertical and horizontal access to policy makers created the institutional possibility for political stalemate, obstructionism, and delay in the nuclear policy process, but particularly in implementation arenas. Most participation by opponents of nuclear energy occurred in these arenas because participants were often unable to gain access to the inner circles of policy formation.

The State-Civil Society Intersection

Government intervention into the nuclear sector was usually indirect in the United States. Although the AEC and the Joint Committee on Atomic Energy initially had total control over the ownership and development of nuclear power, they relinquished most of it in 1954 when Congress amended the Atomic Energy Act, turning most ownership privileges over to the private sector (Green and Rosenthal, 1963:123–58). Uranium enrichment, part of the process of creating reactor fuel, was one exception. The AEC retained title to its enrichment facilities, but subcontracted their operation to private corporations.

The government owned only a few of the nation's one hundred operating commercial nuclear plants. Therefore, it relied on two sets of relatively indirect policy tools for sectoral intervention. First, it tried to promote the nuclear sector's initial development during the 1950s and 1960s with titillating incentives, such as state-corporate financing of demonstration reactors, massive infusions of research and development funds, free fuel fabrication schemes, training opportunities for reactor operators, waivers of fuel use charges (until 1964), and an insurance indemnification program limiting private operator liability in the event of an accident (Nader and Abbotts, 1979; Meyers, 1977). It also offered a variety of incentives to develop the fuel cycle industries, such as attractive procurement policies, import tariffs, enrichment policies, and tax breaks (Battelle, 1978:119–25).[13] Although the subsidization was extensive, in most cases the government did not provide investment capital directly to the industries or participate directly in production. Instead, and with few exceptions, incentives came in the form of infrastructure and contractual agreements that defrayed costs to the companies. Second, the government took responsibility for regulating activities throughout the nuclear sector. Congress instructed several agencies, including the AEC and its heir, the Nuclear Regulatory Commission (NRC), to ensure that nuclear operations did not compromise the public health and safety. Policy makers have used regulation as their primary policy tool since the mid-1960s. As noted earlier, regulation permits the government to act only as a referee of industrial activity, not as a player with extensive powers for directing the general flow of economic activity in a sector.

However, some state policy makers did possess a more direct regulatory tool. State-level public utility commissions directly established the profit rates of electric utility companies. This was one of the few opportunities policy makers had since 1954 to exercise direct control

[13] For a brief review of the AEC's direct involvement in promoting the sector, see Campbell (1986).

over the investment decisions of firms in a nuclear industry.[14] Nevertheless, this was not an effective tool for coordinating *sectoral* activity inasmuch as it involved fifty autonomous state utility commissions without any obligation to cooperate with each other in policy making. The government did not control the allocation of capital in the capital and credit markets where firms in nuclear and other industries often competed for financing. In short, state policy makers had a weak and indirect set of policy tools—an institutional condition that would seem to have severely limited their ability to coordinate planning in the sector.

STRATEGIC POLICY AREAS

Planning failures in four important policy areas caused many of the problems that were pivotal in the sector's collapse.

Reactor Standardization Policy

Escalating plant costs and lead times were two of the major stumbling blocks to the U.S. nuclear sector. Electric utilities, reactor manufacturers, architect-engineering firms, the federal government, and other actors in the nuclear sector recognized since the 1960s that one way to reduce these problems was to standardize nuclear plants— build plants as identical to each other as possible and minimize design changes across plants during construction. The idea was similar to mass production: achieve production efficiencies and economies of scale by avoiding design changes with each unit produced. Despite several attempts, the sector did not effectively standardize the plants. Manufacturers commonly marketed two different kinds of reactors, boiling water and pressurized. Reactor sizes varied widely and generally became bigger and more powerful over time (Bupp and Derian, 1978:73). Furthermore, architect-engineering firms offered a variety of designs for the nonnuclear side of the plant that included different kinds of turbines, control rooms, and auxiliary power and safety systems. As a result, almost every nuclear power station built in the United States was unique (OTA, 1981a:3). The lower costs and other

[14] The Federal Energy Regulatory Commission regulates the price of electricity produced at federal facilities, produced privately and transmitted across state borders, and sold wholesale. However, this amounts to only 12 percent of all the electricity produced annually in the United States and, therefore, is not particularly relevant to the nuclear sector's history (GAO, 1981a).

benefits that might have been achieved through standardization scarcely materialized at all.

Reactor Safety Policy

Antinuclear groups in the United States saw reactor safety policy as a major bone of contention since at least the late 1960s. They argued that private ownership led to a sectoral interest in profits at the expense of public health, safety, and the environment and that this interest permeated the policy process and undermined safety planning (e.g., Ford, 1982; Gyorgy et al., 1979; Nader and Abbotts, 1979). Concerns over reactor safety spilled into licensing hearings, the courts, electoral referenda, and legislative bodies in Washington, D.C., and around the country. Reactor safety policy was one of the most important issues triggering the legitimation problems the nuclear sector encountered. Many agree that the issue's development was so important that it catalyzed the antinuclear movement's escalation in the early 1970s (Nelkin and Fallows, 1978).

Finance Policy

Escalating plant costs were often cited as one of the most important reasons why electric utilities cancelled and eventually stopped ordering nuclear plants. In fact, the problem was not so much rising costs per se but the trouble utilities experiencing cost increases had in raising sufficient capital either to finish nuclear projects already under construction or to begin new ones. State-level public utility commissions refused to grant the rate increases necessary to cover these costs. As a result, investors in the capital markets became very reluctant to risk their money on nuclear projects. Without sufficient capital nuclear projects could not proceed.

High-Level Radioactive Waste Policy

By 1987 the United States had not developed an operating facility to permanently manage the high-level radioactive wastes the nation's commercial reactors were producing. This policy failure raised havoc within the sector during the 1970s and 1980s. Private corporations tried to reprocess nuclear waste commercially in the late 1960s and 1970s but failed. Reprocessing separated uranium and plutonium chemically from other radioactive waste and, if those elements were recycled as new reactor fuel, reduced some of the problems of waste

27

disposal. Years ago the AEC encouraged reprocessing as the first step in its waste management plan. When it did not develop, utilities, with limited temporary storage capacity for their wastes, faced the threat of having to close down their reactors. Finally, Congress instructed the Department of Energy in 1982 to seek and develop permanent storage sites, but as implementation began it was not clear whether or when that task would be accomplished. As a result, the absence of a permanent waste management program continued to be a heavy burden for the sector. The Supreme Court ruled in 1983 that public utility commissions were within their rights to refuse utilities permission to build new nuclear capacity until the federal government provided an acceptable and working waste management system. In fact, antinuclear groups had advocated this policy in licensing proceedings, utility commission hearings, and the courts since 1976, further disrupting the licensing process and undermining whatever hopes there were for the sector's recovery during the mid-1980s.

PART II

THE FAILURE OF COMMERCIAL NUCLEAR ENERGY POLICY

CHAPTER THREE

Competition and the Absence of Standardization

Eli Whitney was one of the first inventors to recognize the benefits of standardization. He discovered in the late eighteenth century that if a series of muskets could be manufactured to the same detailed specifications, rather than building each one differently, parts could be mass produced and stockpiled, production could be sped up, quality control could be increased, and the cost of producing each musket could be reduced. Since then thousands of industries have standardized their products and achieved similar benefits. Standardization never materialized in the U.S. nuclear sector, however, even though many believed that it could solve some of the sector's most serious problems. More important, the failure to standardize the nation's nuclear plants reflected the sector's inability to plan effectively.

The degree to which a nuclear sector may standardize its plants varies across two dimensions. First, the sector may adopt one or more basic nuclear technology *concepts*. The United States builds two conceptually different types of nuclear plants, pressurized and boiling water systems.[1] Other countries, such as France and Canada, rely on single systems and, therefore, have outstandardized the United States at this very fundamental level. Second, once the concept is chosen, the sector may standardize, in varying degree, different aspects of the

---

[1] The boiling water reactor allows water, passing through the hot reactor core, to boil, produce steam, and drive a turbine to produce electricity. The pressurized system keeps water from the core at higher pressures to prevent boiling. Its heat is transferred to another water coolant system that is allowed to boil and run the turbine.

plant's *design*. The depth of design standardization may vary tremen-
dously. For example, at a general level manufacturers may agree to
build either one, or several sizes of reactors. At a more detailed level
they may decide either to precisely specify (standardize) the design
down to the last nut and bolt, or to leave such details to the individual
project managers. In both cases, the first choice produces a more
standardized design. The more features plants have in common, the
more standardized they are.

Representatives from the nuclear industries, antinuclear groups,
regulatory agencies, and electric utilities have maintained for years
that standardization is an effective way to avoid design changes during
construction, reduce licensing delays, minimize shortages in the supply of components, and, therefore, cut construction times and plant
costs (e.g., JCAE, 1974a; Walker and Lönnroth, 1983:67). They have
also argued that standardization improves quality control and plant
safety (U.S. House, 1978; OTA, 1981a; U.S. Senate, 1978b). Ironically,
while both advocates and critics of nuclear power agree that standardization is necessary, the United States is the only major nuclear
country in which almost every nuclear plant is largely custom built
(NRC Special Inquiry Group, 1980:45). This is even more perplexing
in view of the fact that corporations have tried to standardize plants
since the mid-1960s and federal regulators have tried since 1972.
Some claim that the AEC and NRC frustrated the standardization
effort by constantly changing regulatory requirements. The implication is that government mismanagement is to blame. However, this
explanation is questionable. It was not excessive, but *insufficient* state
intervention that contributed to the problem. Furthermore, although
the state played a role, competition within several nuclear industries
was just as important in undermining standardization. The plan failed
because the economic and political institutions created imperatives
that were antithetical to the stable, cooperative atmosphere necessary
for successful standardization planning.

THE AMBIVALENT QUEST FOR STANDARD DESIGNS, 1965–1971

The mid-1960s was a time of great optimism within the nuclear
energy sector. Because electric utilities around the nation enjoyed
increases in electricity demand of about 7 percent annually, many
planned to build new generating capacity (Arthur D. Little, Inc.,
1968:15). Nuclear reactor manufacturers benefited from that expansion. Orders for nuclear power plants began to surge in 1966, hitting
a record peak of thirty units in 1968 (Table 3.1).

Table 3.1. Sales of nuclear steam supply systems by year and by vendor

	Number of Sales						
Year	General Electric	Westinghouse	Babcock and Wilcox	Combustion Engineering	General Atomic Corporation[a]	Other	Total
pre-1965	5	5	1	—	1	8	20
1965	3	3	—	—	1	—	7
1966	9	6	3	2	—	—	20
1967	7	13	5	5	—	—	30
1968	7	4	3	—	—	—	14
1969	3	3	—	1	—	—	7
1970	3	5	2	4	—	—	14
1971	4	10	2	—	4	—	20
1972	14	11	5	2	—	—	32
1973	8	13	2	11	—	—	34
1974	11	7	7	6	2	—	33
1975	—	4	—	—	—	—	4
1976	—	—	3	—	—	—	3
1977	—	—	—	6	—	—	6
1978	—	2	—	—	—	—	2
1979	—	—	—	—	—	—	—
1980–85	—	—	—	—	—	—	—
Total	74	86	33	37	8	8	246

[a]General Atomic Corporation dropped out of the market in 1975.
SOURCE: Adapted from NRC (1980a).

However, problems loomed on the horizon. One study, funded by the AEC, estimated that between 1966 and 1968 actual plant costs rose 50 percent over those originally expected (Arthur D. Little, Inc., 1968:23). In several early cases where utilities bought whole plants for a guaranteed fee, plants cost 90 to 110 percent more than anticipated—a serious problem for the reactor manufacturers who sold them and had to absorb losses of about $75 million per plant (Perry et al., 1977:35). There were several reasons for these cost overruns. First, utilities kept building bigger plants in the hope of achieving economies of scale. However, building large plants from the extrapolations of smaller designs, rather than from full-scale prototypes, created a host of expensive and unexpected engineering difficulties. Second, production costs were uncertain at a time when many components were just coming off the drawing boards. Third, production facilities were still not perfected for the larger plants. Many of these troubles had common origins in market competition and the absence of standardization (Arthur D. Little, Inc., 1968:24).

General Electric manufactured boiling water reactors, while Westinghouse, Combustion Engineering, and Babcock and Wilcox each sold different versions of the pressurized water reactor. Because of the intense competition among them and their assumption that larger reactors would benefit from economies of scale, a major sales pitch at the time, they all kept selling different and increasingly larger models (Hertsgaard, 1983:63). Thanks to the pressures of competition, utilities could choose from a wide selection of reactor concepts and designs.

In addition to cost overruns, limited engineering and construction capabilities confronted reactor manufacturers as orders poured in for new plants. Manufacturers also worried that the AEC would soon face an unprecedented wave of construction permit applications following the ordering boom—a workload that would tax the agency to the limit, create regulatory bottlenecks, and prevent the steady flow of nuclear plants through the construction permit and subsequent operating license reviews (Gartman, 1968:48).[2] Reactor manufacturers felt that they could reduce production and licensing times, and, therefore, overall project lead times if they standardized plants. Shorter lead times would also make plants less expensive to build and help reduce cost overruns. Westinghouse took the first step by developing a Standard Information Package defining technical details for what they planned would be their standard reactor design (Arnold and Grain, 1972). By 1967, Westinghouse and General Electric had submitted packages to the AEC for preliminary safety review and approval. The idea was that a utility could buy one of their reactors later and, since it had already been approved by the AEC, avoid the long and expensive part of the agency's construction permit review that involved evaluating the reactor design's safety.

Even though this was supposed to cut licensing time, the AEC rejected the idea (Ward, 1973). During an interview for this study one NRC official intimately involved with the standardization program reported that those in charge at the AEC were concerned that reactor technology was still in a developmental phase, particularly because manufacturers were scaling it up so rapidly without much previous operating experience. Regulators did not want to freeze a reactor design and remove it from the safety review until they were convinced that it was problem free. Furthermore, the market for nuclear plants was expanding rapidly. One researcher at the OTA informed me that AEC officials apparently did not think licensing delays or cost in-

[2] The utility needs a construction permit to build a nuclear plant. Later, after most of the construction is finished, it applies for an operating license required to run the plant. The NRC is responsible for awarding both of these.

creases posed a significant threat to the sector's development at that time.

In 1970, Westinghouse announced that it had developed standard design packages for each size plant it offered. It planned to cut production costs for both itself and its utility customers by mass producing and stockpiling inventories of components in advance for each standard design (Lester, 1970). Babcock and Wilcox had already started pursuing this idea with the sale of two reactors to the Tennessee Valley Authority for their Bellefonte project that year. As it turned out, these were the first of nine identical reactor designs Babcock and Wilcox would sell (Hamilton, 1975).

Architect-engineering firms were also interested in standardizing the nonnuclear portion of the plant they supplied. This part of the plant included the turbine generators, some cooling systems, the control room, and emergency generators among other things. In 1970, Stone and Webster started developing standard designs for the nonnuclear portion of the plant to complement those the manufacturers developed for the reactors. They wanted to reduce licensing time and improve plant reliability and operation (Kennedy et al., 1976). However, unlike the reactor manufacturers, architect-engineering firms did not seem to be extremely concerned with reducing production costs directly. They saw standardization primarily as a way to help utilities move plants through the regulatory bureaucracy faster and build a better quality product. The reason for this difference lay in the kinds of contracts utilities had with both the architect-engineers and reactor manufacturers. Architect-engineers contracted with utilities on a cost-plus basis guaranteeing the architect-engineer a set profit above whatever production costs they incurred. On the other hand, manufacturers agreed to provide the reactor for a fixed fee, so their profits varied depending on their production costs. Under fixed-fee contracts they could not pass higher costs along to the utility as architect-engineers could, but had to absorb them through lower profits.

Perhaps more important, a few utilities began to cultivate a taste for standardization; the concept was beginning to become commercially appealing. In addition to the Tennessee Valley sales, the Duke Power Company ordered duplicate designs for its three Oconee plants in 1966, filed a single preliminary safety review application covering them all with the AEC, and received construction permits the following year. A company spokesperson noted later that this duplication strategy reduced engineering time, construction time, and, therefore, costs (Owen, 1974:238). However, these were exceptional cases. Most utilities still refused to accept standard designs, insiting instead on specific design changes (Gartman, 1968:49). When asked why this was the case, a spokesperson from the Atomic Industrial Forum, the nuclear sector's trade association, informed me that most utilities continued to seek increasingly larger and presumably more cost efficient reactors. They also kept buying state-of-the-art technology at a time when it was evolving rapidly. Because most utilities did not have any in-house nuclear expertise at the time, they had to rely on the reactor manufacturers for technical advice in many nuclear matters. It is likely that if utilities wanted state-of-the-art designs it was because manufacturers stressed the importance of being at the technological forefront. After all, manufacturers were competing with each other on the basis of design. Each had an interest in convincing utilities that they should buy the latest equipment, especially if it was equipment the manufacturer was ready to sell. The same strategy applied to offering larger reactors.

In short, manufacturers and architect-engineering firms began to cultivate an interest in standardizing nuclear plant designs with mixed emotions. Their ambivalence stemmed from the contradictory interests of facilitating the sector's prolonged development by reducing regulatory review time and costs, on the one hand, and competing against each other for sales and profits in the short term by offering newer, bigger, state-of-the-art designs on the other. As a result, most utilities bought the latest models and avoided standardization, believing, for example, the reactor manufacturers' promises about increasing economies of scale with larger plants. Furthermore, the AEC refused to freeze design requirements until the sector gained enough operating experience with the larger, more complex versions to be sure that they were safe—something that was difficult to do while designs still vacilated with the rigors of competition. Although movement toward standard designs started to develop, two concepts and a wide range of designs were still available.

A PLAN EMERGES, 1972–1975

A dramatic turn of events occurred between 1972 and 1975 in the nuclear sector. First, utilities ordered thirty-four reactors in 1973, another record, and almost as many the following year (see Table 3.1). However, orders plummeted to only four units in 1975. Part of the reason was that electric utilities had experienced a critical deterioration in financial health since the mid-1960s. (The indications, causes, and consequences of this crisis are discussed in detail in chapter 6). By 1972 finance capital was becoming so expensive for electric utilities that their ability to finance new generating capacity had, for the first time, started to become a problem (Gandara, 1977:33). This had severe consequences for nuclear projects because they were much more capital intensive than conventional generating systems. Second, construction permit and operating license reviews swamped the AEC in the late 1960s. The number of applications the AEC received annually between 1966 and 1971 tripled the number received during the previous ten years (Table 3.2). Reports from utilities that many more could be expected in the early 1970s made matters look even worse (NRC, 1978b:V–1). A federal appeals court exacerbated these problems in 1971 by ordering the AEC to consider the environmental effects and potential radiological dangers of nuclear plants in its reviews. The decision forced the AEC to review sixty nuclear projects a second time (AEC, 1973c). Both the regulatory backlog and the increasing financial strain on utilities had important implications for standardization policy.

The AEC acknowledged the licensing problem in 1972 and proposed standardization as a possible solution. The agency worried that the licensing delays and higher costs utilities faced as a result of the bureaucratic logjam might undermine reactor sales at a time when the utilities' financial troubles threatened their pursuit of the nuclear option (AEC, 1972). Officials felt that standardization would make the regulatory review process more effective and efficient (AEC, 1974c:C–1). Furthermore, according to interviews conducted for this study with NRC officials, the agency had apparently decided by 1972 that the technology was finally mature enough to standardize for short periods of time.

In March 1973, the AEC released a statement placing a 1,300 megawatt upper limit on reactor size and offering several licensing options it hoped would encourage the industry to pursue design standardization. The first was called *referencing,* an idea like the one reactor manufacturers had proposed when they submitted reactor designs for preliminary regulatory approval. Referencing provided both manufacturers and architect-engineers a chance to have their designs reviewed and approved for safety by the AEC before utilities bought them. When utilities used these designs later in their plants, they would be exempt from parts of the AEC safety review. *Duplication* was the second option, a carbon copy of the procedure Duke Power had followed with its Oconee project. A utility would plan to build

Table 3.2. Applications received by the AEC and NRC for construction permits and operating licenses, 1955–1977

Year	Number of Applications		
	Construction Permit	Operating License	Total
1955	2	0	2
1956	2	0	2
1957	0	0	0
1958	0	1	1
1959	7	1	8
1960	2	2	4
1961	0	5	5
1962	1	3	4
1963	2	0	2
1964	2	1	3
1965	4	2	6
1966	12	1	13
1967	18	3	21
1968	10	7	17
1969	8	6	15
1970	11	8	19
1971	6	12	18
1972	4	4	8
1973	20	6	26
1974	19	4	23
1975	6	3	9
1976	2	2	4
1977	2	2	4

SOURCES: NRC (1978b) and NRC (1981a):41.

several identical nuclear plants and submit a single design plan for them all as part of its construction permit application. The program would save both time and money in the safety review process.[3] About a year and a half later the AEC added another option called *replication,* whereby a utility could submit a design for AEC safety approval that had already been accepted for another plant. As an incentive, the AEC promised to give scheduling and review priority to applications submitted under these options, claiming that the program could cut two years off the time required to bring a plant into commercial operation (AEC, 1973c:92).

Replication and duplication were not much different from each

[3] The AEC offered a third option at the time, but with no significance for this story. It was a manufacturing license issued to companies building identical plants at a common location and shipping them elsewhere. The agency offered it as encouragement for the development of floating nuclear power plants, an idea that never matured. No utility ever bought such a plant either in the United States or abroad.

other or from the normal licensing procedure. In all three cases the utility absorbed the cost of preparing the preliminary safety report about the plant's design and submitted it for safety approval *during* the AEC's construction permit review. Of course with duplication the utility filed a single preliminary safety report on its design for all the plants to be built. With replication it submitted a safety report previously available for another plant. In both cases the utility was supposed to save time and money. As the number of plants a utility proposed to build with a single design increased, the costs and time involved with the safety review declined accordingly. However, referencing was a unique and truly innovative approach. The AEC reviewed the plant's design for safety *before* the utility applied for its construction permit. The manufacturer or architect-engineer submitting it bore the costs of preparation and having it approved, not the utility that eventually used it. Hence, even if the utility built just one plant and referenced the design, its savings would be greater than under replication, duplication, or normal procedures.

Referencing also had other benefits. For example, reactor manufacturers and architect-engineers, expecting to sell their designs to several utilities, could stockpile standard components. Subsequently, the utility would know that components would be ready when needed and that construction delays related to late delivery of these parts would be avoided even on single plant projects. Under replication or duplication only large multiplant projects, generally limited to the largest utilities, could stockpile. As such, referencing could appeal to all utilities interested in building nuclear plants. It also promised the greatest benefits to reactor manufacturers interested in reducing their own production costs because they could produce components in bulk and stockpile them even without multiplant projects in hand. Furthermore, referencing increased the possibility of standardizing designs more precisely. Manufacturers and architect-engineers could submit very detailed final designs for regulatory approval under the referencing option. If a utility used that design as part of its construction permit application, it would reduce the chances of expensive construction delays later due to unfinished design and engineering work, a problem that frequently besieged projects with design plans less precisely specified when construction began (Atomic Industrial Forum, 1978). In short, regardless of the number of plants ordered in a project, referencing offered tremendous benefits.

Reactor manufacturers grew more interested in standardizing designs for several reasons. First, they were still struggling to eliminate cost overruns of at least $1 million per plant—overruns they had to absorb because they contracted with utilities on a fixed-fee basis (*Commerce Today*, 1974:14). As a result, manufacturers pursued standardization to reduce both design and construction costs (MacMillan and Johnson, 1974). Second, reactor manufacturers worried that their utility customers were losing money as a result of longer licensing times. The average review time for construction permit applications tripled between 1967 and 1973 and nearly doubled for operating licenses (Table 3.3). According to a vice-president and general manager from General Electric's nuclear division, this was one of the sector's worst problems because the long and uncertain time required for starting a plant created serious financial problems for the utilities (*Chemical and Engineering News*, 1973:7). For example, General Electric reported that delaying the initial operation of nuclear plants ready to be used could cost a utility from $100,000 to $200,000 per day in interest charges and supplementary power costs alone (*Business Week*, 1973). Therefore, standardization, particularly through referencing, also appealed to the manufacturers as a way to reduce licensing times and keep utilities interested in nuclear power. As a result, each manufacturer submitted at least one reference design (a total of eight) to the AEC for preliminary approval by late 1975 (NRC 1980a:1–11).

The principle of standardization also appealed to architect-engineering firms. They were also interested in reducing licensing time to the extent that it would make the nuclear option more attractive to utilities (Ward, 1973). However, as noted earlier, the interests of architect-engineers and reactor manufacturers diverged for contractual reasons that reduced the architect-engineers' relative bullishness over standardization. Architect-engineers had cost-plus contracts with utilities that guaranteed them a set profit. Reactor manufacturers did not. Hence, manufacturers, having a greater economic incentive to minimize their costs, should have pursued standardization more vigorously, for the money they saved would have increased their profits. These divergent interests seem to have had significant effects. All the manufacturers referenced some designs, whereas only two out of twelve architect-engineering firms applied for preliminary approval of reference packages during the first three years of the AEC program (NRC, 1980a:1–11).

By this time, utilities were ready to try standardization. Six utilities submitted a total of eight construction permits between 1973 and 1975 for twenty-one power plants under the reference option (OTA, 1981b:297). The AEC and, later, the NRC received sixteen construction permit applications involving at least one of the standardization options (Table 3.4). Over half of the construction permits

40

Table 3.3 Average review time for construction permits and operating licenses, 1956–1980.

Year	Construction Permits		Operating Licenses	
	Number Issued	Time in Months	Number Issued	Time in Months
1956	2	13.1	0	0.0
1957	1	6.9	0	0.0
1958	1	15.8	0	0.0
1959	6	10.5	1	15.6
1960	2	12.7	1	9.7
1961	0	0.0	0	0.0
1962	1	18.9	5	14.7
1963	1	4.8	3	19.9
1964	2	10.7	2	23.3
1965	2	10.4	0	0.0
1966	3	2.9	1	22.9
1967	8	9.7	3	16.7
1968	10	12.7	0	0.0
1969	12	14.6	3	24.3
1970	9	19.0	3	22.4
1971	6	21.7	4	28.8
1972	0	0.0	9	31.3
1973	11	32.6	8	36.9
1974	9	33.1	14	42.1
1975	8	28.8	5	38.5
1976	9	26.3	8	51.5
1977	6	39.5	4	51.8
1978	7	44.7	4	52.8
1979	2	40.2	0	0.0
1980	0	0.0	0	72.1[a]

[a]Although it is not clear from the government's data, this figure must represent average months per applicant in certain applications completed but not yet issued in light of the Three Mile Island accident and subsequent licensing suspensions.

SOURCES: NRC (1980a): 14, 17, and NRC (1981a): 39–41.

received in 1974 and 1975 involved some form of standardization. The reasons for the enthusiasm were obvious. Reports from the trade journals (e.g., Ward, 1973) and professional meetings (Falkin, 1975; Arnold and Grain, 1972) promised utilities that standardization could reduce their licensing times and costs. Furthermore, according to the head of the Atomic Industrial Forum, the nuclear sector's trade association, standardization could reduce the number of design changes ordered by regulators, something that would cut costs even further (*Energy User's Report,* 1974e:A–27). However, while utilities were complaining that these design changes caused expensive construction and operating delays (*Energy User's Report,* 1974f:C–2), not all of them jumped on the standardization bandwagon. After all, almost half of

Table 3.4. Use of standardization in construction permit applications, 1973–1980

Year	Total Construction Permit Applications	Construction Permits Using Standardization Options			
		Duplication	Replication	Reference	Total
1973	19[a]	2(4)	—	—	2(4)
1974	19	6(11)	1(2)	6(17)	11(24)[b]
1975	6	—	1(2)	2(4)	3(6)
1976	2	—	1(2)	1(2)	2(4)
1977	2	—	—	1(2)	1(2)
1978	na	—	2(4)	1(2)	3(6)
1979	0	—	—	—	—
1980	0	—	—	—	—

NOTE: The number outside the parentheses is the number of construction permit applications. The number inside the parentheses is the number of units ordered.

[a] This number does not include one construction permit application for a floating nuclear power plant.

[b] Two applications for six units fall into both the duplicate and the reference categories. Hence, this total is less than the sum of the parts.

SOURCES: OTA (1981): 297–302, NRC (1980a), and NRC (1981a).

the construction permit applications submitted in 1974 and 1975 were *not* for standardized plants. In fact, according to a vice-president for the Rochester Gas and Electric Company, a utility building a major duplication project, some utilities were really quite hesitant to participate in the program (*Energy User's Report,* 1975a:D–1).

By 1972 the AEC realized that licensing delays and cost escalation were adding to the nuclear utilities' already severe financial headaches. The agency also felt that nuclear technology was ready for standardization and that it would improve plant safety. Regulators offered a standardization plan to relieve the pain and sustain growth in the nuclear sector. Reactor manufacturers pursued standardization to reduce their own costs, increase profits, and reinforce their market by providing a more bureaucratically streamlined, economical, and, therefore, attractive product to their customers. Architect-engineering firms were also interested in the plan because they were concerned with the utilities' welfare, not because costs and delays threatened their own profit margins. The utilities began to standardize, but less enthusiastically than might have been expected. As it turned out, their reluctance was one reason why architect-engineers balked at the standardization program while manufacturers embraced it.

THE FAILURE OF STANDARDIZATION, 1976–1981

New orders only trickled in for nuclear plants after 1974. No utility ordered a plant or applied for a construction permit after 1978.

Furthermore, a wave of project cancellations shocked the sector. During this period the standardization program met serious resistance from the reactor manufacturers, architect-engineering firms, and utilities. For financial reasons, manufacturers stopped seeking preliminary approval for their reference designs after 1976 (NRC, 1980a:1–11). Westinghouse, for example, had submitted three reactor designs for preliminary approval under the AEC's referencing program. However, only one utility had purchased any of them and then for use in only two plants (OTA, 1981b:297). Combustion Engineering was more fortunate inasmuch as utilities referenced its most popular design in fifteen plants. Nonetheless, according to company officials it was still not worth the investment (*Electric Light and Power*, 1978:26).

However, reactor manufacturers remained dedicated to referencing, at least in principle. A vice-president in Westinghouse's water reactor division told a congressional committee that referencing was still desirable but that reference designs with preliminary approval should remain valid for ten years, rather than expiring after five as they did then. This would allow utilities to reference them more often and make referencing profitable for manufacturers (U.S. House, 1978:678–79). Despite these problems, Combustion Engineering applied to the NRC for *final* approval of a reference design in 1980. It was the first manufacturer to do so. The NRC granted final approval only to designs specified in enough detail to meet the requirements of an operating license review—an examination that required much more precision and detail in the design than the construction permit review. Utilities could reference designs with preliminary approval in their construction permit applications but not when they applied for an operating license later because designs with only preliminary approval were not defined precisely enough.

Architect-engineers sought preliminary approval for their designs longer than manufacturers, but stopped after 1978 (NRC, 1980a:1–11). Significantly, none of them ever submitted a detailed design for final approval, another indication that they were not as interested in the program as the manufacturers were. Only half the sector's architect-engineering firms ever chose to participate in the reference program, a rate much lower than the manufacturers', all of whom were involved.

Not all utilities pursued the standardization options, but many did. Sixty percent of the construction permit applications submitted between 1975 and 1977 included either the replication or reference options (Table 3.4). Half of the construction permit applications filed under the standardization program after 1972 used referencing.

However, only one utility ever referenced an architect-engineer's design for the nonnuclear portion of the plant (OTA, 1981b:337). Except for that single case, utilities standardized only their reactors, a small part that constituted just 10 percent of the nuclear plant's entire design (OTA, 1981a:26). Ironically, despite their verbal support for design standardization, the utilities' behavior indicated that they still had strong reservations about the government's program.

Regardless of the problems and the publication of several gloomy reports about the failure of standardization, the sector still generally *believed* in the plan's virtues. The NRC (1977c; 1978) and the U.S. General Accounting Office (1977a) found that referencing had not yet significantly shortened licensing reviews. Nevertheless, the NRC, remaining optimistic, believed that referencing was at a breakeven threshold and that benefits would materialize soon if utilities continued to reference their designs. Additionally, it noted that review time was much shorter when an entire plant was standardized than it was for plants only partially standardized (NRC, 1978b:III.6–4). Experience from a large multiplant project using the duplication option corroborated that conclusion. The utilities involved in that project reported savings of $600,000 per construction permit application (Nuclear Projects, Inc., 1978).

Several observers recognized that the NRC was not completely to blame for licensing and lead time delays (e.g., Atomic Industrial Forum, 1978; Messing, 1978; GAO, 1978; 1977a; NRC, 1977c). For example, the Congressional Budget Office (1979) reported that government intervention caused only about 20 percent of these delays. Problems in the private sector, such as financing, materials shortages, and labor difficulties, caused the rest. However, the Congressional Budget Office saw standardization as a solution even for these problems, arguing that it would encourage component stockpiling and help avoid delays in delivering construction materials and components. Evidence from other multiplant projects including the duplication effort showed that labor costs were cut as construction crews gained experience from one identical plant to the next (e.g., Keith and Karner, 1978; Nuclear Projects, Inc., 1978; U.S. House, 1978:137). The Atomic Industrial Forum maintained that standardization could make financing nuclear projects easier by bringing stability and predictability to licensing, design, and construction (Atomic Industrial Forum, 1978:3). The point is that the sector remained convinced that standardization was a good idea, yet it failed to pursue the plan wholeheartedly. As a result, the benefits of standardization did not materialize. What explains this ironic failure?

44

THE INSTITUTIONAL BARRIERS TO SUCCESS

The logic of referencing dictates that architect-engineers and reactor manufacturers eventually seek *final* approval for their designs, a certification awarded only after the NRC has examined a design specified in much greater detail than that required for preliminary approval. Utilities can only reference a design when they apply for an operating license if the design has been granted final approval. Otherwise, the NRC must examine a detailed description of the design from scratch as part of the operating license review. This comprehensive examination defeats the purpose of referencing by prolonging the licensing review, giving the NRC a chance to impose design changes and increasing the application preparation and review costs the utility incurs.

Manufacturers started applying for final design approval in 1980. However, for institutional reasons architect-engineering firms had no intention of doing so. The level of detail required for final approval raised antitrust problems. If an architect-engineer specified its reference design as precisely as the NRC required for an operating license application, it would virtually have to name components manufactured by specific suppliers. According to a representative from the Atomic Industrial Forum, a utility referencing an architect-engineer's design with final approval would have to buy components from those suppliers, a practice that would restrict competition (U.S. Senate, 1978b:377). The law required that utilities solicit competitive bids from component suppliers. If a utility used an architect-engineer's reference design, suppliers whose components were not specified in the design could sue the utility for violating antitrust laws (O'Donnell, 1977:4). Additionally, according to an executive from the Long Island Lighting Company, the utilities feared that restricting competition could lead to monopoly pricing (Falkin, 1975:36). For example, once an architect-engineer specified a particular pump in its design, and, therefore, a single pump supplier, the absence of competitive bidding among those suppliers could inflate the price a utility referencing that design had to pay for the pump (OTA, 1981b:304).

From the utility's point of view it made little sense to reference an architect-engineer's design with preliminary approval because the more detailed version, with final approval, could not be used later during the operating license review without running into these problems. As a result, the utilities almost never referenced the architect-engineer's design. In turn, architect-engineers were hesitant to seek preliminary approval and, recognizing the antitrust and monopoly pricing problems involved, refused entirely to submit designs for final approval (Saldarini, 1979:605). In short, the standardization plan failed dramatically with respect to the nonnuclear portion of the plant because regulatory authority was fragmented between conflicting antitrust and nuclear energy policies.

Two questions remain. First, if they knew about these problems, why did architect-engineers seek preliminary approvals at all? They hoped that the NRC would eventually accept a less precisely defined design for referencing in the operating license application, a design somewhere between the broad description required for preliminary approval and the exact details necessary for final approval. They pushed the NRC to adopt that approach during the late 1970s (NRC, 1978b). Second, if the architect-engineering firms refused to pursue final design approvals, why did any reactor manufacturers try to get it? Manufacturers moved ahead cautiously in their applications for final design approvals despite the possibility of antitrust complications because the nature of their relationship with the utility tempered the risks (Sherwood, 1979). Unlike architect-engineers, manufacturers bought or produced most of the reactor components themselves before they sold the system to a utility (NRC, 1978b:VI–4). As a result, the utility was not involved in purchasing individual reactor components and, therefore, was not subject to antitrust statutes as it was with architect-engineers.

Industry representatives have argued that the NRC undermined standardization by constantly ordering utilities to change their designs, even after approving them under the standardization options (e.g., Atomic Industrial Forum, 1978; *Nuclear News*, 1981:40). They have claimed that these alterations caused scheduling delays, delivery delays, replacement of work already completed at the site, and other problems that standardization is supposed to help prevent. As a result, it is argued that although utilities submitted standardized applications, they still faced a variety of escalating costs due to the unpredictable and unstable nature of the regulatory climate. In fact, representatives from the Atomic Industrial Forum told me that constantly shifting regulations actually deterred companies from attempting standardization in the first place.

It is true that the NRC has increased both the number and strictness of its regulations over the years, particularly since the accident at Three Mile Island in 1979 (e.g., Komanoff, 1981). However, there are several reasons why regulation is a questionable explanation for the failure of standardization. First, one well-informed NRC official reported during an interview for this project that although regulatory changes have affected all plants, the NRC imposed fewer changes on plant designs with either preliminary or final approvals under the standardization program. As a result, fluctuating regulations should have stimulated, not deterred, the pursuit of standardization. Second, even if we accept that regulators did impose major changes on previously approved standard designs, this did not apparently undermine the standardization program itself. Manufacturers continued to participate in the program through 1980 when Combustion Engineering requested final approval for one of its reactor designs. Architect-engineering firms applied for preliminary design approvals through 1978, the last year a utility ordered a nuclear plant in the United States. Most important, utilities continued to use the replication and reference options to standardize portions of their plants until they stopped ordering completely (see Table 3.4). Although regulatory changes were a problem, they did not discourage most companies from following the standardization plan. The point is that institutional factors subverted the plan more than the vacillating requirements of government regulators.

The Effects of Competition and the State

None of these attempts to achieve standardization by controlling nuclear plant designs ever really cut to the heart of the problem. A more far-reaching solution would have limited the sector to a single nuclear plant concept as some other countries have done. Although the idea was recommended, there were never any serious attempts to build just the boiling or pressurized water reactor in the United States. Again, competition was an important reason.

According to an internal staff memorandum, the NRC recognized that utilities could operate nuclear plants more safely if the industry produced a single standardized concept but that competition prevented this from happening (Heltemes, 1979). Not much could be done to alter the situation. According to the OTA (1981a), limiting the sector to a single standardized concept would reduce manufacturers and architect-engineers to mere suppliers of components and engineering services. If the sector abandoned the boiling water reactor, its manufacturer, General Electric, would be eliminated. If the sector chose to drop the pressurized concept, Westinghouse, Combustion Engineering, and Babcock and Wilcox would probably have been forced from the market. The costs of retooling and reeducation necessary to switch from one concept to another would surely prohibit manufacturers from remaining. Similarly, utilities could not band together and demand a single standardized concept. The laws guarding against the formation of trusts and collusion in the market would specifically prohibit such behavior.

Government policy makers would also have had a difficult time trying to force one concept or another on the sector because they lacked the institutional means for industrial restructuring. First, they did not have direct control over the allocation of credit and capital that could be used to entice utilities to buy one reactor concept rather than another. Second, any attempt the government made to reduce competition would probably have conflicted with antitrust laws. Third, under the 1954 Atomic Energy Act only the private corporations could develop most parts of the sector including the manufacture of nuclear plants. Hence, Congress prohibited the government from using either partial or full state ownership anywhere in the nuclear sector as a tool for standardizing reactor concepts. In short, state policy makers lacked the capacity to compel the sector to standardize at this level. The OTA (1981b:68) concluded that these institutional constraints in both the public and private realms posed substantial, if not insurmountable, barriers to this kind of standardization. Private competition and a state incapable of direct intervention were the two structural stumbling blocks.

Not only did competition among manufacturers prevent the standardization of plant *concepts* from becoming an agenda item receiving serious consideration, but it also constrained the subsequent search for standardized *designs*. With two plant concepts, the best anyone could hope for were two different designs, one for each concept. However, design-based competition among reactor manufacturers shattered those hopes as manufacturers continued to offer, and utilities continued to buy, a variety of different sized plants. This was not so much a problem of poor judgement or mismanagement on the parts of either the manufacturing or utility companies as it was a problem of institutional constraints. Manufacturers had to keep changing designs to survive competitively in a situation that required paying attention to short-term sales and profitability goals. Utilities could only choose from the selection available in the marketplace, and, at least initially, they lacked the technical expertise to realize the problems they would encounter if they continued to buy bigger, state-of-the-art designs. Antitrust statutes, preserving competition, further limited the possibilities of standardizing the architect-engineers' non-nuclear side of the plant. As a result, the industries did not have the institutional capacities to develop or follow a standardization plan that would effectively solve the sector's licensing and cost problems. Of course the AEC and NRC, lacking effective policy tools other than the promise of minimizing design changes and granting privileged position to standardized applications in the licensing review queue, faced institutional constraints of their own that prevented them from helping the private sector overcome these problems. The best that regulators could do was to help reduce the number of designs to a manageable handful and then have them specified more precisely than in the past. In short, the rigors of short-term competition, reinforced politically by antitrust law and a regulatory apparatus incapable of overcoming the obstacles involved, contradicted and undercut the attempt for far-sighted sectoral planning.

CHAPTER FOUR

Legitimation and the Reactor Safety Crisis

Philip Sporn, president of the American Electric Power Compnay, testified before the Joint Committee on Atomic Energy in 1968 that nuclear energy would suffer a serious set back if any incident impaired complete public confidence in the safety of nuclear power plants (JCAE, 1968:27). He had no idea that events unfolding at the AEC were already making his prediction come true. The imperatives of short-sighted economic competition helped subvert the nuclear sector's plans for standardization—plans designed to relieve problems jeopardizing the sector's economic viability. In conjunction with a conflicting set of policy goals institutionalized within the AEC, these imperatives also threatened the sector's *political* viability. The AEC faced an apparently irreconcilable policy dilemma that constrained the agency's ability to plan a reactor safety policy that was both politically and economically acceptable. On the one hand, in keeping with the interests of nuclear corporations and high-ranking government officials, the agency wanted to promote the sector's development as quickly as possible. On the other hand, it also had an obligation to protect the public's safety. When it became clear that the AEC allowed its interest in immediate development to undermine the planning necessary for ensuring that reactors were built and operated safely, both the agency and the sector suffered a massive legitimation crisis.

In the early 1970s many individuals and groups accused the AEC of licensing commercial nuclear plants without being sure that the safety systems in those plants could prevent catastrophic accidents. The ensuing controversy had extensive effects. Antinuclear activity escalated dramatically, reaching a new level of struggle and public intervention into the policy process that continued into the 1980s. Several observers have argued that this caused extended licensing delays and expensive regulatory changes (e.g., Bupp et al., 1975; Montgomery and Quirk, 1978; U.S. House, 1981b:3; Ward, 1977:124). In an attempt to resolve the crisis, AEC officials convened the longest rule-making hearings in the government's history, overhauled their entire safety research program, and watched as Congress abolished their agency.[1]

These events developed in four stages. First, a legitimation problem began to fester *within* the AEC as its technical staff (scientists and technical experts) started to doubt the integrity of the safety policy decisions the agency's administrative managers and their bureaucratic staff were making. Second, that problem erupted into a full-blown legitimation crisis as members of the technical staff began to struggle against current safety policy by posing alternative policy-making criteria to those their administrative superiors were using. Third, when publicity exposed the internal crisis, public doubts and a new legitimation problem developed *outside* the agency. Finally, this triggered an external legitimation crisis as antinuclear groups increased their opposition to current policy and tried to impose alternative policies and policy-making criteria on the AEC.[2]

THE INTERNAL LEGITIMATION PROBLEM DEVELOPS

During the late 1950s and early 1960s, reactor manufacturers and the federal government realized that unanticipated cost increases were undermining initial attempts to sell nuclear plants to utilities (AEC, 1967:4–5; JCAE, 1958:3–7). Manufacturers and utilities took two steps to promote commercial acceptance and cut costs. First, to gain economies of scale reactor manufacturers started offering plants

[1] The point of this chapter is not to provide a history of the antinuclear movement. That has been done elsewhere at great length (e.g., Barkan, 1979; Barkenbus, 1984; Camilleri, 1984; Campbell, 1982; Ebbin and Kasper, 1974; Kitschelt, 1986; Lewis, 1972; Mitchell, 1981; Nelkin and Pollak, 1981a).

[2] I have discussed the conceptual distinction between legitimation problems and crises, and the theoretical implications of this story for theories of political legitimation, especially Weber's (1978) ideas on internal legitimation crises, elsewhere (Campbell, 1987). Here it is important to understand that a legitimation problem develops when individuals subject to legitimate political domination, domination based on their voluntary consent to the rule of others, begin to question *cognitively* the authority of their superiors. However, a legitimation crisis develops only when those individuals begin to pose alternatives *actively* to that authority. These distinctions are conceptually discrete, but are far more continuous at the empirical level.

four and five times larger than those sold previously. Between 1962 and 1972 the mean generating capacity per reactor sold skyrocketed from 313 to 1,141 megawatts (Bupp and Derian, 1978:73). Until 1974 manufacturers felt that the size and, therefore, the cost efficiency of their reactors determined their competitive position in the market to a great extent. Those securing the most sales at any time were those offering the largest models (Hertsgaard, 1983:63). However, manufacturers sold larger plants not just to win business away from each other, but also to convince utilities to buy nuclear rather than coal-fired plants, nuclear power's biggest competitor (Gandara, 1977:58–59). Economies of scale appeared to be much greater for nuclear plants than they were for coal-fired plants, an important selling point because nuclear plants were more expensive to build (AEC, 1962a:11; 1962b:51). Second, economics also inspired utilities to try building nuclear plants closer to their metropolitan service areas. Utilities wanted to reduce the costs of electricity transmission—costs of about $250,000 per mile (Rolph, 1979:60). Siting a plant four miles instead of twenty miles out of town meant saving about $4 million. According to a member of the Advisory Committee on Reactor Safeguards, a panel of AEC scientists and engineers that reviewed and made recommendations on all reactor license applications, utility pressure for less remote siting increased significantly during the early 1960s. In the interests of safety, the advisory committee approved many of these applications on the condition that manufacturers and utilities would counterbalance siting closer to cities with improved reactor safety systems (Okrent, 1981:20).

The advisory committee recognized that selling bigger plants had facilitated commercialization, but at a price. Bigger plants meant hotter, more radioactive reactor cores and, therefore, greater danger in the event of an accident. Isolated siting had been a key safety precaution for the earlier plants. Now that utilities wanted to build plants closer to cities, engineered safety features became more important (Lawson, 1968:1). The danger was particularly acute for loss-of-coolant accidents. The boiling and pressurized water reactors sold in the United States needed water circulating constantly over the reactor core to prevent it from getting too hot. If the cooling system failed, the core could overheat to several thousand degrees Fahrenheit, triggering a core meltdown where the reactor fuel burned through the bottom of the plant into the earth below. If it came into contact with groundwater or any other liquid along the way, the interaction would create steam that could explode up through the top of the plant spewing radioactivity across the surrounding area (Hendrie,

1976:673; Perrow, 1984:40–43). Manufacturers installed emergency core cooling systems on the new large reactors to prevent such a catastrophe in case the primary cooling system failed. However, according to an AEC report, the agency was not sure how well these emergency systems worked (AEC, 1967:27).

The AEC was on the horns of a dilemma. On the one hand, policy makers wanted to maintain an environment conducive to the sector's immediate expansion. To reduce the costs of nuclear power, they allowed utilities to build larger reactors closer to cities. On the other hand, this policy posed an increased risk to public safety. Hence, improved safety systems were necessary. To the extent that new systems also increased plant costs at a time when the competition between nuclear and coal was fierce, the two policies conflicted with each other. However, if the AEC did not take appropriate steps to guarantee the public's safety, it would create a situation that, if exposed, could undermine its external legitimacy. In fact, the 1954 Atomic Energy Act directed the agency to simultaneously facilitate the sector's commercial success and protect the public from the dangers of nuclear power. As a result, the act institutionalized those contradictory policy goals.

By 1965 part of the AEC's regulatory staff became concerned that the agency should proceed more cautiously and pay more attention to safety research. The head of the Advisory Committee on Reactor Safeguards wrote to the AEC's chair warning him of the dangers associated with scaling up reactors without either sufficient operating experience or experimental data to verify that safety systems were adequate for the new plants. In that letter he urged the AEC to initiate a research program to test and improve reactor emergency core cooling systems (JCAE, 1967:119). The advisory committee was worried about approving applications for two, large, centrally located reactors, both in the 800 megawatt range, without enough data to confirm the effectiveness of their safety systems.

According to a member of the advisory committee at the time, the industry pressured the AEC not to delay construction of those plants (Okrent, 1981:114). The commission openly admitted its sensitivity to the problems of delays stemming from the regulatory process (Mann, 1966:296). Waiting for the requested safety research to be finished would exacerbate those delays and increase construction costs at a time when the sector was just beginning to achieve commercial success. Not wanting to stunt the sector's growth, the AEC's chairperson persuaded the advisory committee to approve the new applications if the reactor manufacturers would agree to improve the emergency cooling systems on those plants and if the AEC would accelerate its emergency cooling system research. Furthermore, he convinced the advisory committee not to send a formal letter to the AEC advising that more stringent emergency cooling criteria be adopted. He was concerned that such a letter would generate public relations problems for the sector and undercut the current ordering boom. Instead, he offered to form a special task force to study the acceptability of current emergency cooling system designs. The advisory committee acquiesced to both requests and approved the plants in 1966 (Okrent, 1981:chap. 8).

This was not the only time the AEC tried to quiet the safety controversy brewing within its ranks. In addition to the advisory committee, other members of the AEC's technical staff were worried about the adequacy of emergency cooling systems. In 1965 a report from one of the AEC's national laboratories urged a massive testing program to confirm computer models predicting emergency cooling system performance on large reactors (Bright et al., 1965). AEC officials classified the report immediately and kept it under wraps until 1974 (Webb, 1976:108). A year earlier the agency suppressed and shunned a similar recommendation by an internal staff study group (Primack, 1974).

In short, members of the regulatory staff were concerned over the safety issue and were agitating for corroboration of the emergency cooling system criteria (Rolph, 1979:86). Technical staff members were upset that no one could accurately determine the safety of the new larger reactors without further safety research. They felt that the technical merits of current safety criteria, upon which the AEC based its licensing policy, should be reviewed. If the criteria were found deficient, they wanted the agency to revise them. A legitimation problem had developed within the agency over the means used to make safety and licensing policy. The early signs of an internal legitimation crisis were emerging as staff members started posing alternative approaches to the safety research problem. Administrators were anxious that internal dissent might jeopardize the AEC's credibility. They tried to prevent that from happening. Despite these concerns, the licensing of plants continued.

THE INTERNAL LEGITIMATION CRISIS DEVELOPS

The problem of insufficient data persisted for several reasons and increased the legitimation crisis in the AEC. First, the agency decided to bolster the nuclear sector's commercial future in 1962 by developing a more advanced reactor. This was an effort to improve the economics of nuclear power and, therefore, its advantage relative to coal by increasing reactor efficiency and reducing operating costs. Officials chose the fast breeder reactor concept for development (AEC, 1962a; JCAE, 1958).[3] Milton Shaw, the head of the AEC's Division of Reactor Development and Technology, reported that by 1965 "the introduction of safe, reliable, economic breeder reactor plants into the utility environment became the Commission's highest priority reactor development program" (Shaw, 1968:178).

This had a major impact on the safety research program for conventional reactors. The Reactor Development and Technology Division managed both reactor development and safety research. Because they emphasized the need for breeder development and because the federal government's Budget Bureau was pressuring the AEC to reduce research into conventional reactors now that they were believed to have achieved commercial acceptability, officials minimized safety research budgets (Del Sesto, 1979:97–100; Okrent, 1981:313; Rolph, 1979:70). Despite the clear need, safety research became a low priority at the division. After 1965 safety research budgets declined in proportion to breeder development funds (Table 4.1). The safety budget, about 70 percent as large as the breeder budget in 1965, shrank to only 16 percent by 1974. This was mainly due to the increase in funding for breeder research from about 1 percent of total AEC expenditures in 1965 to over 9 percent by 1974 while safety research budgets remained relatively stable in proportion to overall AEC spending.

A second reason for the delay in acquiring safety system data involved management of the research itself. In response to recommendations by the AEC's long-awaited task force report, initiated earlier to appease the Advisory Committee on Reactor Safeguards, the AEC launched a major research project to corroborate emergency cooling system criteria. The U.S. General Accounting Office (1976a:10) reported later that it was also a response to the corporations' worrying that nonverified emergency system codes were creating expensive licensing delays.[4] However, the project's development

---

[3] The breeder reactor's appeal was that it could burn fuel much more efficiently than conventional reactors. Theoretically, it could actually produce more fuel than it consumed, hence the name breeder. Advocates of nuclear power were quick to point out that it would provide an extremely inexpensive source of fuel, a major advantage in the competition with coal.

[4] The Atomic Industrial Forum and reactor manufacturers complained to Milton

Table 4.1. AEC budgets for fast breeder reactor development and safety research and development, 1965–1974 (in thousands of dollars)

Year	Total AEC Budget	Fast Breeder Reactor		Safety R&D		
		Budget	Budget as % of Total Budget	Budget	Budget as % of Total Budget	Budget as % of Breeder Budget
1965	2,624,966	33,116	1.2	23,225	0.9	71
1966	2,402,925	41,950	1.7	24,942	1.0	59
1967	2,263,749	54,596	2.4	32,878	1.4	59
1968	2,466,588	81,099	3.3	37,733	1.5	48
1969	2,450,360	97,898	4.0	38,381	1.6	38
1970	2,454,970	104,055	4.2	43,054	1.8	42
1971	2,274,661	105,840	4.5	40,261	1.8	38
1972	2,392,073	138,801	5.8	49,056	2.0	38
1973	2,393,144	160,965[a]	6.6	57,390	2.3	36
1974	2,307,465	211,884[a]	9.1	33,493	1.4	16

[a] Includes only budgets for the liquid metal fast breeder reactor. Previous years also included budgets for other advanced types of breeder reactors. All those involved in this category were high-gain breeders.

SOURCES: AEC (Financial Reports, 1966–74, 1975).

was a clumsy affair and results were slow to materialize. Milton Shaw, the project's director, was convinced that careful quality assurance was just as important as engineered safety features in ensuring reactor safety.[5] Others on the AEC agreed, but also recognized that quality assurance could improve plant reliability and, therefore, profitability for utilities. Again, this was a very important consideration because the competition between nuclear and coal was intense (Liberman, 1966:308; JCAE, 1967:57). As a result, the project became a huge showcase for proving the possibility of meticulous quality assurance techniques (Gillette, 1972c; AEC, 1970a:ii).

The obsession with quality assurance in the AEC's major emergency cooling system test, the loss-of-fluid test, undermined other projects also designed to produce the necessary data. According to scientists at the AEC's Oak Ridge National Laboratory, where much of the agency's safety research was conducted, as budgets for the test became inflated out of the concern with quality assurance, they cut deeply into other important safety tests (Gillette, 1972c:870). The loss-of-fluid test consumed 40 percent of the entire AEC safety budget by 1973, almost twice as much as it had in 1966 just before officials marked it as a major safety research project (Table 4.2). By 1969 the Advisory Committee on Reactor Safeguards complained to the Joint Committee on Atomic Energy about the drain the test and its showcase effect were having on other crucial safety projects (JCAE, 1974b:43).

The showcase idea and the general problems of developing a massive research project led to extensive scheduling delays (GAO, 1976a:chap. 3; JCAE, 1974a:38; 1974c:458). By 1969 the AEC admitted that its emergency cooling system project, originally scheduled for completion in the late 1960s, would only begin initial tests sometime during the middle of the next decade (AEC, 1970b:102). Interests in

---

Shaw in 1967 that in the absence of appropriate safety data and, therefore, clearly defined safety standards, the regulatory staff was imposing excessively conservative safety requirements on plants. They felt this created an unpredictable licensing process that undermined utility efforts to plan nuclear systems, increased the amount of time required to bring plants on line, and led to higher plant costs. Reactor manufacturers felt that safety research should focus on confirming the codes and reliability of safety systems such as the emergency cooling system. They were convinced that the results would persuade the regulatory staff to stabilize or ease safety criteria. This would expedite licensing accordingly (JCAE, 1967:436). The Joint Committee on Atomic Energy also recognized the problem and told the AEC that whatever could be reasonably done to streamline matters ought to be done (JCAE 1967:37).

[5] According to officials at the Oak Ridge National Laboratory, resistance by General Electric and Westinghouse, the nation's two largest reactor manufacturers, in adhering to rigid quality assurance techniques was partially to blame for Milton Shaw's obsession with demonstrating the virtues of quality assurance (Gillette, 1972c:870).

Table 4.2. Annual loss-of-fluid test (LOFT) budget as percentage of total annual AEC safety research and development budget, 1965–1974 (in thousands of dollars)

Year	Total LOFT Expenditures	Total AEC Safety R&D Budget	Percentage of Total AEC Safety R&D Budget Spent on Loft
1965	4,393	23,225	19
1966	6,102	24,942	24
1967	10,272	32,878	31
1968	13,745	37,733	37
1969	14,910	38,381	38
1970	13,171	43,054	30
1971	12,714	40,261	31
1972	16,477	49,056	33
1973	23,420	57,390	40
1974	23,272	33,493	71

SOURCES: AEC (*Financial Reports,* 1966–74) and NRC (1977a).

pushing the breeder and demonstrating the economic advantages of meticulous quality assurance caused much of the delay. According to personnel involved with the program, timeliness was clearly a distant secondary priority (GAO, 1976a:25). The anticipated data were still years away from being available.

There was a third reason why acceptable data were not in hand. Following commercial acceptance of the light water reactor and plans to develop the breeder, Congress, the federal Budget Office, and nonnuclear utilities convinced the AEC to leave a lot of the conventional reactor safety research to the private sector. The commission was already subcontracting many important safety research programs to the manufacturers through its national laboratories, but stepped up that program in 1970, exacerbating an already obvious conflict of interest (GAO, 1976a:37–38). The AEC was asking corporations to provide data that might eventually lead to tougher regulations and higher construction costs—something the corporations wanted to avoid. As early as 1968 the Joint Committee on Atomic Energy recognized that manufacturers were reluctant to approach the agency with safety improvements because they feared regulators would order them to add the new features to plants, thus increasing costs (Okrent, 1981:184). There was no reason to expect that things would be different now.

Nevertheless, given the absence of independently generated data from the national laboratories, the regulatory staff had little choice but to use the manufacturers' results. According to the director of safety programs at the Oak Ridge National Laboratory, by 1971 the regulatory staff at the AEC had to rely heavily on data provided by the same corporations they were supposed to regulate. Both Oak Ridge and the Advisory Committee on Reactor Safeguards complained that this seriously compromised the AEC's ability to evaluate reactor safety (Cottrell, 1974:49; Ford and Kendall, 1975:19; Okrent, 1981:184), especially with regard to the computer codes designed to predict emergency cooling system performance. In short, the AEC's technical staff questioned the legitimacy of policy made in what they considered to be a scientifically unacceptable manner. The AEC's research community viewed this situation with alarm (JCAE, 1974c:278).

The legitimation crisis grew as fears developed within the AEC and national laboratories that emergency cooling systems were not as effective as the manufacturers and utilities claimed. A 1970 AEC staff report argued that much work was still urgently needed to demonstrate the effectiveness of emergency cooling systems (AEC, 1970a). The Oak Ridge laboratory had discovered unforseen technical problems that could prevent adequate emergency cooling in the event of a loss-of-coolant accident. Staff scientists occasionally published these and other disparaging results in *Nuclear Safety,* an Oak Ridge technical journal available to the public (e.g., Rittenhouse, 1971). Experts at the national laboratory in Idaho Falls, Idaho, began to wonder if some AEC experiments were too small to model accident sequences accurately in large reactors (Bright, 1971). They also suspected that the reactor manufacturers had distorted their research results about emergency cooling systems either out of incompetence or willful deception (Ford, 1982:106). Finally, instead of forcing emergency coolant into the reactor core as intended, an important loss-of-coolant simulation pumped the water out of the original rupture, leaving the core completely exposed (Primack and von Hippel, 1974a). If this had happened at a real reactor, a meltdown would have occurred.

In April 1971 members of the Idaho laboratory circulated a report internally concluding that good data simply did not exist for evaluating emergency cooling system capabilities. This prompted two AEC task force members evaluating the available data to issue a memorandum stating that the system's performance could not be defined with sufficient assurance to provide a clear basis for licensing (Ford, 1982:108). Now, in the absence of adequate confirmatory data with which to make technically informed licensing decisions, the staff was beginning to oppose not just research policy but also licensing policy. The legitimation crisis was widening.

Milton Shaw moved to stifle the emergence of any other evidence that might fuel the crisis. According to officials in the national labora-tories, administrators slashed budgets for loss-of-coolant tests and related research. They suppressed the Idaho report and censored other damaging research reports. Some of the most critical research results bearing directly on emergency cooling systems were never passed on to the licensing staff at all. The idea was to contain the conflict within the AEC's research community (Ford, 1982:chap. 2; Gillette, 1972b; 1972a).

To summarize, the 1960s were times of increasing concern within the AEC over the direction and scope of safety research policy. A legitimation problem developed as technical groups within the AEC's staff began to suspect that research was inadequate to justify the further licensing of large-scale commercial reactors. That problem escalated into a crisis when staff members objected within the agency and in scientific publications to the technical legitimacy of research and licensing policies. Administrators, fearing the development of external legitimation problems, tried to silence that opposition.

The direction of safety research policy and, therefore, the subse-quent lack of confirmatory data stemmed from the AEC's concern with promoting the nuclear sector's growth. The policy had deep institutional roots. Reactor manufacturers, facing stiff competition in the short-term from both each other and coal plants, pushed for larger, more centrally located nuclear stations, which raised safety concerns with the AEC technical staff. This created the possibility of licensing delays, regulatory changes, and further cost increases. To avoid these economic problems, the AEC tried limiting the number of regulatory obstacles to the sector's development. In particular, the AEC continued licensing despite the blatant absence of crucial safety data. By law the AEC was supposed not only to promote development but also to ensure the public's health and safety. The conflict between AEC administrators and technical staff reflected those contradictory yet institutionalized policy imperatives. However, under pressure from those interested in the sector's immediate growth, such as the manufacturers, utilities, and the Joint Committee on Atomic Energy, the commission chose to favor a policy promoting the sector's de-velopment rather than one granting highest priority to the more distant goal of ensuring reactor safety. For example, it favored breeder research over safety research. As a result, a legitimation crisis developed within the AEC.

It is important to recognize two things. First, technical staff mem-bers did not object either to the development of nuclear power or to the licensing of nuclear plants per se. They just opposed the criteria or *means* regulators used to make safety and licensing decisions. Perhaps some of them suspected that officials neglected safety considerations because the AEC was trying to reconcile its dual mandate. However, I have no evidence that this was necessarily so. Second, whether they realized it or not, the agency's contradictory policy *goals*, protecting public safety and facilitating the development of a profitable nuclear sector, caused the internal legitimation crisis over policy-making means. The cover-ups, censorship, and other attempts to ignore the technical staff's advice indicate that administrators were willing to favor one policy goal, immediate development, at the expense of another, securing important information through a prolonged safety research program.

THE EXTERNAL LEGITIMATION PROBLEM DEVELOPS

Publicity about the escalating internal crisis contributed to the breakdown of the AEC's legitimation externally. In the late 1960s and early 1970s the Union of Concerned Scientists, an independent group of scientists concerned with the dangers of nuclear power, started asking questions about emergency cooling systems at AEC licensing hearings. The AEC convened these hearings locally as part of the construction-permit and operating-license reviews to provide citizens and their representatives a chance to express concerns about the plant under consideration. They raised the issue in virtually all of these hearings by 1972 (Rolph, 1979:114). According to those involved from the Union of Concerned Scientists, information published by members of the AEC technical staff in *Nuclear Safety*, indicating that the safety system might not be effective, first provoked their concern (Ford, 1982:111–15). Later, members of the Oak Ridge technical staff leaked information about cooling system problems to the group both anonymously and in secret meetings, knowing that the Union of Concerned Scientists would publicize the situation, oppose continued licensing on those grounds, and try to get improved safety criteria implemented. According to one activist involved at the time and interviewed for this study, when people from the Union of Concerned Scientists visited Oak Ridge to gather more information, members of the technical staff there told them specifically about the dissent within the AEC.

The timing here is important. When satisfaction was not forthcoming from within the agency, the initial response of technical staff members was to alert the outside scientific community by engaging in scientific debate. They published articles in *Nuclear Safety* trying to raise concerns among their colleagues and arguing the technical and scientific merits of their case in an explicitly scientific forum—an extension of the strategy they had pursued earlier within the agency. Only later did they recognize that a *scientific* confrontation was not enough and that an overtly political one was necessary. At that point they began leaking information to sources not just scientifically astute but, more important, adept at confronting the agency *politically*. They had changed strategies and were now pursuing their objectives in an explicitly political manner, an indication that they realized political pressure rather than somewhat more objective scientific criteria was guiding AEC licensing and safety research policy. Hence, they transformed what began as a scientific debate over a set of technical differences into an attempt to initiate a political confrontation. The idea now was to provide someone with the technical weapons necessary to wage a successful political battle from the outside.[6] In the process, the staff's goals had subtly shifted from raising issues through proper channels within the agency to deliberately politicizing them externally.

The Union of Concerned Scientists began publishing a series of reports in July 1971 revealing that experimental data were lacking, that some tests failed to confirm the adequacy of emergency cooling systems, and that administrators had suppressed dissent within the AEC and national laboratories (e.g., Forbes et al., 1971; 1972). With this information members of the organization leveled a scathing attack on the AEC's recently promulgated Interim Acceptance Criteria for emergency core cooling systems (Ford et al., 1972). They substantiated their criticisms with evidence from personnel at the AEC's national laboratories and several government documents (Ford and Kendall, 1972). The AEC issued the new, more conservative criteria in June 1971 in an attempt to defuse concerns within its research community and among interveners who were using the issue as an effective inroad to licensing hearings (Cottrell, 1974:38).

From the commission's point of view, the situation was getting out of hand. According to the deputy director of the AEC's Directorate of Licensing, the AEC convened special rule-making hearings to address the new criteria in a sweeping effort to absolve the local licensing

---

[6]This was not an unusual strategy. Expertise is often used as a political weapon in debates in which the management of technology and science is at issue. Nelkin (1984:17) and Primack and von Hippel (1974b) discuss this at length.

boards of further delays associated with the issue (JCAE, 1974b:527). They lasted over a year and reconfirmed the allegations made previously about the AEC. Under cross-examination by members of the Union of Concerned Scientists, AEC technical staff revealed even more information damaging to the credibility of emergency cooling systems and the commission policy itself. They exposed the history of censorship, cancelled research, inadequate data, and internal dissent in detail (Ford, 1982). Prompted by these events, the Joint Committee on Atomic Energy held its own investigation into reactor safety. Again AEC experts pointed the incriminating finger at the AEC and its emergency cooling system programs (JCAE, 1974c). The hearings and the controversies received lots of publicity. For example, the *New York Times* ran twenty-seven articles directly related to the reactor safety controversy between 1972 and 1973.

THE EXTERNAL LEGITIMATION CRISIS DEVELOPS

Public recognition of the problem soon translated into action. Even before the AEC hearings were finished, antinuclear forces redoubled their political efforts to guard the public from what they perceived as the dangers of nuclear power. In May 1973 Ralph Nader and a major environmental group sued the AEC in an attempt to shut down two-thirds of the nation's operating reactors charging that the utilities had built them and the agency had licensed them without adequate emergency cooling system standards. Nader also announced plans for suits against several specific plants for similar reasons and a massive lobbying campaign against the sector (Barfield, 1973). Later, Dixie Lee Ray, the AEC's new chairperson, reported that Nader's congressional lobbying effort was so successful that even Senator John Pastore of Rhode Island, head of the Joint Committee on Atomic Energy and an avid nuclear advocate in Congress, did nothing to push pronuclear legislation because of the extreme pressure constituents placed on him (Burn, 1978:91).

Within a year Dixie Lee Ray complained to the joint committee that interveners were challenging several AEC licensing decisions in federal courts by arguing that the Interim Acceptance Criteria were inadequate (JCAE, 1974c:27). Opposition at licensing hearings also increased. According to the Federal Energy Administration (1974:3.7–4) and the AEC (1974d:14), citizens, worried about reactor safety, were having their greatest impact at licensing hearings where they created serious licensing delays. They caused most of these delays through 1976 by raising questions about emergency safety, core cooling, and major reactor accidents (Cohen, 1979a).[7]

Perhaps the most important outgrowth of the emergency cooling system controversy for the antinuclear movement was the qualitative change it generated in the movement itself. It caused a massive transformation of public consciousness. One of the participants from the Union of Concerned Scientists told me that for the first time the devastating possibilities of a reactor meltdown received public attention in a politically dramatic way. The director of another antinuclear organization reported during an interview with me that the episode clearly demonstrated how the AEC was acting as part of a "good old boys" network, rather than as a scientifically objective and politically neutral regulator. Antinuclear groups recognized that the issue involved more than just the adequacy of safety policy-making criteria as it had during the internal crisis. It was also a matter of overall policy goals. They saw that there was a conflict between the agency's interests in promoting the industry's development and protecting the public's safety, and that the conflict over safety criteria was a manifestation of that deeper contradiciton. Undoubtedly, revelations of AEC cover-ups, designed to keep the internal conflict over contradictory policy means quiet and out of public view, underscored this more fundamental contradiction between the policy goals of safety and economic growth, and fueled the crisis.

As a result, groups began to organize and cooperate together at the local, state, and national levels in new and innovative ways (Hertsgaard, 1983:70). Most notably, Ralph Nader formed the Critical Mass organization, which held major rallies and strategy sessions in 1974 and 1975 attracting representatives from groups around the nation. The focus was not so much on the technical aspects of nuclear power as it had been previously, but on the political strategies required to slow or halt the sector's growth. This politicization marked a turning point in the movement's history and an upswing in its level of activity (Nelkin and Fallows, 1978:285). Furthermore, the goals of the movement were different from those of the AEC's dissenting staff

7 In retrospect, the extent to which citizen interventions have actually caused the majority of licensing delays and cost increases is subject to debate (cf. Bupp, 1981; Bupp et al., 1975; Komanoff, 1981; Montgomery and Quirk, 1978; AEC, 1974d; GAO, 1977a). However, both the AEC and the nuclear industries believed at the time that interventions were part of the problem. They took steps to rectify the situation. In 1971 legislators in Congress introduced a bill that would have limited public intervention at local hearings (Lewis, 1972:259–67). Congress heard similar proposals throughout the 1970s, but failed to enact any of them (e.g., U.S. House, 1978).

members. Nader's organization adopted much more extreme aims than did the AEC dissenters. Nader's people wanted to shut down *operating* reactors. Dissenters in the AEC only wanted to delay further licensing long enough to examine and, if necessary, adjust the safety criteria.

The stimulus for the activists' reinvigorated activities, Nader said, was the reactor safety issue (*Energy User's Report*, 1974d:A13). A stream of legislative and electoral proposals appeared at all levels of government calling for a moratorium on further nuclear expansion until the technical problems were resolved (*Energy User's Report*, 1974b). By late 1975 legislators raised the issue in both houses of Congress. For example, twenty members from the House of Representatives sponsored a bill in 1975 calling for a five-year suspension of licensing for all nuclear plants until the OTA could study the unresolved safety problems (*Energy User's Report*, 1975b). There were antinuclear bills pending in twenty-eight states (Burn, 1978:91). A vice-president from Stone and Webster, an architect-engineering firm, told the Atomic Industrial Forum in 1974 that "the level of opposition has increased enormously during the last year, . . . there are now a great number of organizations and individuals whose full time efforts are directed toward convincing the public that nuclear power plants constitute a clear and present danger to the health and safety . . . of the population" (*Energy User's Report*, 1974a:A3).

I do not mean to suggest that the development of the internal legitimation crisis over reactor safety was solely responsible for the entire antinuclear mobilization. The antinuclear movement had complex historical roots including, among other things, the development of the environmental and antiwar movements during the 1960s, and several other important technical controversies about nuclear power raised at various times during the previous decade (see note 1). What I am suggesting is that this was the most serious legitimation crisis the AEC had ever experienced either internally or externally. Furthermore, the emergency safety system crisis galvanized the antinuclear movement, pushing it to new, unprecedented levels of action. The transformation of the internal crisis into an external one fanned a situation that had been smoldering for years. As a result, it finally burst into political flames.

PUBLIC CONFIDENCE DETERIORATES

The crisis had a dramatic effect on public confidence. As noted earlier, survey data collected and analyzed by the Battelle Human

Affairs Research Center indicate that although public support for nuclear power in general was positive and constant until the accident at Three Mile Island in 1979, people had begun to express opposition to the idea of actually living near a reactor much earlier. Opposition to the idea of living near a nuclear plant climbed from 28 percent to 45 percent between 1973 and 1978 at a steady pace (Figure 4.1). According to Battelle researchers, the increased salience of nuclear safety as a public issue after 1970 contributed to that increase (Melber et al., 1977:154; Rankin et al., 1981). These data are enlightening. Attitudes about nearby plants are just as important as those about nuclear power in general. After all, it is local concern that often turns into licensing interventions when utilities propose nuclear projects for an area.

Events surrounding the emergency cooling system crisis were partially responsible for these attitude changes. By 1975 55 percent of those who opposed nuclear power in general reported that they did so because they felt reactors were simply not safe enough. Although that percentage declined until 1979, reactor safety remained the single most frequent complaint these people had about nuclear power (Rankin et al., 1981:95). Furthermore, these concerns were three to four times more influential in affecting their attitudes about building nuclear plants nearby than any others (Rankin et al., 1981:96–104). Finally, the public's concern with reactor safety was positively related to an absence of confidence in both the government and the experts' abilities to handle the technology safely. According to Battelle, 58 percent of the public believed in the government's ability to manage nuclear power safely in 1977, and the proportion declined gradually to 42 percent by 1980. The percentage having confidence in the abilities of scientists and engineers dropped from 64 to 54 during the same period. Both trends began *before* the accident at Three Mile Island (Rankin et al., 1981:113–15). Comparable data are not available for the period before 1977, but the U.S. Federal Energy Administration (1974:IX20–23) reported that by 1974 public acceptance of nuclear power had become a serious problem for the sector not only because the public felt that reactors were dangerous but also because they suspected corporate and government decision makers were not concerned enough with safety.

THE INSTITUTIONAL ROOTS OF THE CRISIS

The AEC had suffered both an internal and an external legitimation crisis. Internally the crisis developed out of a contradiction

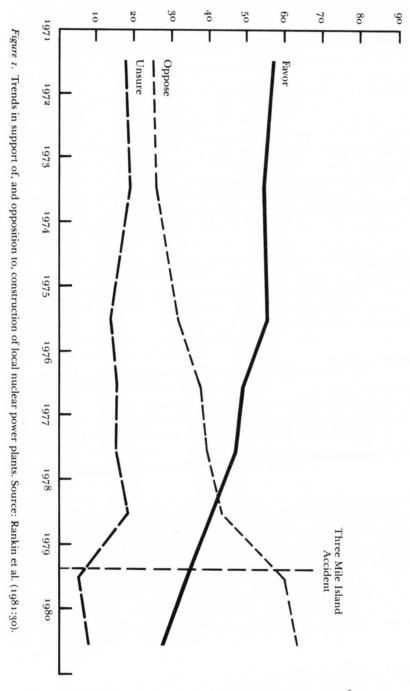

Percentage of Respondents

Favor

Oppose

Unsure

Three Mile Island
Accident

Figure 1. Trends in support of, and opposition to, construction of local nuclear power plants. Source: Rankin et al. (1981:30).

67

between the state's responsibility for maintaining a regulatory posture conducive to both the nuclear sector's growth and profitability on the one hand and, on the other, its duty to take appropriate steps to protect the public's health and safety. That contradiction became manifest in the struggle between top-level bureaucratic administrators pressing for the industry's rapid development and technical experts urging caution and a more thorough, far-sighted, and time-consuming approach to safety policy. Eventually, public recognition of that crisis created an external legitimation problem and crisis for the agency and the sector. The external crisis was simply the last in a series of four conceptually distinct stages.

In fact, it is impossible to empirically disentangle the link between internal legitimation crisis and external legitimation problem. The leaking of inside information to outside sources who would use the information to oppose AEC policy was the most severe manifestation of the internal crisis. This was a way for members of the AEC's technical staff actively to oppose the policy of their superiors and force consideration of alternative policy approaches when satisfaction was not forthcoming from within the agency. In other words, the final expression of the internal legitimation crisis was the deliberate creation of an external legitimation problem.

The development of both legitimation crises revolved around what David Dickson (1984:293–300) has called the tension between technocratic and democratic policy-making paradigms. The technocratic approach assumes that the government should not intervene into the economy unless there is overwhelming scientific evidence that it is necessary. It is a rationality that, justified by claims to scientific and technocratic expertise, obeys the demands and values of private capital rather than democratic interests. Democratic policy making assumes that it is better to be safe than sorry because the public's interests, rather than those of corporate elites, should receive top priority. Policy makers should intervene when they recognize a potential threat to the public interest even if the evidence justifying that action is not totally conclusive. The tension between technocratic and democratic paradigms directly reflects the more general institutional contradiction between the imperatives of capitalism and democracy discussed in chapter 2 to the extent that the technocratic view tends to grant pride of place to the pursuit of private economic growth while the democratic approach considers the public interest more important. Dickson and others (e.g., Nelkin, 1984:14; Primack and von Hippel, 1974b) have maintained that the power accruing to those controlling scientific and technical information can threaten democratic principles by reducing the public's role in policy making and creating an opportunity for the technocratic perspective to prevail. That is precisely what happened here and, once revealed publicly, precipitated the external breakdown of legitimacy. As a result, the tension between policy-making paradigms was the manifestation of a more fundamental institutional contradiction between capitalism and democracy.

The 1954 Atomic Energy Act, specifying the AEC's dual mandate, institutionalized the tensions between these two paradigms and between the different interests they represented. Ironically, members of the AEC's technical staff opposed the technocratic policy-making logic. Instead, they followed the democratic paradigm, advocating a conservative approach to the safety problem whereby the AEC would slow down licensing until they collected the necessary safety information. On the other hand, administrators and bureaucrats, not wanting to jeopardize the sector's continued development, adopted a technocratic approach, and, therefore, gave the safety issues secondary priority. They soft peddled the policy option that would have delayed licensing precisely because they believed the wait would jeopardize the sector's immediate economic viability. When disgruntled staff members revealed that choice to the public and, in effect, exposed the capitalism-democracy contradiction, the external legitimation crisis developed because people felt that the agency had not served the public interest. They questioned both the specific policy involved and the agency's mission.

That crisis was not simply the result of poor judgment by AEC officials. Those decisions had deep institutional roots. The law was ambiguous about which goal, promotion or safety, should receive top priority. This provided an opportunity for a select group of political and economic elites favoring the technocratic perspective to dominate policy making.[8] Furthermore, AEC administrators often made decisions like these in very insulated policy-making forums where elites favoring the sector's rapid development generally had privileged ac-

---

[8] I do not mean to imply that policy making involving scientific or technical issues is ever politically neutral. Even in areas like occupational health and safety or environmental protection, where legislative mandates are less ambiguous than they were here, politics plays the major role (e.g., Dickson, 1984; Nelkin, 1984; Primack and von Hippel, 1974b; Szasz, 1984). The point here is that in the AEC's case the institutional opportunity existed for policy makers virtually to ignore technical arguments counter to existing agency policy and justify their position on legal grounds if necessary. The decision to reduce safety research on conventional reactors at the AEC in favor of developing the breeder reactor was a good example.

cess.[9] Hence, it was even more likely, given the institutional structure of the policy process, that the goal of quick development, couched within a technocratic policy-making perspective, would receive top priority.[10] I am not denying that the AEC made some bad decisions that contributed to the legitimation crisis. For example, the cover-ups and suppression of research by agency administrators had significant effects. The point is that institutional and political conditions existing at the time created a situation in which it was likely that regulatory officials would choose the technocratic option despite internal pressure for a democratic policy approach favoring safety first. Even the decisions to promote the breeder at the expense of safety research and to delay key safety testing in the interests of demonstrating the advantages of quality assurance were at least partially linked to economic imperatives: increasing the efficiency and reducing the costs of nuclear plants relative to coal.

The government's attempts to regain legitimacy and correct its mistakes highlighted the conflicting policy goals and underlying paradigms. Congress abolished the AEC in 1974 under the Energy Reorganization Act, partially in an attempt to recoup regulatory legitimacy but also to coordinate all energy research during a national energy crisis. The NRC assumed responsibility for regulating all nuclear matters pertaining to the public health and safety, and the Energy Research and Development Administration had responsibility for nuclear research and development. This was a deliberate attempt to separate institutionally the AEC's two contradictory policy goals into different agencies. It was an effort to cleanse the agency of what outsiders perceived to be an obvious institutionalized conflict of interest (Mazuzan and Trask, 1979).

The AEC and NRC also revamped safety policy to stem the tide of criticism rising against regulators. First, in 1973 the AEC reduced the number of joint safety research projects it conducted with nuclear corporations, such as the reactor manufacturers, because agency officials wanted to prevent any further appearance of conflicting interests (GAO, 1976a:38). Second, officials issued new emergency core

9 Chapter 5 discusses in detail these insulated policy-making arenas and their effects on planning and the sector's development.

10 Primack and von Hippel (1974b) found the same pattern in several policy areas where scientific expertise informed policy making. When the public did not have the institutional opportunity to contribute either directly or through their representatives, decision making often boiled down to serving short-term bureaucratic or corporate interests. They reported many cases in which policy makers ignored advice from technical and science advisors because it was in their political or economic interests to do so.

70

cooling system criteria the same year. They were more conservative than the Interim Acceptance Criteria and included some of the technical recommendations critics had raised in the rule-making hearings, although the Union of Concerned Scientists, Ralph Nader, and independent experts from the American Physical Society and the Rand Corporation still complained that they were not conservative enough (Brand, 1975; Emshwiller, 1973:16). Third, the NRC mounted a massive safety research program to address many of the issues raised during the rule-making hearings, especially the need to confirm emergency cooling system criteria (Kouts, 1975). Half of the NRC's entire budget was devoted to safety research by 1977. Over 60 percent of that was poured directly into emergency cooling and loss-of-coolant accident work (NRC, 1978a:S1–3). However, the Advisory Committee on Reactor Safeguards reported in 1978 that the NRC put so much attention into this research that it was neglecting other safety problems, equally important, but not related to the emergency cooling crisis (NRC, 1978a:2–9). Why?

According to a government report on reactor safety research, there were several reasons for this. NRC officials wanted to reduce the public's concern that there was insufficient data on emergency cooling system problems. They also hoped that the research would ease both emergency system design requirements and manufacturing costs for the sector by showing that current emergency cooling system criteria were too conservative, something corporate representatives had wanted since 1967 (see note 4). Finally, administrators wanted the research program to confirm emergency cooling system performance capabilities so that reactors could run at higher temperatures, burn fuel more efficiently, and, therefore, operate more economically for utilities (GAO, 1976b:16). Moving into new research areas would have delayed achieving these goals. As a result, this research choked off funds to other important safety research areas for nearly a decade (Reactor Safety Research Review Group, 1981; NRC, 1980b:219). In short, by trying to satisfy the interests of both the public and the corporations in the nuclear sector, administrators continued to tread a very fine line between the promotion of capitalist growth and the public interest.

In a fascinating analysis of the development of capitalism, science, and technology, David Noble (1977) argues that science typically helps legitimize and reproduce the power of the dominant political and economic interests in society. He shows how science and science policy is often far from a value-free enterprise. To an extent, the case of the nuclear sector supports his analysis. The AEC and NRC used science to help achieve the nuclear sector's immediate economic interests. However, science was not simply a slave to capital. Others seeking an approach to reactor safety policy informed more by a democratic than a technocratic perspective also used science to their advantage. In this case science was a double-edged political sword. Activists forced the government to improve its regulatory and safety research policies, even if officials intended those changes primarily to restore public confidence in both the sector and the government's ability to regulate it effectively. Of course, administrators did not surrender entirely. They designed their relegitimation effort to favor the sector's development as much as possible. The irony was not that activists had succeeded at the expense of other important safety needs. Instead, it lay in the ability of government administrators to turn the activists' victory to the sector's advantage by developing a research program that would not just relegitimize but also help sustain nuclear power both politically and economically.

Chapter Five

The Politics of Nuclear Power, the Power of Nuclear Politics

The reactor safety crisis was a catalyst for the antinuclear movement in the United States. But what effects did the movement have on the nuclear sector? How did the policy process influence the movement and contribute to its effects? Observers agree that antinuclear groups gained access to that process and created political stalemates over key policy issues. Some argue that this contributed significantly to the nuclear sector's collapse (e.g., Bupp, 1979; Golay, 1981; Kemeny, 1980). Others disagree (Komanoff, 1981). Without an analysis of political institutions, it is difficult to answer these questions. In the United States the institutional arrangements governing the politics of nuclear power tended to limit the access of different groups to different policy arenas. In addition to raising new concerns about the appropriateness of specific policies, differential access also reinforced public doubts about the legitimacy of the policy process itself. Political struggle continued to erupt and flowed into policy arenas particularly conducive to obstructionist politics. This created policy stalemates, undermined planning, and dealt new blows to the sector's viability.

POLICY ARENAS

There is a long-standing debate among policy analysts about the nature of policy making in the United States. Many have argued that political authority has become more diffused among federal, state, and local governments, that administrative arrangements have grown more complex, that the number of opportunities for different groups

73

to participate in policy making have increased, and that the achievement of policy goals has become more difficult (e.g., Advisory Commission on Intergovernmental Relations, 1981; Reagan and Sanzone, 1981:4). As a result, they claim that competition among various agencies, policy-making elites, and special interest groups has often bred policy failure and a crisis of confidence in the government's ability to implement policy (Advisory Commission on Intergovernmental Relations, 1980; Pressman and Wildavsky, 1979; Walker, 1981:16). However, others have argued that political and corporate elites with privileged access to the most important policy-making arenas at least *formulate* policy consistently (Domhoff, 1983; 1978b; Lindblom, 1977; Mills, 1956). According to this second perspective laissez-faire attitudes among elites and a distrust of the government's ability to plan effectively undermine political planning in the United States more than excessive competition over policy or flaws in the structure of the planning process (Vogel, 1978).

Despite their differences, both sides recognize the importance of specifying the degree to which policy arenas are hierarchically centralized and insulated from public pressure. Furthermore, those arguing for the decentralized pluralist model tend to focus on policy implementation while those suggesting a centralized elite model tend to concentrate on policy formation. As a result, there is room for agreement about the amount of access that different groups have to the policy process and the effectiveness of the process in the United States. Policy formation often occurs in arenas relatively insulated from public pressure, while policy implementation, the interpretation and application of substantive policies developed elsewhere (Lundqvist, 1980:6), tends to occur in more decentralized, accessible forums (Domhoff, 1978a; O'Connor, 1973:chap. 3; Pressman and Wildavsky, 1979).[1] This does not mean that there is an ironclad separation between the policy formation and implementation processes. In some cases there are important reciprocal influences that create a seamless web connecting the two (Bardach, 1977; Pressman and Wildavsky, 1979:178). The problems of implementation may limit the range of policies policy makers choose from. Policy goals may shift as administrators struggle to find pragmatic ways to implement them. Nevertheless, it is useful to maintain the conceptual distinction while remaining sensitive to the interrelationships.

Not only different phases of the policy process but also different

---

[1] Theoretical support for this view is found in Alford (1975), Alford and Friedland (1985), Bachrach and Baratz (1962), Domhoff (1978b), and Lukes (1974).

kinds of policy making develop in different policy arenas. For example, policy makers often create programs designed to facilitate capital accumulation in relatively insulated agencies restricted to powerful political and corporate elites. The Federal Reserve Board and the Council of Economic Advisors are classic examples of insulated economic policy making (Lindberg, 1982b). On the other hand, policy makers develop programs with less explicitly economic goals, such as education and welfare policy, in more publicly accessible forums, which have the added benefit of legitimizing the state's activities (e.g., Habermas, 1973:36; Miliband, 1969:165; O'Connor, 1973:chap. 3; Offe, 1974:47; Poulantzas, 1978). As a result, the relative influence of different groups of political participants often varies according to the type of policy under consideration (Sahr, 1985:141).

We can make three important conceptual distinctions about the policy process which are useful for understanding how the antinuclear movement helped undermine the viability of the nuclear sector. First, specific policy arenas are either centralized and insulated from public pressure or decentralized and accessible. It is tempting to equate this *centralization* dimension with federal, state, and local levels of government where the federal level is the most centralized. However, this is not always the case. There are some important policy arenas that are decentralized, highly accessible to all interest groups, but within the jurisdiction of the federal government. One example is the Atomic Safety and Licensing Boards, which must approve individual construction permit and operating license applications for nuclear power plants before federal regulators may grant them. Other examples are the federal district and appellate courts. Second, different phases of the policy process and different types of policy are often *segregated* within the state apparatus. On the one hand, we can distinguish between the state's policy formation and implementation functions. On the other hand, we should differentiate between policies that address primarily economic or noneconomic goals. Most of the government's involvement with nuclear energy has involved the latter. The 1954 Atomic Energy Act instructed the AEC to protect the public health and safety and to encourage private corporations to commercialize the technology. Therefore, except for electric utility and antitrust regulation, the act prohibited the government from directly regulating capital formation within the nuclear sector.[2]

---

[2] The government does influence the sector's economic condition. Health, safety, environmental, and other kinds of regulation obviously have economic effects, although not always as intentional policy goals. Furthermore, the government provided economic support for the nuclear sector through research and development programs,

Third, the formation and implementation of different policies is often institutionally *fragmented* among any number of agencies or branches of government within a particular vertical level of centralization. The greater the number of agencies, the more fragmented decision making becomes within a level of government. Pressman and Wildavsky (1979:141) argued that the more fragmented the policy process is among either policy makers or implementors, the more opportunities there are for different decision makers to exercise control over the policy process. Such fragmentation, they claimed, tends to make the policy process less efficient and effective.[3]

POLICY FORMATION, IMPLEMENTATION, AND THE NUCLEAR STATE

Centralized administrative agencies and congressional committees at the federal level have historically had most responsibility for nuclear policy formation regardless of the desires of less centralized, state and local governments. The doctrine of federal preemption prevented lower governments from superseding the rules and regulations that the AEC, the NRC, and the Energy Research and Development Administration, later the Department of Energy, promulgated in promoting and regulating the nuclear sector. For example, a federal district court ruled in 1971 that Minnesota officials could not legally force utilities to keep radiation emissions around nuclear plants lower than the levels the AEC prescribed (Nader and Abbotts, 1979:338). The ruling reinforced the federal government's right to regulate the safety and health aspects of nuclear power without interference from state governments. In Congress, the Joint Committee on Atomic Energy enjoyed similar control over policy formation, serving as legislative and conference committees to both houses of Congress in all nuclear matters. It proposed, advocated, and then advised Congress on all nuclear legislation without interference from other congressional bodies. In practice the joint committee was usually a

---

insurance schemes, fuel subsidies, and uranium enrichment services. The point is that the government is not responsible for supervising or establishing policy concerning the sector's economic health per se except insofar as antitrust and electric utility regulation is concerned.

[3] This scheme is similar to that offered by Friedland, Piven, and Alford (1977), who suggest that power struggles determine the institutional structure of government by segregating different kinds of policy (economic and noneconomic) into different institutional arenas at either centralized or decentralized levels. My scheme offers two refinements. It adds a third dimension, fragmentation, and also recognizes that policy makers may segregate policy formation and implementation into different arenas.

strong ally of the AEC. For these reasons the joint committee and the AEC nearly monopolized the formation of nuclear energy policy during their lifetimes (e.g., Clarke, 1985; Hertsgaard, 1983:255; Lewis, 1972:chap. 2).

Policy-making autonomy began to crumble in 1974 with the organizational fracturing of the AEC. Afterward the NRC formed most regulatory policy and the Department of Energy was responsible for most development policy. Furthermore, the newly elected Democratic majority in Congress abolished the joint committee in 1977 because they felt that members of the committee were too close to the industry, had a terrible public image, and did not understand nuclear technology well enough (Ford, 1982:226). As a result, the NRC and the Department of Energy had to work with twenty-eight congressional committees and subcommittees that inherited various oversight responsibilities from the joint committee (Barkenbus, 1984). However, while policy formation became much more fragmented among these new agencies and congressional bodies, it remained centralized at the federal level and relatively autonomous from lower levels of government. This did not mean that state and local governments were completely powerless. They often shared regulatory responsibility with the federal government over the environmental and siting aspects of nuclear projects (OTA, 1984:151). They gained additional regulatory influence through new legislation, such as the 1982 Nuclear Waste Policy Act, that provided for state participation in the management of radioactive waste. Beginning in the mid-1970s state governments also learned to influence the nuclear policy process by exercising their right to regulate the economic behavior of utilities through public service commissions. However, much of this lower-level participation came during the implementation rather than the formation stages of nuclear policy.

Implementation has been much more decentralized than policy formation. The AEC's Atomic Safety and Licensing Boards routinely held public hearings that provided an opportunity for concerned citizens to raise questions, gather information, and express their views about nuclear projects under consideration for construction permits and operating licenses. Critics and advocates of nuclear power have also asked the courts to interpret policies as part of the implementation process. State, county, and municipal governments have had jurisdiction over parts of the implementation process, often with significant results. For example, Suffolk County in New York State blocked operation of the Shoreham nuclear station on Long Island, at least temporarily, by refusing to approve the utility's emergency evacuation plan, required to protect nearby residents in the event of a reactor accident (OTA, 1984:150). Massachusetts threatened to do the same thing to the Seabrook plant (Wald, 1986a). Furthermore, several state governments refused utilities permission to start new nuclear projects for economic reasons. Some city and state officials have tried to block implementation of federal law allowing utilities to use their highways for shipping nuclear waste.

In fact, control over implementation has given lower-level governments a limited amount of indirect, de facto influence over policy formation, another indication of the intimate relationship between these two phases of the policy process. For example, in the early 1970s Kansas officials fought implementation of the AEC's plan to locate a national radioactive waste storage system in their state. Eventually, their resistance helped convince the agency to abandon the plan and search for a new policy. Later, when the Department of Energy was developing another waste management plan, the Interagency Review Group on Nuclear Waste Management, an administrative committee established to help form the policy, recommended not granting states a chance to veto the storage sites chosen. The committee worried that any state selected would exercise its veto and block implementation if given the chance (Interagency Review Group on Nuclear Waste Management, 1979). In both cases concerns about implementation informed the policy formation process. As a result, policy formation was only *relatively* autonomous and centralized from lower-level government and interest-group pressures. Nevertheless, implementation was much more decentralized and accessible, a critical point that provides the key to understanding how the antinuclear movement influenced both the policy process and the fate of the nuclear sector.

Who Had Access and Why?

Corporate, political, and technocratic elites advocating nuclear power had privileged access to the most insulated and centralized interiors of the policy process. The intimate relationship between the nuclear corporations, AEC, NRC, and Joint Committee on Atomic Energy was well known (e.g., Green and Rosenthal, 1963:169; Hertsgaard, 1983; Metzger, 1972:29–30). Although criticism forced the AEC to start paying more attention to public concerns by the early 1970s, one observer wrote that "the AEC was [still] dominated by the demands of industry and was subservient to the will of the proindustry Joint Committee" (Lewis, 1972:259). That intimacy developed and continued into the 1980s through lobbying, advisory committees, and informal consultations between regulators and corporations about proposed regulations, licensing, and other policy matters. For example, according to one NRC senior staff member interviewed during this study, after the accident at Three Mile Island in 1979 utilities and reactor manufacturers, concerned that they would have trouble meeting new safety regulations, consulted with the NRC regularly to develop and administer regulatory changes in mutually acceptable ways. Informal consultations like these also occurred constantly during the licensing review process. In fact, these contacts were so prevalent that they raised doubts about the NRC's ability to regulate the sector impartially (President's Commission on the Accident at Three Mile Island, 1979:20; Weinraub, 1983:1). Moreover, pronuclear technocrats and scientists, employed or funded through the federal agencies charged with managing nuclear technology, provided most of the technical advice to policy makers, a situation that bolstered these suspicions (e.g., Metzger, 1972:26; Steinhart, 1978).

Nuclear critics did not have the same access. The NRC viewed them as outsiders and, according to one staff member I interviewed at the Union of Concerned Scientists, did not often invite them to the daily discussions between regulators and corporate officials. Instead, Critical Mass, Friends of the Earth, and other opposition groups lobbied in Congress or, more often, worked through decentralized arenas. Of course, all of these forums were equally accessible to nuclear advocates.

Differential access also characterized functionally segregated policy arenas. Nuclear advocates had consistent access to places where policy was formed and implemented while opponents remained confined primarily to the latter (Golay, 1981:30). For example, the Joint Committee on Atomic Energy and the AEC consulted directly with nuclear corporations and utilities when developing emergency core cooling system research policy, the largest safety research program in AEC and NRC history. Corporations provided much of the experimental data and computer modeling that formed the basis for the policy (Cottrell, 1974; GAO, 1976a; JCAE, 1967:18). The Advisory Committee on Reactor Safeguards often experienced pressure from corporations and utilities when making its decisions (Okrent, 1981). Opponents of the government's policies frequently found themselves excluded from these arenas and confined primarily to licensing board hearings and the courts—forums reserved for ensuring proper implementation and removed from actual policy making (JCAE, 1974b:527; 1974c:27). More recently, the National Research Council

79

(1984), the U.S. General Accounting Office (1986; 1985b), and officials in several state governments (GAO, 1985c:34) have criticized the Department of Energy for selecting waste disposal sites and for developing siting guidelines without input from the people potentially affected. Generally citizens were able to express their views on these matters only in forums such as public hearings and the courts where they tried to block implementation of decisions the department made behind closed doors.

There are several reasons why there was such differential access. Part of the explanation is the amount of resources available to the different groups involved. Nuclear advocates had much more money, legal expertise, and other assets necessary for influencing the policy process than did environmentalists, citizen groups, and activists critical of nuclear policy (Ebbin and Kasper, 1974:194; U.S. Senate, 1977:19–22). Critics spent about $4 million annually during the early 1980s on lobbying, public education, and other activities. Nuclear corporations planned to spend $27 million in 1983 just for public relations campaigns (OTA, 1984:214). Technical and scientific expertise was also a particularly important, yet unevenly distributed resource. Most nuclear scientists and engineers had continuing relationships with either regulators or corporations that they risked by associating with opponents of nuclear power. For example, during the emergency core cooling system controversy several dissenting staff scientists in the AEC's national laboratories lost either their research funds or their jobs (Ford, 1982). As a result, it was often difficult and expensive for antinuclear groups to engage scientific help (Ebbin and Kasper, 1974:15). Although the formation of groups like the Union of Concerned Scientists, comprised of scientists and other nuclear experts, reduced the gap somewhat, one senior staff member from that organization told me that they were still at a tremendous disadvantage in resources for influencing the policy process.

Perhaps more important, the commercial nuclear sector in the United States emerged from military programs shrouded in secrecy. Only a few private contractors, military personnel, scientists, and powerful congressmen involved with the technology's military development during the 1940s created the original government bureaucracy and its early policies. Whatever access critics and nuclear opponents have gained to the policy process since then came through political struggle. For example, AEC administrators began holding public licensing hearings in 1957 because critics found that the agency had issued a reactor construction permit despite recommendations to the contrary by its own regulatory staff and the Advisory Committee on Reactor Safeguards, one of the first scandals to rock the agency. Similarly, AEC officials established routine Atomic Safety and Licensing Board hearings open to the public in 1962 to improve the agency's credibility, to absorb political conflict, and, therefore, to facilitate indirectly the AEC's promotional efforts (Mazuzan and Trask, 1979:48–50). Occasionally, the AEC and NRC convened public rulemaking hearings to review controversial regulations and issues for similar reasons. They usually convened the hearings when nuclear critics persisted in raising objections at licensing hearings that caused or threatened protracted licensing delays. The emergency core cooling system controversy was a classic but not unique example. Rulemaking hearings were a convenient way to circumvent objections and avoid delays at licensing hearings because they removed contested issues to another arena for public debate (JCAE, 1974b:527). Once removed, interveners could not raise them during individual licensing hearings. However, because rule-making hearings served only an advisory role in the promulgation and establishment of regulatory policy, critics charged that they provided more formal than substantive input into policy making. Nevertheless, critics did raise technical issues there that led to new, more stringent safety regulations. Again, the emergency core cooling system case was one where criticism produced tougher standards through rule-making hearings. There were others (e.g., Reactor Safety Research Review Group, 1981). Access to the electoral arena did not come easily either. During the 1970s antinuclear groups put referenda and electoral initiatives to stop the construction of nuclear projects on state ballots only after heated political struggles. Even then pronuclear forces usually beat them at the polls spending at least twice as much as the critics did on referenda campaigns (Gyorgy et al., 1979:384; Olson, 1976; Wasserman, 1979:59). The same was true of court cases. In short, differential access developed because nuclear critics, systematically omitted from the policy process initially, usually only secured access to relatively decentralized implementation arenas through political struggle.

CHANNELS OF INFLUENCE

Differential access influenced the trajectory of political struggle in the sector. Critics objected to several nuclear policies that they felt did not adequately protect the public safety and health. Usually focusing on specific plants, they initially used decentralized implementation forums to raise many of their concerns about reactor siting, potential earthquake damage to plants, safety, and environmental impact (Caldwell et al., 1976; Mitchell, 1981). This tactic was not surprising in that such forums provided the easiest access. Moreover, public opinion polls showed that concerns with nuclear power were more pronounced and more consistently linked to political activism when they pertained directly to the respondent's community or locale (Melber et al., 1977:154). If satisfaction was not forthcoming there, activists usually moved the struggle to more centralized arenas through whatever channels were available. This also contributed to the erosion of the policy process's legitimacy.

Citizens argued at an Atomic Safety and Licensing Board hearing in 1969 that the AEC should consider all of the environmental effects that two reactors then under consideration for construction permits would have on the Chesapeake Bay. The AEC refused, arguing that it was responsible for examining the plants' radiological impacts, but not the broader environmental effects such as thermal pollution. A regional coalition of environmentalists went to court. The U.S. Court of Appeals in Washington, D.C., upheld their complaint in 1971 and instructed the agency to obey the 1969 National Environmental Policy Act by considering the other environmental impacts during licensing. Similarly, critics raised the struggle over emergency cooling regulations to federal courts and centralized rule-making hearings when Atomic Safety and Licensing Boards refused to withhold permits and licenses until more data were available and the AEC examined the problem.

Perhaps the most graphic illustration of the channeling process involved nuclear waste policy. Beginning in 1976, states began to pass referenda, legislation, and public service commission declarations that restricted future nuclear expansion within state borders until the federal government developed a working program to manage nuclear waste (Atomic Industrial Forum, 1982; NRC, 1982a; 1981b). Some states also restricted the in-state disposal and storage of used reactor fuel. Communities, including New York City, passed laws forbidding the transport of high-level radioactive waste on their thoroughfares, making temporary solutions to the waste problem more difficult to achieve (Saiter, 1983). The conflict over nuclear waste finally worked its way to Congress, where, after a two-and-a-half-year legislative battle, legislators passed the 1982 Nuclear Waste Policy Act, ordering the Department of Energy to develop waste repositories. One reason it took so long to pass the bill was that several states, concerned that the department would pick them as disposal sites, demanded provisions in the bill that guarded against their selection

(Barlett and Steele, 1985:chap. 5). Ironically, Congress did not pass the bill until it included a provision granting any state the right to veto its designation as a waste site—a clause that created another institutional opportunity for states to block the implementation of federal policy.

The struggle over waste policy highlights the tendency for political struggles over nuclear policy to flow toward more centralized arenas. During an interview for this project, one member of the Union of Concerned Scientists reported that national organizations like his, which were once content to work through more decentralized implementation arenas, now, thanks to the fragmenting of the Joint Committee on Atomic Energy, try to influence both the formation and implementation of policy by *initiating* many of their struggles at the federal level. They lobby Congress, testify at congressional hearings, consult directly with federal regulators when possible, and work through the courts. They realized that they could accomplish very little at state and local levels, particularly in implementation arenas such as licensing hearings, that would help them change most NRC regulatory policy. In effect, activists learned to channel their dissent through whatever institutional opportunities they felt would lead to success.

Critics also began to question the legitimacy of the policy process because they recognized that the most accessible channels strictly limited their ability to influence policy makers. Interveners in Vermont, dissatisfied with the way things were going at their Atomic Safety and Licensing Board hearings, began complaining in 1970 that the AEC was favoring the promotion of nuclear power at the expense of safety and the environment (Ebbin and Kasper, 1974:99). Going one step further, groups in Michigan filed a lawsuit charging that their licensing board did not pay enough attention to their concerns and was biased in favor of the nuclear utilities it was supposed to help regulate. As more groups began to intervene in these proceedings around the country, they began to believe that the hearings were a charade; an attempt to create the appearance, but not the reality, of effective public input into the policy process. Even some AEC staff members conceded off the record that the hearings were a process for questioning decisions already made elsewhere (Ebbin and Kasper, 1974:141). A Senate investigation discovered in 1977 that regulators made most of their licensing decisions before ever holding hearings. Typically, by the time officials announced that they would convene hearings, the NRC staff and the utility applicant had already worked together for a year or two pounding out the technical details of the application to ensure that the licensing board would grant the construction permit or operating license (U.S. Senate, 1977:54).

Exacerbated by the crisis over emergency cooling systems, the legitimacy of the AEC's policy process continued to deteriorate. In 1972, six groups filed suit in federal court, arguing that the AEC's roles were contradictory, that its bias in favor of nuclear power rendered it incapable of performing its regulatory duties properly, and that Congress should relieve it of those responsibilities altogether (Ebbin and Kasper, 1974:234). In short, when public interest groups involved with implementation began to define their participation as primarily an exercise in symbolic politics, conflict spread to new and often more centralized arenas, such as rule-making hearings, electoral referenda, and higher courts. Furthermore, disenchantment with legitimate procedural channels caused a split in the antinuclear movement in 1975. Groups fed up with legal strategies turned to nonviolent civil disobedience, including public protests, sit-ins, and the occupation of nuclear power plant construction sites (Mitchell, 1981). For those who remained committed to legal channels, there were eventually many institutional points of access to the policy process at various levels of government. Ironically, although officials created forums such as licensing and rule-making hearings that facilitated participatory politics in order to neutralize nuclear opposition, these mechanisms later contributed to the escalation of antinuclear activity.[4]

In addition to citizen groups, lower-level governments objected to the policy process, worrying that officials in Washington were forcing policies on them without seriously considering local or state interests and without allowing them sufficient opportunities to contribute to the policy-making process. Conflict emerged among different levels of government. For example, the NRC ruled in 1986 that emergency planning at the Shoreham plant on Long Island should proceed even though state and county government officials protested that they could not develop an adequate evacuation plan. Representative Edward Markey, who chaired a congressional subcommittee with jurisdiction over NRC activity, called the decision "the groundwork to ram a nuclear power plant down the throats of state and local authorities who have made it clear they do not want the plant to operate" (Wald, 1986a:5). In Ohio, where a similar conflict over evacuation plans developed, the governor's office suggested that they were reviewing options to fight the NRC's decision (Wald, 1986a). It is unclear who

[4] Habermas (1973:96) suggests that policy makers often resolve legitimation problems by providing more democratic access to the policy process.

will win these intergovernmental fights. As noted earlier, Kansas defeated federal attempts to build a radioactive waste repository within its borders in 1970 without allowing state representatives to participate in the decision-making process. However, Minnesota failed to toughen the AEC's radiation emission standards.

In sum, the institutional structure of the policy process contributed to the politicization of various policy issues and the policy process itself. More important, political institutions provided opportunities for activists and policy makers from all levels of government to channel their conflicts into decentralized policy arenas devoted primarily to implementation. Later, because critics saw that struggles waged there were futile, conflicts began moving toward more centralized arenas, such as Congress, rule-making hearings, and higher courts. Many of these were closer to the sources of policy formation.

OBSTRUCTIONIST POLITICS, PLANNING, AND THE SECTOR'S DECLINE

All of this affected the nuclear sector's planning capabilities and, therefore, its continued viability. By centering conflicts around implementation, institutional arrangements facilitated the development of obstructionist politics, something that became the rule rather than the exception (Bupp, 1979). The repercussions for the sector were severe, yet in some cases quite subtle. For example, struggles over safety, environmental, and other policy issues often caused licensing delays that some observers argued increased costs for nuclear construction, one of the major stumbling blocks for the nuclear sector in the United States (e.g., Bupp et al., 1975; Montgomery and Quirk, 1978). The appellate court's 1971 decision requiring a complete environmental review of all plant applications contributed to an expensive eighteen-month hiatus in licensing at the AEC (Mazuzan and Trask, 1979:70). Officials at the Seabrook station reported that the state of Massachusetts objected to the utility's evacuation plan, causing a six-month delay that cost operators $300 million (Wald, 1986a).

On the other hand, in an extremely sophisticated and insightful statistical analyses of the problem, Charles Komanoff (1981) argued that regulatory changes from the AEC and NRC, not nuclear critics delaying licensing, caused most of the escalation in plant costs during the 1970s. Representatives from the Atomic Industrial Forum agreed, adding that regulators were too quick to make changes and that such overregulation helped kill the nuclear option (Szalay, 1984). Komanoff's data show that as regulatory changes increased, so did the costs of building plants. However, he did not recognize that the identification and politicizing of issues such as safety in licensing hearings and other implementation forums by activists often contributed to the promulgation of new regulations in the first place. One NRC commissioner told me that individual antinuclear licensing interventions and their associated delays were relatively inconsequential in directly affecting the costs of specific plants but that groups like the Union of Concerned Scientists used the interventions to identify safety problems common to many plants, and the disclosures led to the promulgation of the major regulatory changes central to Komanoff's argument. The emergency cooling system controversy is a case in point. Although Komanoff's analysis is insightful as far as it goes, many of the political and institutional pressures are just too subtle for his statistical model to capture (Bupp, 1981). Therefore, it seems that obstructionist politics had at least a subtle, indirect effect on nuclear plant cost escalation and, therefore, the sector's viability, if not a more direct impact on a plant-by-plant basis. Others I spoke with at the OTA agreed with this assessment. This reciprocal yet institutionally segregated relationship between policy makers and activists also underscores the important interplay between the policy formation and implementation processes.

However, obstructionism also affected planning and the sector's viability more directly. The most important example was the fight over nuclear waste. Beginning in 1976, antinuclear groups began to convince state public service commissions not to approve new nuclear projects until the federal government was ready to receive the plants' radioactive waste and used reactor fuel, a service that will probably not be available until at least 1998 (Barlett and Steele, 1985:151). Critics argued that until then utilities could not accurately forecast all of the plant's operating costs because the expense of waste management was unknown. Because public service commissions were responsible for regulating utility rates, determined in part by considering utility operating costs, and because it was impossible to predict these costs for nuclear plants without a solution to the waste problem, critics claimed that commissions should not approve new nuclear projects. By defining the issue in *economic* terms before public service commissions, nuclear opponents avoided the threat of federal preemption, for the federal government had only minimal responsibility for regulating the economics of nuclear generated electricity.[5] The U.S. Supreme Court upheld this argument in 1983 (Greenhouse, 1983:1).

5 See chapter 2, note 14, for details.

According to spokespersons from two national antinuclear organizations interviewed for this study, success like this and the ability to avoid federal preemption convinced activists to begin rephrasing their arguments in economic rather than safety terms and to present them before state public service commissions in order to block further nuclear development.

Obstructionism and the conflicts surrounding the sector also contributed to the deterioration of investor confidence in nuclear power. A financial analyst for the Edison Electric Institute, the utility trade association, informed me that declining public confidence helped undermine the utilities' ability to raise capital for nuclear construction. First, citizens urged public service commissions not to increase rates or otherwise help provide the investment capital necessary to build new nuclear plants because they felt the costs were unknown and the safety questionable. The degree to which a public service commission is willing to provide rate relief directly affects the utility's ability to raise capital in the capital markets. When that relief is not forthcoming, investment capital becomes more difficult and more expensive to obtain. As discussed in chapter 6, the ability to raise investment capital became an increasing problem for many nuclear utilities, a problem facilitated by the unique and institutionally accessible structure of utility regulation. Second, individual citizens themselves held almost 70 percent of all the utility equity in the United States. If these people did not support nuclear power, they could withhold their investment capital from utilities planning or trying to finish nuclear projects.

The point is that obstructionist politics tended to undermine the planning required for the sector's development. Obstructionism helped foil the government's plans for the development of a nuclear waste management system. Obstructionism helped make it difficult for utilities to plan nuclear projects requiring large amounts of capital over long periods of time because the availability of capital was uncertain. Obstructionism contributed to licensing delays, instability in the regulatory process, and the escalation of project costs—factors that made it even more difficult for utilities to plan for nuclear projects.

The multiplication of agencies and congressional committees responsible for nuclear policy also inhibited smooth planning in the sector and raised doubts about the government's ability to formulate and implement policy (Bupp, 1979:151). The problem of policy coordination increased because several agencies began exercising control over the same policy where a single agency was once responsible. For example, following the dissolution of the AEC, both the NRC and the

87

Energy Research and Development Administration had some control over the national laboratories. Bureaucratic in-fighting, squabbling, and turf wars delayed several projects from generating the data necessary for important regulatory policy decisions (GAO, 1976a; 1976b). The problems of fragmented policy jurisdiction became more important, but they do not seem to have been as significant in undermining planning and the sector's development as those stemming from decentralization and segregation. However, this may change, particularly if more fragmenting occurs. For example, observers feel that management of nuclear waste has become especially difficult since the NRC, Department of Energy, Department of Transportation, and the Environmental Protection Agency started sharing responsibilities for managing it (Barlett and Steele, 1985:51).

THE SIGNIFICANCE OF POLITICAL INSTITUTIONS

In democratically decentralized systems, when many interest groups cannot gain access to policy formation, their consent may not be forthcoming, the legitimacy of the policy process becomes suspect, political struggles over policy emerge in implementation arenas, and obstructionist politics ensue, making implementation difficult (Mayntz, 1975:262; Rein and Rabinovitz, 1977:6). This is precisely what happened with nuclear policy in the United States. Antinuclear groups had great difficulty gaining access to places where government and corporate elites created policy. This bred distrust and suspicion among those excluded, which led to deliberate confrontations in implementation arenas. Conflict flowed to whatever arena seemed most promising in terms of changing or blocking policy. When one channel failed to produce results, nuclear critics tried another, carrying the struggle to new parts of the state apparatus in a more centralized, federally oriented direction toward the policy source.

Dorothy Nelkin (1984:18) described the institutional channeling of political conflict in other technology policy areas in the United States. She noted that it usually involved litigation, referenda, public hearings, lobbying, and political demonstrations because these were the forums readily available to all the interested parties. The analysis presented here is consistent with her observations, but offers a more refined three-dimensional view of the processes. By distinguishing among different types of policy arenas, we understand why controversy tends to flow systematically in certain ways through the policy process. Initially it appears in decentralized implementation arenas, where access is easiest, but later moves toward centralized places closer to policy formation if implementation struggles prove unsuccessful and the losers wish to continue the fight. In short, not only are there institutional reasons why conflicts emerge in the arenas she mentions, but, more important, there are institutional reasons why the conflicts shift among arenas in certain directions.

Several observers recognized that the nuclear policy process in the United States became more pluralist, particularly after the fragmentation of the AEC and the Joint Committee on Atomic Energy. They found that this exacerbated implementation problems and created more obstructionism than there was in the past (Barkenbus, 1984; Bupp, 1979). The analysis presented in this chapter supports this important insight to the extent that it considers policy implementation. However, the need for conceptual refinement appears again. If we do not distinguish among types of policy arenas, this description of growing pluralism becomes oversimplified and confusing. Although the policy process became more inclusive, groups previously excluded gained access primarily to policy implementation, not policy formation, circles. Unless we note this critical distinction, it is difficult to understand why obstructionism developed at all. If activists had gained access to policy formation as well as implementation circles, there would have been no reason for obstructionism to develop. Why would participants who contributed to policy formation and whose agreement was required to establish policy in the first place try to block that policy's implementation later?[6]

Antagonism and conflict tend to characterize the regulatory process in the United States in areas besides nuclear power. For example, Lennart Lundqvist (1980) found that there was tremendous conflict over air pollution regulation in the United States because the policy process was intimately linked with institutions such as litigation, adversarial hearings, and electoral competition that facilitated conflict and a winner-take-all attitude among participants. In Sweden the courts were reluctant to hear complaints, administrative autonomy was greater, and, as a result, the regulatory politics of air pollution were more consensual. He also found that air pollution regulations were more extreme in the United States, at least initially, because citizens had more institutional opportunities to influence the policy process. The more insulated and centralized Swedish system pro-

---

[6]This point is elaborated in chapter 8, particularly with respect to the Swedish case, where there was more access to policy formation for citizens and where obstructionist politics were less common.

duced more moderate, conservative standards. In a comparison of United States and Swedish occupational safety and health regulation, Steven Kelman (1981) found many of the same institutional biases but also corresponding ideological slants. He argued that for historical reasons a self-assertive value system permeated the consciousness of United States citizens, which contributed to the adversity and conflict over policy. In Sweden accomodationist institutions and deferent values produced more negotiation, cooperation, and consensus among those involved.

It also appears from their descriptions (Kelman, 1981:150–58; Lundqvist, 1980:123) that the more insulated Swedish model produced what Dickson (1984) described as a technocratic policy paradigm, a more conservative, cautious approach designed not to undermine economic growth, while the relatively accessible U.S. model generated a democratic policy paradigm more responsive to the general public.[7] What is interesting about the U.S. nuclear regulatory process is that it involved *both* models and paradigms simultaneously. Policy formation was usually insulated and consensual, although rarely involving citizen participation. Policy implementation was accessible and adversarial. Furthermore, those involved in policy formation pushed a technocratic approach from above, while citizens involved with policy implementation advocated a democratic approach from below. When the two paradigms collided, conflict and policy stalemates occurred. Contrary to what Kelman might expect, struggles over policy did not spring from a general set of self-assertive values but from political institutions that fostered conflicts over policy paradigms and the policy process itself. If the institutional opportunities had been available in the United States for nuclear critics to participate during the earlier stages of the policy process and push it in a more democratic direction, they might not have engaged in so much obstructionism later.

It is also possible that antinuclear criticism and obstructionism would not have developed in the first place, or at least not to the extent they did, if regulators and nuclear corporations had built safer plants initially, solved the waste problem earlier, standardized plants more thoroughly, and paid more attention to the environmental impacts of nuclear power—things that might have happened if policy makers had adopted a more democratic policy paradigm. Similarly, utilities

7 It is questionable how responsive occupational safety and health policy was to the workers' concerns. Empirical evidence exists indicating that Kelman seriously overstated the victories of U.S. workers in this area. See Szasz (1984; 1982).

and architect-engineers building nuclear stations might have avoided many of the problems, delays, and expenses usually attributed to project mismanagement (e.g., Cook, 1985) if they had been more attentive to the long-range implications of their activity, a perspective central to Dickson's democratic policy paradigm. However, as suggested in previous chapters, institutional imperatives—both political and economic—helped stifle the development of such farsighted planning. When antinuclear activity emerged, the political institutions that provided links between civil society and the government's policy process were ripe for the development of obstructionist politics. As a result, not only did institutional arrangements facilitate the manifestation of the contradiction between technocratic and democratic policy paradigms, but they also mediated the effects the ensuing struggles had on policy outcomes and, therefore, the sector's viability.

CHAPTER SIX

Financial Crisis

Political struggles, legitimation difficulties, and the absence of standardization each took its toll on the nuclear sector through licensing delays and vacillating regulations, which in turn contributed to escalating plant costs. Inflated costs are not necessarily lethal to a sector's growth, however, unless the financial environment makes it difficult to raise additional investment capital. Such difficulties become extreme in the nuclear sector. The relationship between the state and civil society, specified by the institutional arrangements among the public utility commissions, utilities, and suppliers of finance capital, prevented electric utilities from raising enough money through revenues to continue building nuclear plants without relying heavily on the capital markets. Utilities found it difficult to finance nuclear projects during the 1970s and 1980s because they could not compete effectively for investment capital. Government officials were unable to help because they lacked the institutional means for controlling the allocation of capital in the capital markets. This made it very difficult for utilities to plan capital intensive projects with long lead times. Although other factors, including the decline in electricity demand during the 1970s, contributed to the uncertainty surrounding planning, utilities stopped ordering new nuclear plants and cancelled orders for old ones primarily because they could not raise the extra capital required to cover rising costs. In effect, the nuclear sector's financial crisis was the *culmination* of its other problems. In an interview in the *Wall Street Journal*, Carl Walske, chairperson of the Atomic Industrial Forum, admitted that "the number one reason for the lack of new orders is not the NRC, but utility financing" (Large, 1982).

The Institutional Structure of Capital Formation

John Zysman's (1983) work on industrial finance provides an excellent starting point for studying the relationship between the state and the firm's ability to raise finance capital externally. He argues that in market-based economies, such as the United States, private, competitive capital markets allocate most capital. The state generally controls capital allocation only in the aggregate through monetary, fiscal, and welfare policies. As a result, the responsibility for planning industrial development rests largely with individual firms. Since the firm's access to capital through the markets is based on its immediate profitability, the potential for unified, farsighted planning at the levels of either industrial sectors or the national economy is minimal. The state is not able to coordinate long-range planning because of the policy constraints imposed on it by the centrality of private capital markets to finance (Zysman, 1983:chap. 6). On the other hand, in credit-based, statist economies, such as France, the state has direct control over capital allocation because it dominates the banking system that supplies most of the economy's finance capital. The role of capital markets is minimal. The state is able to plan national industrial strategies by entering directly into the life of companies because it has several instruments for the selective allocation of credit between industries and firms, including the preferential distribution of government loans, loan guarantees, subsidies, and the discretionary manipulation of interest rates (Zysman, 1983:76).

Like other institutionalists (e.g., Krasner, 1978; Shonfield, 1965) Zysman is concerned with the institutional constraints impinging on the firm's ability to secure finance capital from *external* sources, not with those that facilitate or limit the firm's ability to generate investment capital *internally*. Although he recognizes the ability of national governments to manipulate profitability through indirect mechanisms such as wage and price controls, he rarely sees that the state may also gain *direct* control over the rate of profit through some degree of ownership or other control mechanism at the level of the firm itself.[1]

---

[1] The preoccupation of Zysman and other institutionalists with processes of external capital formation does not detract from the importance of their work. Nor does it stem from some theoretical oversight on their part. Their work focuses on advanced capitalist nations and economic sectors where the state generally does not have control over internal capital formation. As a result, they devote most of their attention to the external allocation of finance capital as the key policy tool. Most of the institutional variation for the cases they choose is in external capital formation. In contrast, those comparing capitalist and state socialist societies emphasize the state's capacity to control

Direct state control over profit rates is commonplace in industries that constitute "natural monopolies," such as electric utilities. To ensure that the public has access to electricity at a relatively fair price, the state intervenes directly into the electricity rate-making process. In some countries this is done through nationalization. In the United States this is done through utility regulation. In each case the state has an important policy tool—the ability to control utility capital formation by directly manipulating the rate of profit. Therefore, when studying the institutional constraints that the state encounters when trying to participate in utility planning, including the decision whether or not to promote a nuclear expansion, it is important to consider two institutional factors: (1) the structure of internal capital formation—the manner in which the determination of profit rates generates investment capital—and (2) the structure of external capital formation—the manner in which utilities raise investment capital through the financial markets. In the U.S. nuclear sector the federal government's ability to control both sources of investment capital was very limited. As a result public officials were not able to provide the financial predictability and stability necessary for long-range planning. The utilities were likewise unable, for they had to raise much of their investment capital in capital markets governed by short-term price signals.

The Structure of Utility Capital Formation

Because investor-owned utilities produce 78 percent of all the electricity sold in the United States, it is their story that is important here (Council of State Governments, 1977: chap. 2). They have two sources of capital. First, they accumulate revenues as retained earnings. This is a process of internal capital formation that each state's public utility commission strictly regulates by establishing the price and, therefore, the profit rates for all the electricity private utilities generate and sell within the state. The public is guaranteed access to the legal proceedings where these decisions are made, a situation that often leads to heated political conflict among utilities, citizens, and regulators. Be-

---

both sources of finance because in these comparisons there is more variation on both dimensions. In capitalist society allocation and the initial appropriation of the economic surplus tend to be controlled privately. In state socialist countries both are increasingly state controlled (e.g., Wright, 1979; Szelenyi, 1980; 1981).

cause utilities are regulated in the public interest, retained earnings are usually relatively small and not sufficient to cover the construction of new plants. When utilities need new generating capacity, they must tap a second capital source, where the state has no direct control over allocation: capital markets. There utilities may sell either bonds or stocks.[2] If the utility competes against other firms that appear to be more profitable or safer investments, capital may become so expensive that the utility has to forego its expansion plans. This institutional structure of accessible, decentralized, political regulation and capital markets guided by relatively short-term profitability signals can severely undermine the planning required for the execution of projects like nuclear plants that require the steady infusion of large amounts of capital over a ten- or twelve-year period (Council of State Governments, 1977:6–15).

As noted earlier utilities built new generating capacity during the 1960s and early 1970s to meet a 7.3 percent average annual growth rate in electricity demand (GAO, 1981a:4). They benefited from this because new plants increased the size of their capital investment, often referred to as the rate base. After allowing for the utility's operating costs, the utility commission calculated the rate of return it would allow the utility to earn on its rate base. As a result, while not affecting the rate of profit per se, a larger rate base did increase the absolute profits accruing to a company (GAO, 1981b:5). Because capital was available at reasonable prices then, there was a structural incentive encouraging utilities to maximize capital investments (Willrich, 1975:24). This led utilities to increase their investments in new plant capacity at an enormous rate. (See the Appendix for a more detailed discussion of utility rate making and the investment incentives involved.) From 1964 through 1972 utility investments doubled as a percentage of the total capital invested by all industries in the United States (Table 6.1). Electric utilities were responsible for 15 percent of the nation's annual industrial investments by 1973.

From the standpoint of rate base expansion, the incentives to build nuclear capacity were especially strong because nuclear stations were the most capital intensive of all generating plants (U.S. Senate, 1974:23). This was a major factor stimulating the nuclear expansion during the 1960s and early 1970s (Gandara, 1977:82). In addition utilities believed that the lower fuel costs for nuclear power would

---

[2] Bank loans are another source of finance capital, although one much less desirable in that they are usually only available for relatively short periods of time and at higher costs.

Table 6.1. Capital outlays in electric utilities and other industries, 1964–1973 (in billions of dollars)

Year	All U.S. Industries	Investor-owned Electric Utilities	Investor-owned Utilities as % of Total U.S. Industry
1964	47.0	3.6	7.6
1965	54.5	4.0	7.4
1966	63.5	5.0	7.8
1967	65.8	6.1	9.4
1968	67.8	7.2	10.6
1969	75.6	8.3	11.0
1970	79.7	10.2	12.8
1971	81.2	11.9	14.7
1972	88.4	13.4	15.2
1973	99.7	15.0	15.0

SOURCE: U.S. Senate (1974): 462.

offset its comparatively high front-end capital costs and, therefore, produce cheaper electricity over the plant's lifetime than any other type of plant (AEC, 1973c:15; U.S. Senate, 1974:199). This second advantage increased during the late 1960s as fossil fuel prices rose and uranium prices declined (Gandara, 1977:54). As a result, the nuclear sector's share of all the steam-generated electricity capacity ordered rose 8.5 percent annually between 1965 and 1972, reaching an annual market share of 68 percent (Table 6.2).

However, the expansion in nuclear capacity eventually helped undermine the utilities' financial health. Not only were nuclear plants more expensive to build, but both real and estimated capital costs were escalating *faster* for nuclear than for coal-fired plants, nuclear energy's biggest competitor (Bupp et al., 1975; DOE, 1983a:20). Between 1968 and 1977 capital costs rose at a real annual rate of 11 percent for nuclear plants, but only 5 percent for coal (Neese, 1982:14). As we have seen, chronic delays in construction and licensing, changing regulatory requirements, and the lack of standardization contributed to the difference. Rising project costs exacerbated the utilities' need for capital. Since 1965 utilities had been investing capital at an increasing pace, primarily for new generating capacity. The proportion of that overall increase spent on nuclear power was rising at an accelerating rate (Gandara, 1977:27–28). This was happening precisely when the general cost of capital in the market place was also rising. As early as 1968, investment bankers worried that both the demand for nuclear power and its projected costs were rising. They hinted that this situation might eventually compromise the financial standing of the utilities involved (*Morgan Guarantee Survey*, 1968). They were right.

THE INTERNAL CAPITAL FORMATION CRISIS

Rising costs and capital requirements undermined the utilities' ability to generate capital internally. The amount of the nation's electric utility capital representing construction work in progress quadrupled from $4.4 billion to $16.6 billion between 1967 and 1972. As a percentage of the utilities' total investment, it rose from 8.3 to 18.2 percent (GAO, 1980b:18). The problem was that utility commissions would not allow most of the utility industry's investments for construction work in progress into its rate base until the plants were producing electricity for the public (CBO, 1982:6). Hence, while utilities were increasing the amount of capital invested in new construction, they were not realizing a corresponding increase in earnings with which to cover the cost of that capital.

This was not a serious problem until the cost of capital started becoming prohibitively expensive in the capital markets. It was then that utilities began pressing public utility commissions to allow investments for construction work in progress into the rate base (Gandara,

Table 6.2. Orders for steam-generated electricity plants, 1962–1979

Year	Generating Capacity Ordered (Megawatts)			Nuclear as a % of Total Capacity Ordered
	Total	Nuclear	Fossil	
1962	8,971	628	8,343	7.0
1963	16,633	2,495	14,138	15.0
1964	na	0	na	0.0
1965	28,466	4,490	21,676	15.7
1966	37,204	16,367	20,837	44.0
1967	50,669	25,522	25,147	50.4
1968	36,066	12,895	23,171	35.8
1969	34,278	7,203	27,075	21.0
1970	44,613	14,266	30,347	32.0
1971	36,244	19,931	16,313	55.0
1972	52,678	35,843	16,835	68.0
1973	64,581	38,687	25,894	60.0
1974	72,476	38,978	33,498	53.8
1975	14,924	4,100	10,824	27.5
1976	9,712	3,400	6,312	35.0
1977	14,355	6,220	8,135	43.3
1978	21,353	2,300	19,053	10.7
1979	5,436	0	5,436	0.0

SOURCES: NRC (1980a), Joskow (1979): 240, and Rolph (1977): 41.

1977:95; Hertsgaard, 1983:147). However, consumers opposed the requests, and as a result commissions usually denied them (GAO, 1980b:3). Many utilities reported later that this failure contributed significantly to their financial deterioration (GAO, 1980c:15). It became especially troublesome for utilities with nuclear projects because they required more capital for longer periods before the plant would come into service (U.S. House, 1982:85).

To ease their earnings squeeze and generate necessary investment capital, utilities tried to gain rate increases from state utility commissions. The commissions began granting much heftier increases in 1969, although at only about 60 percent of the amounts utilities requested (Table 6.3) (Gandara, 1977:33; U.S. House, 1981a:229). Citizens convinced utility commissions to begin holding the line on electricity rates (Gormley, 1983). While commissioners recognized the utilities' plight, they also worried that automatically increasing rates at the utilities' request would jeopardize their political legitimacy. Discussing the problem with a Senate committee in 1974, the chairman of Michigan's public utility commission explained that if a commission granted the utilities a full rate increase each time they requested one, "one of the serious problems you would have is gaining any public confidence that the companies are operating to the interest of the consumer, and that the government is doing its job in assuring that these monopolies operate efficiently" (U.S. Senate, 1974:310).[3] The basic contradiction between public and private interests had materialized, this time in the tensions between decentralized, democratic politics and utility profitability as expressed through the political regulation of internal capital formation. Although the specific issues were different, it was the same contradiction responsible for generating so much conflict over reactor safety policy at the AEC. Because citizens had access to public utility commissions, the contradiction produced political struggles at the state level that prevented utilities from generating enough capital internally to easily underwrite more nuclear projects. Instead, utilities had to move deeper into the capital markets to pursue their nuclear dreams.

THE EXTERNAL CAPITAL FORMATION CRISIS

Electric utilities turned toward the bond market during the late 1960s at an increasing rate to raise the capital necessary for their new

[3] The problem of maintaining their legitimacy was a serious one for these regulators. Their jobs depended on it inasmuch as all but six states chose commissioners either through direct elections or through appointments requiring legislative approval (Council of State Governments, 1977:18).

Table 6.3. Electric utility requests for rate increases, 1965–1980 (in millions of dollars)

Year	Amount of Increase Requested	Amount Approved	% Approved
1965	na	0.0	—
1966	na	33.0	—
1967	na	0.7	—
1968	na	20.0	—
1969	na	145.0	—
1970	790	533.0	67
1971	1,368	826.0	60
1972	1,205	853.0	71
1973	2,125	1,089.0	51
1974	4,555	2,229.0	49
1975	3,973	3,094.0	78
1976	3,747	2,275.0	61
1977	3,953	2,311.0	58
1978	4,494	2,419.0	54
1979	5,736	2,853.0	50
1980	10,871	5,932.0	55

SOURCES: Gandara (1977): 33, and U.S. House (1981a): 229.

projects. By 1970 the industry raised over half of its external investment capital through long-term bonds (U.S. Senate, 1974:453). Initially this was easy, but as the earnings squeeze developed, investors saw the bonds as riskier investments. To attract hesitant investors, utilities started offering higher interest rates on their bonds. As a result, the interest on outstanding debt began to increase through the late 1960s and early 1970s as utilities raised more capital through bond sales. By 1974 interest payments on construction projects in progress had risen to 25 percent of total project costs (FEA, 1974:V26). Exacerbated by inflation, a deteriorating pattern emerged for utilities in the bond market. As the utilities' coverage ratio—the relationship between their annual earnings and their annual interest payments on debt—declined, the quality of future bond issues also dropped (Table 6.4). They became riskier investments. In order to attract investors, higher interest rates were offered on new issues. This reduced coverage ratios further, thus perpetuating the cycle (FEA, 1974:V6). The U.S. Department of Energy found that the more nuclear capacity a utility had in place or under construction, the more interest it paid on its new bond issues (Neese, 1982).

In response to deteriorating coverage ratios, electric utility bond ratings declined. Only 11 percent of the nation's major electric utilities held bond ratings at or below Moody's mediocre Baa rating in 1965 (Table 6.4). The situation gradually eroded and by 1975 half were so rated. As with interest rates, the U.S. Department of Energy found

Table 6.4. Deteriorating financial condition of U.S. electric utilities, 1965–1980

Year	Bond Market Performance			Stock Market Performance		
	Coverage Ratio	Average % Return on Newly Issued A-rated Utility Bonds[a]	% of Companies with Bond Ratings above Baa[a]	Common Stock Market-to-Book Ratio	Common Stock Dividend Yield (%)	Preferred Stock Coverage Ratio
1965	5.5	4.7	89	2.3	3.3	3.0
1970	3.5	9.2	78	1.3	5.9	2.2
1975	2.8	10.3	50	0.8	9.7	1.8
1980	2.6	13.4	37	0.7	12.0	1.7

[a]In Moody's nine-point rating scale, the highest quality bond is Aaa; the Baa rating indicates that the company is developing speculative characteristics.

SOURCE: Adapted from DOE (1983a): 23.

that this erosion was significantly worse for utilities involved with nuclear construction because it was so capital intensive (Neese, 1982). This was a grave situation, for many institutional investors, such as pension funds and insurance companies, were not allowed to purchase bonds with the Baa rating or lower, a rule designed to protect them from later risk (DOE, 1983a:21). Institutional investors were major purchasers of utility bonds. In short, the bond market was drying up for utilities. Institutional investors began pulling out of the electric utility bond market in 1971 because it had become too risky compared with other investment opportunities (Stich, 1971:21). The percentage of new long-term capital raised each year by electric utilities through the bond market began to decline (U.S. Senate, 1974:453).

The possibilities of raising capital in the stock market were diminishing for similar reasons. Since earnings were declining, utilities seeking investment capital there were forced to sell new shares at lower prices to continue attracting investors. However, this diluted the value of their stock. The industry's overall market-to-book ratio—the relationship between a share of common stock's current selling price and the total assets per share on the company's books—declined from 2.3 to 1.3 between 1965 and 1970 (Table 6.4). The situation deteriorated by 1974 to the point where over half the electric utility shares on the New York Stock Exchange were listed below book value, that is, with market-to-book ratios below one (DOE, 1983a:21–23). Selling below book value diluted the value of stock and made it exceedingly difficult to sell.

In 1967 utility stock market-to-book ratios dropped below the average of most other industrials. The price-to-earnings ratio for utility stock, reflecting the amount of money investors were willing to pay for one dollar of earnings, also slipped below the average for most other industrials that year. By 1968 utility stock was earning less than the average industrial stock (Stich, 1971:22–23). The situation continued to deteriorate. Utilities nearly tripled the dividend yield on common stock between 1965 and 1975 to attract investors (Table 6.4). The industry's preferred stock coverage ratio, the ratio of gross post-tax income to interest and dividends payments, slipped steadily as a result of the earnings squeeze that utilities were suffering.

To summarize, by 1972 a capital crisis had developed for the electric utility industry. That year capital outlays by investor-owned utilities peaked as a percentage of total capital investments by all other industries in the United States. Less than 25 percent of investment capital was internally generated, down from 42 percent in 1965 (U.S.

Senate, 1974:462). Utilities tried to cover some of their investments tied up in nonearning construction with rate increases, but after a 1972 peak of 71 percent, the amount public service commissions approved as a percentage of the total dollar amount the industry requested declined. Except for 1975 the percentage approved remained between 10 and 22 points lower than it had been in 1972, reflecting the development of widespread consumer resistance to further rate hikes (U.S. House, 1981a:229). For institutional reasons the state was unable to ease the utilities' internal earnings squeeze.

The need for enormous amounts of capital coupled with internal cash-flow problems stemming from insufficient rate relief had pushed utilities deeper into the capital markets. The situation was bleak. In the bond market, the industry's overall coverage ratio slipped to 3.0 by 1972, a sure sign to investors that utility bonds were risky (Gandara, 1977:30). Furthermore, investors realized that several utilities would face a major debt refinancing at new, higher interest rates in 1973, which would push coverage ratios even lower. They started to withdraw from the utility bond market in 1971 (S. M. Stoller Corporation, 1980:181). By 1972 market-to-book ratios for electric utility stock had dipped dangerously close to one. Coverage ratios were less than a point above the critical 1.5 mark at or below which stock sales were often prohibited to institutional investors (DOE, 1983a:23). Capital markets operating on the basis of the relatively short-term, private, and competitive allocation of capital made it very difficult for utilities to raise finance capital externally. In conjunction with the internal earnings squeeze, the competition for finance capital had led to a cyclical deterioration in both stock and bond values—a reflection of the industry's inability to raise adequate internal revenues.

The Collapse of Nuclear Power

In 1972 utilities began to consider what was necessary to ease their immediate financial dilemma before considering what was good for future service and profitability. Their basic planning strategy shifted from one focusing on future expansion of rate base and generating capacity to one minimizing excessive capital investment in the short term.[4] This came at the risk of having to build new capacity later when it would be more expensive. Nevertheless, the urgency of immediate economic imperatives undermined such long-range planning. The

4 Gandara (1977:26) reaches the same conclusion.

Table 6.5. Cancellations of orders for steam-generated electricity capacity, 1974–1982

Year	Generating Capacity Cancelled (Megawatts)			Nuclear As a % of Total
	Total	Nuclear	Fossil	
1974	18,216	7,216	11,000[a]	39.6
1975	16,596	14,699	1,897	88.6
1976	5,556	1,150	4,406	20.7
1977	12,510	10,814	1,696	86.4
1978	15,670	14,487	1,183	92.5
1979	11,674	9,552	2,122	81.8
1980	21,350	18,001	3,349	84.3
1981	6,706	5,781	925	86.2
1982	na	21,937	na	na
1974–81	108,278	81,700	26,578	75.0

[a] Includes only cancellations for coal-fired capacity in 1974. However, the figure provides a fairly accurate estimate of all fossil-fueled plant cancellations. The General Accounting Office (1980a:6) reports that over 90 percent of all generating capacity cancelled between 1974 and 1978 was either coal or nuclear. Therefore, this figure for coal cancellations is probably a close estimate of all fossil plant cancellations in 1974.

SOURCES: DOE (1983a): 5 and (1983b): 4, and Catalano (1982).

effect of these changing priorities was clear. Although 1972 was an up-beat year with thirty-two new nuclear reactors ordered, utilities also announced that for the first time they were cancelling seven others. The Arab oil embargo of 1973–74 exacerbated this trend by causing electricity rates to skyrocket. Consumers protested and reduced electricity consumption. The growth rate in electricity demand dropped dramatically. This sparked a wave of cancellations beginning in 1974 for all types of recently ordered steam-generated electricity capacity (Table 6.5). However, 75 percent of the capacity cancelled through 1981 was nuclear.

It is clear why nuclear plants were the overwhelming choice for cancellation. According to a prominent utility consultant, in a period when the ability to raise capital was a crucial element in utility planning, nuclear energy was at a distinct disadvantage because its costs were high and the capital invested would be tied up for the longest periods of time before earning a return (U.S. Senate, 1974:33). Ironically, the high capital cost for nuclear power had always been one of its biggest attractions from the standpoint of rate base expansion. Of course having to tie up so much capital in nonearning construction for so long had been an offsetting problem. Now the two worked together to undermine the technology's economic viability. Despite the fact that utility executives were still singing the praises of nuclear power as being cheaper in the long run and an ideal way to displace oil-fired plants (e.g., Dieckamp, 1979:244; Smartt, 1976:100), they continued to cancel their nuclear orders through the 1980s, replacing them in several cases with orders for coal-fired facilities (Utroska, 1982). Furthermore, utilities did not order any nuclear plants after 1978. Wall Street reported that nuclear power was too risky and too uncertain for further investments (*Morgan Guarantee Survey,* 1980:15). The short-term institutional imperatives of capital formation had become antithetical to the long-term planning required to sustain construction of nuclear power stations.

REMEDIAL SOLUTIONS

The utility industry and government made several attempts during the late 1970s and early 1980s to ease the financial crisis that was undermining plans for new generating capacity. However, the institutions involved severely constrained the ability of public and private policy makers to rectify the situation. They were generally unsuccessful.

Utilities continued to press public service commissions for rate increases, convincing some to speed up their rate determinations and grant requests in a more timely fashion. Nevertheless, citizens continued to oppose rate hikes and, as a result, commissions still only granted about 60 percent of the utilities' requests (Gormley, 1983:92). Utilities also kept trying to convince commissions to allow into the rate base more money that was tied up in construction work in progress, arguing that it would improve cash flow, investor confidence, and capital market ratings (*Energy User's Report,* 1981:457; GAO, 1981a:2; U.S. House, 1981a:153). Political opposition was effective again. Most commissions refused to allow investments for construction work in progress, especially for nuclear projects, into the rate base (*Electric Light and Power,* 1982; Shanaman, 1982; GAO, 1980c:23). As a result, internal capital formation problems continued to constrain the development of nuclear power (Reinsch, 1978:18).

In both cases the internal capital formation process, characterized by a decentralized, democratically accessible set of regulatory institutions, provided citizens the opportunity to block the implementation of projects developed elsewhere. Reflecting on this situation, a report by the U.S. General Accounting Office (1980a:24) recognized that consumers did not have access to the meetings where commissions and utilities decided how much and what kinds of new generating capacity they would build. The General Accounting Office suggested that if utility commissions had included citizens in these early policy formation consultations, there would have been less political opposition later because citizens would have felt more a part of the policy process. As we have seen, this was also a problem in other policy areas.

The utility industry often blamed public service commissions for their financial woes, accusing them of unresponsiveness to the need for rate increases and inclusion of construction work in progress into the rate base. Some members of the industry called for deregulation as a solution to their capital formation problems (e.g., Alexander, 1981; Hitch, 1982). They also tried to convince politicians and bureaucrats that federal intervention was necessary. However, institutional constraints prevented that intervention primarily because state-level public service commissions enjoyed a tremendous amount of institutional autonomy from the federal government. Two cases are especially revealing.

First, the Federal Power Commission (FPC) decided in 1974 to allow investments in construction work in progress into the rate bases of utilities under its jurisdiction. However, the FPC regulated only the wholesale and interstate sale of electricity, just 12 percent of the nation's electric power. Hence, although the Federal Energy Regulatory Commission, the FPC's successor, began allowing these investments to earn a return in 1976, the change did not do much to improve the utility industry's financial condition. The only effect it had on state commissions was by way of the example it set. In that respect, the policy was advisory at best (GAO, 1980c; 1981a).

Second, beginning in 1975, various legislators introduced bills in Congress on behalf of the utility industry that attempted to wrench utility regulation out of the hands of state commissions and consolidate it at the federal level. These included proposals concerning the mandatory inclusion of construction work in progress into the rate base, new rate structures, fuel adjustment clauses, and other means to improve the utilities' financial condition (e.g., *Energy User's Report*, 1975d:A12; 1975c:A5; 1976c:A37). Most were defeated, having faced stiff opposition from consumer groups or those advocating the maintenance of state's rights and the sovereignty of public utility commissions. However, Congress did pass the National Energy Act in 1978, a diluted version of the earlier proposals. The legislation encouraged the Department of Energy to participate in utility commission hearings at the state level, but only to advocate, not mandate, that commissions adopt federal policies on such issues as construction work in progress. The act also required that utility commissions consider adopting a variety of federal guidelines on rate making to improve the industry's economic posture. Nevertheless, the new law only granted the federal government an advisory role and, therefore, was unsuccessful in instituting significant changes (*Energy User's Report,* 1978a:3; Gormley, 1983:chap. 1). As the General Accounting Office reported: "The primary authority for regulating electric utilities remains with the states. Federal legislation and policy . . . do not alter the basic charters of state regulatory agencies" (GAO, 1980a:5). The decentralized institutional structure of the policy process undermined all of these rescue attempts.

There were other efforts by the federal government to help improve the utilities' condition during the late 1970s. The Nixon, Ford, and Carter administrations all had advocated direct federal subsidies for the industry through, for example, tax-exempt and government-guaranteed bonds. Ironically, the utilities resisted them for two reasons. On the one hand, they feared that investors would perceive subsidies as an indication that the industry was on the verge of collapse, thereby making it even more difficult to sell utility stocks and bonds. On the other hand, they worried that a gradually increasing range of federal controls over the industry could lead to a government takeover (*Energy User's Report,* 1975a:A33; U.S. House, 1980:6; U.S. Senate, 1974:395–402, 406). This time the structure of external financing foiled the government's attempts to help. As long as utilities were dependent on private capital markets for investment capital, direct government allocation was unacceptable because utilities felt it would hurt their ability to compete for capital in the future.

Alternative Scenarios

The financial crisis was firmly rooted both in competitive capital markets, where short-term profitability determined the availability of investment capital, and in public utility regulation, where political pressure at the point of implementation of utility policy became routine. The same institutions constrained the sector's attempts to resolve the financial crisis. It might be argued, however, that utilities cancelled orders for nuclear plants primarily because there was a dramatic decline in electricity consumption following the 1973–74 Arab oil embargo. The average price for electricity nationally jumped over 17 percent between 1973 and 1974 as a result of more expensive oil (*Energy User's Report,* 1976a:G2). Shocked by the increase in their electric bills, consumers began to save energy. In 1974, for the first time ever, the nation actually reduced its total electricity consumption from what it had been a year earlier. Eventually, demand began to grow again, but at annual rates far below those of the previous fifteen years. According to this argument, utilities began to cancel orders for nuclear plants and decided not to order new ones because they were left with more excess generating capacity than they had originally anticipated. While all of this did have severe implications for the nuclear sector, there are several reasons why it should not be considered the chief cause for the cancellations and decline in ordering.

Several studies have asked utility executives why they dropped nuclear plants from their plans. The responses indicate that both declining electricity consumption and financial difficulties were equally important in their decisions (e.g., S. M. Stoller Corporation, 1980; DOE, 1983a; 1978; GAO, 1980c). However, there are indications that they may have used the declining electricity demand as an excuse for reducing capacity that they would probably have dropped anyway. One utility consultant told a congressional panel that when utilities found themselves in financial trouble and wanted to cancel projects, they often justified their decision publicly on the grounds that there was not sufficient demand to warrant new construction (U.S. Senate, 1974:16). Furthermore, according to the Department of Energy (1983a:17), utilities that were strapped with financial problems and wanted to cut nuclear power from their program could cite lower electricity consumption as a legal rationalization to avoid building new plants for future service requirements. In short, utilities may have used the electricity consumption problem to postpone new projects until their financial outlook improved.

More important, the decline in electricity demand does not explain why nuclear power was dropped from utility programs at an enormously higher rate than fossil fuel plants. If a lower growth rate for electricity consumption was the main factor, it would seem logical that utilities would cancel fewer nuclear projects inasmuch as nuclear power offers certain economic advantages over fossil plants for the utility by contributing to a larger rate base and reducing fuel costs. However, just the opposite occurred. Orders for new nuclear generating capacity as a percentage of all new generating capacity ordered peaked in 1972. Sixty-eight percent of all new capacity ordered that year was nuclear (see Table 6.2). During the next three years, the percentage declined at an increasing rate, recovered slightly in 1976 and 1977, but then continued to drop after that. The decline in electricity demand growth rates in 1974 does not explain why nuclear energy was apparently becoming less attractive than other generating sources in 1973.

Finally, the trend toward nuclear cancellations began in 1972, two years before the major drop in electricity consumption growth rates. If fluctuation in demand was the key element in utility decision making, there would be no reason to expect cancellations prior to 1974. However, while many utilities were still pinning their financial hopes on nuclear energy, some were beginning to feel the economic constraints tightening to a point where their planning calculus began to shift to one of capital conservation. Utilities continued to order many nuclear plants in 1973 and 1974 but with an open mind, recognizing that if financing was not available within the next year or two, they would be able to cancel their orders (Jacobs, 1974:30).

This is *not* to say that the decline in electricity demand was irrelevant to the nuclear sector's collapse. It had important effects in *exacerbating* the trends of cancellations and reduced orders for new plants. It was certainly responsible for the push to cut back all types of generating capacity in general. However, it does not appear to have been the principal cause for the proportionally overwhelming number of reductions in nuclear capacity per se. The institutional constraints precipitating the utilities' financial crisis were primarily responsible for that.

Others have recognized the importance of the institutional arrangements of capital formation for utility planning and the nuclear sector's decline. For example, in an excellent international comparison, Måns Lönnroth and William Walker (1979) argued that utilities in the United States could have avoided many of the financial problems that undermined their nuclear plans had the government assumed a more active role providing loans, approving plans, and regulating utility prices. They claimed that such government backing would have allowed utilities "some freedom to invest in a pattern of electricity supply that reflects perceptions of long-term interests, at the risk of some economic wastefulness in the interim, rather than always being prisoners of short-term commercial pressures" (Lönnroth and Walker, 1979:37). They suggested that more government involvement would have reduced short-term economic uncertainty and facilitated planning.

The analysis presented here tends to support this crucial insight. However, two things distinguish my analysis from theirs. First, in the United States utilities were *not* completely at the mercy of short-term commercial pressures, as Lönnroth and Walker suggest. In fact, state regulators mediated the relationship between private utilities and the capital markets, although indirectly, through the public utility commissions' control over utility profit rates. Second, the problem was not so much the absence of state involvement as it was the institutional constraints that prevented existing state regulation from serving the utilities' interests. Citizens struggling through decentralized, democratically accessible, and autonomous regulatory apparatuses stopped public utility commissions from awarding rate increases large enough for utilities to raise the money they wanted through revenues and, later, capital markets—a direct manifestation of the contradiction between public and private economic interests. Perhaps more important, although we need to understand how the state controlled internal and external sources of investment capital insofar as the control affected utility planning, we also need to understand the relationship *between* the two capital sources. The political regulation of utility profit precipitated an earnings squeeze that forced utilities to rely more heavily on external sources of capital and then put them at a competitive disadvantage for that financing. In other words, once the public-private contradiction began to undermine internal capital formation, the institutional structure of external capital formation mediated the effects that the initial contradiction had on the further development of nuclear power by creating a situation in which utilities had to rely more heavily on private financial markets—a source of financing itself driven by the imperatives of short-term profit antithetical to the long-term investment planning the sector needed. An analysis that neglected the story of internal capital formation would not have thoroughly explained the institutional roots of the external capital crisis that contributed to the nuclear sector's collapse.

CHAPTER SEVEN

Indecision over Nuclear Waste

Commercial nuclear reactors produce high-level radioactive waste so deadly that it must be isolated for thousands of years. Yet the nuclear sector in the United States, having generated this material for three decades, will not have a permanent waste management system operating until at least the late 1990s. This is not for lack of effort. The federal government tried to build several systems, but failed each time. Indeed, it remains to be seen whether its current effort, started in 1982, will be any more successful than previous attempts. Moreover, the inability to solve the waste management riddle threatened whatever chances the sector as a whole had for rejuvenation. The situation grew so severe by 1979 that one exasperated utility executive declared that "the history of nuclear waste disposal in this country is nothing short of disaster . . . waste disposal may be the issue that sinks nuclear power" (Smock, 1979:55).

The key to this policy failure lay in the institutional constraints that policy makers faced. The story was complex because, more than any of the other policy areas discussed so far, it involved all of the institutional dimensions explored earlier: the structures of the state, the economy, and the state–civil society intersection. At first, as noted earlier, officials at the AEC decided to develop a private reprocessing industry to chemically separate uranium and plutonium from other radioactive wastes in the spent fuel reactors produced. Part of the plan was that the sector would recycle these two elements as fresh reactor fuel. However, this was only an initial step toward solving the waste problem because reprocessing reduced, but did not eliminate, the material requiring permanent disposal. Nevertheless, the AEC's inability to direct the economic decision making of reprocessing corporations, the corporations' need to compete with each other for business, and the capacity of various political groups to block the policy process destroyed the federal government's reprocessing plan. Other waste management programs followed, but also failed because outsiders impeded their implementation.

LIMITS POSED BY THE STATE–CIVIL SOCIETY INTERSECTION

The 1954 Atomic Energy Act defined and institutionalized the relationship between the state and the rest of the commercial nuclear economy, giving the AEC only minimal, indirect control in planning the development of commercial waste reprocessing. Although legislators had instructed the AEC to promote the commercialization of nuclear power (Clarke, 1985), they imposed strict limits on how the agency could proceed. Most important was the stipulation that the AEC encourage the development of nuclear power in the private sector on a competitive basis. As a result, private firms became the critical decision-making units controlling the nuclear sector's development. In effect, the law made the AEC a junior partner to the private sector with only a limited range of policy tools. The AEC could gently encourage firms to move in certain directions, but private corporations made the final decisions. This introduced a profitability calculus into government planning. The AEC realized that it had to minimize financial risk and maximize the opportunities for profits in the private sector if it was going to entice corporations to pursue nuclear power.

Following this logic the AEC decided to promote the development of a reprocessing industry to help encourage private utility companies to adopt nuclear technology. Reprocessing was not technically necessary for getting rid of spent fuel because waste could, for example, be removed from the reactor and buried directly. However, AEC officials felt that reprocessing offered benefits that would stimulate the sector's overall development because it created the chance to reduce fuel costs by recycling the recovered uranium and plutonium as fresh reactor fuel. Officials bolstered the incentives for reprocessing by offering to purchase the recovered plutonium from utilities, a way they saw to reduce the cost of nuclear fuel even further. This was imperative during the early days of commercialization. According to a spokesman for one reactor manufacturer, corporations and utilities believed that without the plutonium repurchasing program and the possibility of fuel recycling, the cost of fuel would have been high enough that nuclear power would not have been competitive with traditional fossil fuel plants. Hence, there was a strong incentive for the AEC to develop reprocessing (Edlund, 1963). Furthermore, from the utilities' point of view reprocessing essentially solved the waste management problem by providing someone else to take responsibility for the storage and ultimate disposal of spent fuel. This was just as important to the utilities as minimizing fuel costs (Smith and Bigge, 1970:287).

However, the institutional constraints under the 1954 act forced the AEC to promote the development of a *private* reprocessing industry. In 1956 the AEC announced that it would provide reprocessing technology and a guaranteed supply of spent fuel from its military program as incentives for getting firms to build reprocessing plants. The provision of military waste was especially important. Because the nuclear industry was still just developing, commercial reactors were not yet producing enough spent fuel to sustain a private reprocessing industry. The AEC planned to use the military's waste to fill the gap during the interim with waste from the reactors it used to produce weapons-grade plutonium (S. M. Stoller Corporation, 1975:127).

An AEC guarantee for five-years worth of spent fuel helped convince the Nuclear Fuel Services Company to build the first commercial reprocessing plant at West Valley, New York, in 1962 (Lester and Rose, 1977:22). The plant started operating in 1966 using the government's Purex reprocessing technology and could reprocess three hundred metric tons of waste annually (B. Cohen, 1979:26).[1] The facility cost $32 million but would have been much more expensive were it not for two factors. In addition to the company's efforts to cut construction costs in order to maximize profits later, the AEC imposed contractual pressure to keep reprocessing prices low. This was an attempt to make fuel recycling more appealing and, therefore, increase the attractiveness of nuclear power to the utilities (B. Cohen, 1979:26–31; Metz, 1977:44–45). In an effort to preserve future profit margins as best it could, the company cut back on expensive safety features such as adequate ventilation systems and proper shielding around radioactive pipes, decisions that caused important political and economic problems later (Freeman, 1981: chap. 8; U.S. House, 1975:861).

By 1969 the reprocessing industry's success seemed imminent. General Electric had started building a plant at Morris, Illinois, involving a

---

[1] Three hundred metric tons per year was a relatively small amount. Utilities in the United States accumulated about 22,800 metric tons of spent fuel by 1970 (Barlett and Steele, 1985:124–25). If the West Valley plant had operated at full capacity from the time it began operations in 1966 through 1970, it could have reprocessed only about 5 percent of that waste.

new Aquaflour process capable of handling three hundred to five hundred metric tons of spent fuel per year. Allied General Nuclear Services had applied to the AEC for a construction permit to build a much bigger Purex plant, with a capacity of fifteen hundred metric tons per year, at Barnwell, South Carolina. Their hope in building the huge plant was to achieve economies of scale large enough to help them cut prices and capture a major share of the reprocessing market, one that promised to be substantial now that utilities were buying nuclear plants. Atlantic Richfield also filed for permission to begin work on a plant of the same size as the Barnwell facility.

The institutional character of the state–civil society intersection, specified by the 1954 act, had several critical effects on the AEC's reprocessing plan. First, since the state had to encourage the development of nuclear power indirectly in the private sector, reprocessing became a critical part of the AEC waste management strategy. This was not because the AEC saw reprocessing as particularly desirable from a waste management standpoint, although it may have been, but because reprocessing promised certain economic advantages that the agency could use to persuade private utilities to buy nuclear plants. Second, the private sector assumed responsibility for most of the reprocessing industry's development. Hence, the AEC had to depend on the private sector for the ultimate success or failure of reprocessing. The AEC had only a few indirect incentives with which to encourage the participation of private corporations. This severely restricted the agency's ability to control the reprocessing industry's development. If the corporations decided to abandon the industry, reprocessing would die and the AEC could do nothing to stop it. Ironically, although it was the AEC's ultimate *responsibility* to plan for the disposal of the nation's commercial nuclear waste, the 1954 act transferred effective *control* over the reprocessing part of that plan from the AEC to the private reprocessing corporations. Therefore, given the institutional nature of the state–civil society intersection, the government was in the unenviable position of having to plot a waste management strategy but without the tools or leverage to ensure that corporations would necessarily adhere to the plan. This created the opportunity for a second institutional limit, the structure of the economy, to affect reprocessing. The results were disastrous.

Limits Posed by the Structure of the Economy

Intense competition among the four reprocessing corporations for market share and profits forced each to pursue its own immediate economic interests at the expense of the AEC's long-term waste management strategy. As a result, the reprocessing industry began to collapse and the government's plan began to unravel. The first sign of trouble came when Atlantic Richfield withdrew its construction permit application in 1971. The company had not been able to sell nearly as many contracts to utilities for future reprocessing services as Allied General, its major competitor (S. M. Stoller Corporation, 1975:127). Initially, Atlantic Richfield had adopted a technology that left reprocessed spent fuel in a solid form—as opposed to Allied General's Purex process, which left liquefied waste after reprocessing. The Purex plant was considerably less expensive to build and operate as long as it did not have to reconvert wastes into solid form for permanent disposal. However, the Purex process was less desirable from a strictly waste management perspective because the liquid wastes it left were more difficult to dispose of than solids (U.S. House, 1977a:36). Nevertheless, Atlantic Richfield decided to abandon the market. Their solids-only process simply could not compete on a price basis with Allied General, despite its waste management advantages (U.S. House, 1977a:35–36).

General Electric cancelled its Morris facility in 1974 for similar reasons, but announced that its new solids-only Aquaflour process had become a technological nightmare. Many observers felt that competition with Allied General was a contributing factor. *Science* magazine reported that visions of competing with the alleged economies of scale at Allied General's huge Barnwell facility convinced General Electric to quickly expand the size of its own plant in Illinois. Apparently the expansion was premature, for General Electric did not have much experience with its new process (Gillette, 1974:771). The hasty renovation caused technical problems that were too expensive to fix (Resnikoff, 1975).

However, others directly involved argued that technical prolems had had nothing to do with it, that competition was entirely to blame. Because General Electric's Aquaflour process was a more expensive solids-only approach, as long as companies did not have to solidify the wastes left after reprocessing, the company was at a competitive disadvantage compared to Allied General, with its less expensive, yet liquified, technology. According to Cleve Anderson, designer of General Electric's plant and inventor of the Aquaflour process, if everyone had to solidify their final wastes, then Allied General would have had to add solidification facilities to its plant and the tables would have been turned. General Electric could have reprocessed at lower overall prices than Allied General—even after fixing the technical problems on its renovated plant (U.S. House, 1977a:73). In fact, the AEC did rule in 1970 that reprocessors had to solidify final wastes. Nevertheless, despite that decision, Allied General continued to offer lower bids than General Electric for reprocessing services. According to Anderson, Allied General executives believed they could convince the federal government to subsidize their required solidification facility. Their bids reflected that assumption and remained below what General Electric's would have been after renovating the Aquaflour process. As a result, Anderson argued, it was not a technological failure as publicized, but a *competitive* failure that forced General Electric to close its plant.

In any case competitive pressure had eliminated a technology from the market place that was superior for handling radioactive waste. More important, competition had forced another corporation to abandon reprocessing. Despite its wish to see reprocessing flourish, the AEC could do very little other than watch its plan continue to disintegrate. Under the 1954 act, the relationship between government and corporations ensured that private firms would decide whether or not to reprocess. Within those limits economic competition created a situation in which individual, short-term, corporate interests guided the decision making—even at the expense of the nuclear sector in general. This further constrained the AEC's capacity for waste management planning. Both the structure of the state-economy interface and the structure of the economy continued to undermine reprocessing. However, a third limit, the politically accessible structure of the state, also took its toll.

LIMITS POSED BY THE STRUCTURE OF THE STATE

There were several institutional channels of access to government policy makers that affected the reprocessing industry's fate. Political groups, citizens, and government officials used them to influence the AEC's waste management policy, particularly during policy implementation. Because these groups did not always have goals consistent with the AEC's initial reprocessing plan, they helped drive the two remaining reprocessing corporations from the market. This happened first with Nuclear Fuel Services.

Nuclear Fuel Services

In 1972 Nuclear Fuel Services temporarily closed its plant because it had not been able to negotiate enough long-term reprocessing contracts with utilities building new reactors. General Electric and Allied

General's promises of larger and more cost efficient plants had put Nuclear Fuel Services at a competitive disadvantage (Rochlin et al., 1978:21). Furthermore, operations at West Valley had been losing millions of dollars. Therefore, Nuclear Fuel Services closed the plant temporarily to expand its capacity, increase economies of scale, and improve its competitive position (U.S. House, 1975:861). The company filed for a new construction permit from the AEC in 1973 (AEC, 1974a). Following normal procedures, the AEC convened hearings providing an opportunity for public discussion of the permit. The hearings offered outsiders, concerned with how the plant was built and operated, a point of access to arenas where the AEC implemented safety and other regulatory policies. A variety of public interest groups, including the Sierra Club, a national environmentalist organization, intervened at the hearings, raising questions about the plant's environmental impact and arguing that it was structurally incapable of withstanding earthquake tremors that could occur in the area. They convinced the AEC to require architectural changes in the plant. Company employees working at West Valley also participated at the hearings, objecting to inadequate safety systems and dangerous working conditions inside the plant. Again, the AEC agreed to order the necessary improvements (Freeman, 1981:chap. 8). Most important, the commission decided that it would require the company to meet its 1970 guidelines requiring reprocessors to solidify final waste products after it had granted West Valley a special exemption to the rule. These and other necessary modifications would have cost $600 million. Compared to the $32 million first invested to build the plant and the $15 million originally estimated for expansion, managers felt that the project was now too expensive to be profitable. Nuclear Fuel Services announced its withdrawal from the industry in 1976 (B. Cohen, 1979:26).

The interaction among different institutional effects in this case was significant. Competition in the reprocessing industry contributed to cost cutting and, therefore, to the development of many safety problems, which interveners raised later at the construction permit hearings. The company eliminated expensive safety features when the plant was first built and refused to fix resulting problems later because it would have been too expensive to do so at a time when the firm was trying to remain competitive by reducing costs wherever possible (Rochlin et al., 1978). For example, when employees complained that certain ventilation ducts were radioactive and threatened their health, plant officials did not clean them because of the expense (Freeman, 1981:231–36). The company was primarily concerned with maximizing profits and remaining competitive, something they had to do in order to survive in the marketplace (U.S. House, 1975:883). In short, a contradiction had developed, exacerbated by the intense competition prevalent at the time, between the company's interest in profit and employee's concerns with safety. This sparked demands for plant improvements, which interveners pressed on policy makers through public hearings. Had the institutional context been different, plant managers might have made different decisions and avoided some of the problems that flared up later. The plant might have survived as a result.

Of course there were other problems because the company did not adopt a solids-only technology in the first place. This decision created the possibility that the company would have to build expensive solidification facilities as in fact it later did. If the decision to use a liquified technology, not a solids-only process, was simply a matter of poor judgment by company officials, then perhaps the company's downfall was the result of corporate mismanagement rather than institutional factors. However, to understand why the company made this decision we also need to know why the AEC advocated the Purex process. Again, institutional constraints were involved.

Purex was the most developed reprocessing technology available when Nuclear Fuel Services considered building its plant. During an interview for this book one ranking NRC staff member involved with waste management reported that in its haste to promote the industry, the AEC pushed the Purex technology precisely because it was the only one ready for immediate commercialization. AEC officials did so despite the fact that it was not the best technology for ultimate waste disposal. After all, it left liquefied, not solid, wastes. The AEC knew this and even thought about developing a solids-only process. Nevertheless, the agency finally decided to promote Purex for the Nuclear Fuel Services plant instead (U.S. House, 1977a:34–65). Hence, the decision to pursue Purex and drop the solids-only technology was not just an accident of poor judgment by Nuclear Fuel Services or the AEC, but a product of institutional imperatives. The AEC wanted to facilitate the commercialization of nuclear power according to the 1954 act and saw Purex reprocessing as a quick means to that end. Nuclear Fuel Services had no other technological options, accepted the AEC's offer, and proceeded with the Purex process. This created the possibility for the AEC's later solidification decision and the massive expansion costs associated with it.

Allied General

The effects of policy-making accessibility, which dovetailed with those of the other institutional limits in the Nuclear Fuel Services story, were more dominant in the demise of Allied General's plant. This time political forces made demands contrary to the AEC's reprocessing plan through several institutional channels, including environmental hearings, the courts, and the White House, and destroyed what was left of the reprocessing industry.

Construction began on Allied General's Barnwell plant in 1970, but eventually ground to a halt as a result of expensive regulatory changes and delays. In addition to its earlier requirement that reprocessors solidify final wastes, the AEC ruled in 1974 that companies had to solidify the plutonium they recovered through reprocessing. Now Allied General had to build another solidification facility (*Nuclear Energy Policy Study Group,* 1977:322; Tannenbaum, 1976:21). However, construction soon stopped on the project. The NRC announced in 1975 that it would not decide whether to permit plutonium fuel recycling in nuclear reactors until hearings investigating the environmental impacts of the process were finished. Plutonium recycling had been a hotly contested political and environmental issue since the AEC released its preliminary environmental impact statement a year earlier. Following the provisions of the National Environmental Policy Act, the NRC was conducting public hearings to review the report— hearings required under the act. The hearings dragged on for several months. Meanwhile, at the request of environmentalists and others concerned with the problems of plutonium proliferation, a federal court ordered the NRC to suspend licensing and construction permits for all commercial facilities associated with plutonium recycling until the hearings were finished (*Energy User's Report,* 1976b:A-9).

The effect was devastating for the Barnwell plant. Allied General's president complained that until the hearings were done it made no sense for his company to begin reprocessing because there was no place to put the recovered plutonium. Having expected to ship it shortly after extraction, Allied General had built only limited storage for liquefied plutonium at Barnwell. If the plant started to reprocess, storage would soon be full and it would have to shut down because the NRC would not allow them to expand storage until after the hearings (U.S. Senate, 1978a:824). He told a group of industry leaders in 1976 that the lack of a clear policy on plutonium recycling was preventing his company from finishing its plant and starting operations. He also said that it was deterring others from entering the business (Schubert, 1976:117). This did not bode well for the reprocessing industry. A study commissioned by the AEC concluded that in 1975 reprocessing was in a state of commercial disarray (S. M. Stoller Corporation, 1975:13). The only remaining plant, Barnwell, faced serious delays, while utilities grew skeptical about the merits and possibilities of reprocessing altogether.

Interveners, such as the Natural Resources Defense Council and the Sierra Club, had taken two opportunities of access to the policy process and inflicted serious delays on the development of reprocessing in this case. First, they extended resolution of the environmental impact statement review by participating in the hearing process. Then they worked through the courts, forcing suspension of construction on the Barnwell project until the hearings were finished (Nader and Abbotts, 1979:331). In effect, they had taken advantage of the opportunities for participation provided by the institutional structure of the state to bring what was left of the reprocessing industry to its knees. This created the preconditions for the last fatal blow to reprocessing—an executive order from the White House banning reprocessing in the United States.

In 1976 President Ford declared a three-year moratorium on reprocessing so that the government could study the risks associated with nuclear weapons proliferation arising from the extraction of plutonium from spent fuel. Ford's decision was partially rooted in the growing realization that reprocessing was not as economically attractive as originally believed (Hill, 1976). With the change in administrations, Jimmy Carter announced in 1977 that he would defer reprocessing *indefinitely* in the interests of controlling proliferation. Carter's policy completely demolished what was left of the government's reprocessing plan. As a result, the NRC suspended the construction permit reviews for the Barnwell facility and the environmental impact hearings on plutonium recycling (NRC, 1978c). Soon thereafter Allied General announced that it would abandon the business (U.S. House, 1979:47). Commercial reprocessing was dead in the United States.

The crux of the matter was that the AEC's plan for reprocessing had now succumbed to the influence of political forces operating through yet another channel of access within the government. Those interested not so much in the management of nuclear waste per se as in preventing the spread of nuclear weapons material by ending waste reprocessing had effectively used the administration's preemptive control over policy in the executive branch to achieve their goals. The White House shared jurisdiction over waste policy with the NRC and, therefore, provided opportunities for new political actors to influence policy making. Accessibility to a rather fragmented policy process had facilitated their mobilization and eventually undermined the remains of the AEC's reprocessing plan.

However, it was not just this accessibility that killed the reprocessing industry. Nor was it just the proliferation issue, although it was the publicly announced rationale for Carter's decision. The entire history of the reprocessing debacle up to that point also played an important part as did the effects of the institutional limits posed by the structures of the reprocessing industry itself and the intersection of the AEC and the industry. According to NRC Commissioner Victor Gilinsky, the dubious economic merit of reprocessing was at least as important in setting the stage for Carter's policy as were any concerns the president may have had regarding international proliferation (Gilinsky, 1978:378). The rising costs of reprocessing, due in part to the interventions and delays discussed earlier, contributed to this concern. It would have been extremely difficult for Carter to shut down an *operating* industry. Hence, the institutional effects that forced three reprocessors from the market and left the fourth unable to operate had established the preconditions for the Carter decision. This is not to say that the proliferation issue was unimportant. But the fact that reprocessing had already ground to a halt created the possibility for this final and most devastating political blow. In any case, the sector needed a new plan for the disposal of waste that did not include reprocessing as an intermediate step. Subsequent attempts to find a plan were generally unsuccessful for two interrelated reasons. First, the government had assumed that reprocessing would materialize and had procrastinated in developing a final disposal policy. Second, political groups took advantage of other institutional opportunities to penetrate the policy process and block the implementation of new proposals designed to solve the waste management problem.

POLITICAL PROCRASTINATION

After it appeared that reprocessing would develop, the AEC stopped much of its planning for the long-term management of spent fuel on the assumption that this responsibility now rested with private reprocessing companies (*Energy User's Report,* 1974c:A19; *Nuclear Energy Policy Study Group,* 1977:249). Instead, the agency devoted most of its attention to figuring out how to store wastes *after* reprocessing. However, the agency's interest in these matters was very limited. AEC officials decided to store liquid reprocessed wastes temporarily in steel tanks until they could develop a more permanent disposal system (NRC, 1976:D-3). The agency did investigate the possibility of burying the waste permanently in underground salt caverns, but this was a low priority project that continued sporadically and with only limited funds (DOE, 1981:48). It was not until 1970, after the AEC discovered several leaky storage tanks, that officials began to take their responsibility for waste management more seriously. Staff members recommended that reprocessors solidify wastes, and the AEC promulgated regulations to that effect requiring solidification within five years of reprocessing and shipment of those wastes to the AEC within ten (AEC, 1974b:1.2–9). This was the AEC's first systematic attempt to develop a policy to deal with waste after reprocessing (NRC, 1976:D-3).

The new policy required that officials plan how to store waste upon delivery. Pursuing their earlier strategy, they decided to bury it in salt caverns near Lyons, Kansas. However, a series of geological problems and engineering errors at the site, followed by an unsuccessful AEC cover-up of the difficulties involved, created a political backlash from citizens, the governor, the Kansas Geological Survey, and the state attorney general, all of whom objected to both the site and how the AEC had tried to force the project on them while ignoring their concerns. As a result, the AEC's legitimacy suffered a serious blow and Congress gutted the project's funding in 1971.[2] The agency abandoned the project in 1972 and developed a plan for building a temporary storage facility above ground from which they could retrieve the waste later. Officials hoped that this plan would buy time to search for another more permanent disposal system (GAO, 1977b:8). However, while the AEC's chairperson promised Congress that the agency was going to move vigorously to develop that system (AEC, 1973a:63), AEC funding for waste management remained stable at only 3 or 4 percent of the agency's annual budgets. Furthermore, the agency never developed either a staff assigned specifically to waste management or any greater priority for the problem than it had before (House, 1977b:29–31).

Why did the AEC continue to procrastinate? The agency was preoccupied with the promotion of commercial nuclear power for most of its existence. The waste management problem did not seem to have much bearing in the short run on commercializing nuclear technology except insofar as reprocessing could reduce fuel costs and provide a place for utilities to get rid of their spent fuel. According to high-ranking officials at both the NRC and the American Nuclear Energy Council, the nuclear sector's primary lobbying organization, interviewed for this study, once it appeared that reprocessing would

---

[2] For a more detailed account of the Lyons history, see Lewis (1972:chap. 6).

develop and provide a place to put spent fuel temporarily, the AEC assumed that it would have plenty of time to develop a permanent disposal plan later, and it delayed working on the problem.[3] Again, this was not a problem of mismanagement on the AEC's part. At the time, there was every reason to expect that private reprocessing would develop and provide the anticipated leeway. Instead, the problem was that, for institutional reasons, the AEC had to rely on a competitive market system over which it had very little control to provide this interim waste storage before final disposal. Furthermore, agency officials had no control over White House edicts suspending reprocessing.

It was not until 1975 that the government began to suspect that it might have to build a waste management system sooner than expected. By then General Electric and Atlantic Richfield had abandoned reprocessing, Nuclear Fuel Services had closed its plant for renovation, and Allied General's project faced long delays. Temporary storage capacity for spent fuel at nuclear stations was beginning to fill up, and there was no place to ship the excess. In response the NRC began granting utilities permission in 1975 to modify and expand their temporary storage facilities at reactor sites to accommodate more spent fuel (U.S. House, 1979:280–81). The Energy Research and Development Administration (ERDA), heir to the defunct AEC's promotional functions, doubled its budget for radioactive waste disposal research and development in 1976 over what it had been two years earlier at the AEC, from $85.4 to $189.6 million in real terms, a jump that reflected the new agency's growing concern with the problem (DOE, 1981:52). ERDA officials warned Congress that there might not be any reprocessing in the United States and that they should make contingency plans accordingly (JCAE, 1976:47, 59). The agency began moving more quickly to develop alternatives for handling and disposing high-level wastes. However, political forces operating within an institutionally porous policy-making system undermined many of these attempts once again.

POLITICAL OBSTRUCTION AND MORE POLICY FAILURES

The AEC started working on a temporary above-ground storage facility after the Lyons, Kansas, fiasco and issued a draft environmental impact statement for the project in 1974.[4] However, state and local

---

[3] Cochran and Tamplin (1978) and Jakimo and Bupp (1978) also make this argument, but neglect the institutional underpinnings.
[4] The project was called the Retrievable Surface Storage Facility.

governments, the U.S. Environmental Protection Agency, the president's Council on Environmental Quality, and environmental groups, including the Sierra Club, opposed the project, fearing that this allegedly temporary solution would detract from the government's permanent disposal efforts and become a de facto permanent disposal facility (Greenwood, 1982:6–7). Their objections reflected concerns about the government's long history of procrastination. ERDA abandoned the project in 1975 in response to these protests and returned to the initial plan of permanently burying wastes in the ground, but with an important twist. The agency would spend $1.2 billion developing six sites for the disposal of both reprocessed wastes and, for the first time, unreprocessed spent fuel (GAO, 1977b:11).[5] However, political problems struck again. Various state and local governments opposed the notion of locating disposal facilities within their borders. Some even objected to the federal government conducting preliminary in-state geological studies that might lead to such an outcome. For example, when ERDA announced that it would investigate the geological suitability of building a pilot project in one Michigan county, residents throughout the area voted overwhelmingly to stop the project (GAO, 1977b:15). In the face of such opposition ERDA retreated again, this time from the multiple-site strategy to look instead for a single location where citizens would be more accepting (Greenwood, 1982:7).

Nevertheless, concerns at the state level mounted. Beginning in 1976, through referenda, gubernatorial mandates, public utility commission declarations, and legislation, several states prohibited the long-term storage or disposal of high-level waste and spent fuel within their borders (Atomic Industrial Forum, 1982; NRC, 1981b; 1982a). By late 1978, thirty-three states had passed laws controlling some aspect of radioactive waste management (Zinberg, 1982:164). In view of this evidence, the U.S. General Accounting Office (1977b:15) reported to Congress that "public and political acceptance is the biggest political obstacle that ERDA must overcome in resolving the waste disposal problem."

The important point is that the institutional structure of the policy process provided opportunities for several different political forces to block the government's plans repeatedly, thereby forcing federal officials to keep changing policy directions. First, the fragmentation of authority over waste policy among federal agencies created the legal opportunity for one agency to block the planning of another. For example, the Environmental Protection Agency helped force ERDA

5 These projects were called Surface Unreprocessed Fuel Facilities.

to drop its initial temporary storage strategy. Second, there were important channels of access to top-level policy makers for citizens and lower levels of government concerned about the project's implications. The Council on Environmental Quality often provided opportunities for the external environmental community to gather information and influence decision makers (Greenwood, 1982:14). Third, opportunities existed at lower levels of government to try to block federal action through a variety of legislative, electoral, and legal tactics.

All of this began to create serious problems for utilities. While the government vacillated among various policy options, utilities continued to worry about running out of space for storing their spent fuel. They had filed forty-four applications with the NRC by 1977 to increase their on-site spent fuel storage capacity (Meyers, 1978:138). However, citizens, environmental groups, and local authorities protested these expansion proposals at the NRC's construction permit hearings and elsewhere. For example, the Portland Gas and Electric Company asked to expand its spent fuel storage capacity in 1977. They had to endure numerous licensing interventions, three law suits, and several appeals before finally beginning expansion two years later (Frewing and Owens, 1979:678). Political opposition doubled the average licensing time for similar projects between 1974 and 1979 (U.S. House, 1979:165). It became apparent that the government would have to do something. When asked in 1977 how much spent fuel they would send the government for storage if space was available, utilities told the U.S. Department of Energy, successor to the ERDA, that they would be ready to ship forty metric tons within the year. The utilities' more alarming estimates for future shipments are listed in Table 7.1. Utilities reported that as reactors operated longer and the volume of spent fuel increased, they would have 4,270 metric tons ready to ship by 1986 and even more after that.

The Department of Energy realized that storage at reactor sites was filling up and threatening to shut down reactors and undermine the sector's economic viability (GAO, 1979:4). According to one agency official, "The uncertainty concerning the ultimate disposition of the spent fuel . . . significantly increased the financial risks for nuclear plant investment, and adversely affected the nuclear option" (Beckjord, 1978:16). Late in 1977 the Department of Energy responded by announcing that it would begin accepting and storing spent fuel from commercial reactors until either reprocessing or geologic disposal became available. The department intended its new plan to relieve the uncertainty surrounding spent fuel disposition. Ironically, it did the

Table 7.1. Spent fuel that utilities anticipated shipping to government storage (in metric tons)

Year	Amount Discharged by Reactors	Amount Utilities Anticipated Shipping
1978	3,340	40
1979	4,360	120
1980	5,580	300
1981	6,990	430
1982	8,740	680
1983	10,650	1,240
1984	12,830	1,880
1985	15,430	3,200
1986	18,330	4,270
1987	21,360	5,550
1988	24,570	7,000
1989	27,890	8,410
1990	31,330	10,220

Note: $N = 53$ responses to 76 requests for information from utilities by the Department of Energy in 1977.
SOURCE: Adapted from Lawrence (1978): 313.

opposite because the government did not decide how much it would charge utilities to store their spent fuel or when it would be ready to accept shipments (GAO, 1979:4). According to the Atomic Industrial Forum this made it difficult for utilities to plan whether they should wait and ship to the government or try to build new on-site storage capacity for themselves (Gordon, 1978:240). The threat of political opposition during implementation of the government's plan further clouded the issue. Utilities worried that the government would encounter objections and then licensing delays that would prevent it from finishing the project quickly. Their concern was justified. The Department of Energy admitted in 1978 that local opposition had already forced them to abandon their first list of potential storage sites and look elsewhere (*Energy User's Report,* 1978c:2). Moreover, interveners announced that they would oppose the policy in adjudicatory hearings (Atomic Industrial Forum, 1978; Howard, 1978; U.S. House, 1977b:102–13).

Recognizing the need for solutions to these problems, President Carter formed the Interagency Review Group in 1978 to suggest solutions and to develop an implementation strategy. The review group recognized two things. First, it saw that technical solutions to the waste management problem were needed soon. Second, it realized that institutional obstacles could undermine the implementation of any plan. The review group was particularly aware that the federal government's relationship with state and local governments over the issues had deteriorated to a point where the latter were impeding even the earliest stages of site evaluation (Greenwood, 1982:35; Interagency Review Group on Nuclear Waste Management, 1979).

To solve the technical problem, the review group recommended in 1979 that the Department of Energy build a storage facility for the nation's unreprocessed spent fuel as soon as possible (Interagency Review Group on Nuclear Waste Management, 1979:62).[6] This was not surprising, inasmuch as the utility industry had advocated such a facility during congressional hearings (U.S. House, 1977b:103) and lobbied for it with the review group (Interagency Review Group on Nuclear Waste Management, 1979:61). More important, the group recognized that to solve the institutional problem the federal government would have to restore public confidence in its ability to manage the waste problem safely, a legitimation problem that had grown steadily for several reasons. One was the episode at Lyons, Kansas. Another was Congress's discovery in 1970 that the AEC was suppressing a study about the geological problems at many current waste storage sites (Cochran and Tamplin, 1978:14). Ralph Nader, head of Critical Mass, a prominent antinuclear group, underscored public concern in 1974 when he said that one of the major problems his organization saw with nuclear power was the government's inability to resolve satisfactorily the waste issue (Energy User's Report, 1974d:A4). That same year a coalition of 130 public interest groups reaffirmed their opposition to nuclear power for similar reasons (Energy User's Report, 1974b:A14). According to national opinion polls, concern with the waste disposal problem had grown to a point by late 1978 where 76 percent of the public felt that the disposal of radioactive waste was one of the biggest problems with nuclear power (Table 7.2). To gain legitimacy for its own recommendations and to facilitate implementation later, the review group held public hearings across the country and solicited public comment on its draft report to get as much input from citizens and potential opponents as possible (Greenwood, 1982:22). It also recommended that the president form a State Planning Council consisting of several governors, state representatives, and federal officials to encourage an atmosphere of "cooperative

[6] The group made its recommendation only after utility and industry sources refused to provide their own facilities away from reactor sites because they felt it would be an unprofitable investment (Beckjord, 1978; U.S. House, 1979:46), an interesting example of the tension between short-term profitability and economic planning.

Table 7.2. Public attitudes about the disposal of high-level nuclear waste

Date	Major Problem (%)	Minor Problem (%)	Hardly a Problem (%)	Not Sure (%)
April 1979	80	15	3	2
October 1978	76	11	4	8
November 1976	67	14	5	14
May 1975	63	14	7	16

Note: Responses were to the question: "Do you think the disposal of radioactive waste which remains radioactive for many centuries to come is a major problem connected with nuclear power plants, a minor problem, or hardly a problem at all?" The data are compiled from ABC News/Harris national polls.
SOURCE: Adapted from Mitchell (1982):32.

federalism" in decision making over the selection of specific storage locations. Carter established the council in 1980 and asked Congress for legislation to implement the storage facility.[7]

The legislation did not come easily. Congress began considering high-level waste management bills in 1980. However, it was not until late 1982 that it finally passed one, the Nuclear Waste Policy Act. One reason it took so long was that several states were concerned they would become dumping grounds for all the nation's nuclear waste. For example, politicians and officials from Mississippi, Louisiana, and Utah, states the Department of Energy was already considering as likely candidates, were able to add clauses to the bill or cut deals with the Department of Energy that effectively eliminated them from consideration (Barlett and Steele, 1985:160). Furthermore, Congress could not muster enough votes to pass the legislation until it added a clause providing any state or Indian reservation that the Department of Energy selected as a disposal site with the opportunity to veto the decision. The veto would stand unless both houses of Congress could

[7] The review group was very worried that states would block implementation if they did not have significant input during the site selection process. To reassure state officials and citizens, the group initially considered recommending formal veto power to any state picked as a storage site. However, it reconsidered later, fearing that this would ultimately result in vetoes by every state eventually selected. In short, given the level of suspicion for federal policy by state and local authorities, the review group did not want to increase the institutional opportunities for these authorities to block implementation. The decision came despite warnings from a spokesperson for the National Conference of State Legislatures that the federal government "should not attempt to dictate the process by which the state decides whether to accept or disapprove a proposed waste facility. . . . To short circuit this process, especially by federal fiat, would be to raise fundamental questions in the public mind about its legitimacy" (U.S. House, 1979:26).

override it by majority votes, an arduous legislative task.[8] Yet no matter how serious these obstacles seemed to be, by 1986 it appeared that they were not the only ones threatening the new program.

THE CHANCES FOR SUCCESS

Opponents began to employ a variety of institutional opportunities to obstruct implementation of the Nuclear Waste Policy Act. Several states used legislative channels to make it difficult, if not impossible, for the Department of Energy to begin testing prospective sites. For example, Mississippi passed a law forbidding the federal government to put a repository anywhere within its borders where five hundred or more people lived within a five-mile radius of the site, a stipulation that virtually eliminated the entire state from consideration (GAO, 1985a:23). Critics also resorted to litigation. Following the Department of Energy's announcement in 1984 that it was considering Mississippi, Utah, Nevada, Texas, and Washington state as candidates for its first waste repository, environmentalists and officials from some of the states filed eight law suits challenging the government's selection criteria. After the Department of Energy announced another list of candidates for a second repository in 1986, two of the states cited, Maine and New Hampshire, sued the department to allow them more time to review and comment on their selection (GAO, 1986). The use of administrative channels also undermined the Department of Energy's efforts. Under the Nuclear Waste Policy Act the department was required to engage in formal agreements with any state it considered for a site in order to ensure that it recognized and met the state's interests. These agreements proved difficult to negotiate. For example, the state of Washington insisted that the federal government guarantee unlimited compensation in the event of a waste management accident, something the Department of Energy was unable to do given the stipulations of another law, the Price-Anderson Act. A negotiating stalemate resulted (GAO, 1985b:iii). Even if these kinds of problems were resolved, the capacity for a governor, state legislature, or affected Indian tribe to veto the Department of Energy's siting decision could still permanently derail implementation. Governor Richard Bryan and the entire Nevada congressional delegation said

[8] For a discussion of the special interests involved in shaping the 1982 Nuclear Waste Policy Act, see Barlett and Steele (1985).

they would do just that if federal officials picked their state for the first repository (Reinhold, 1986). Because 70 percent of Washington's residents reported not wanting the nation's waste, a veto also seemed likely there (Nappi, 1985). Similarly, the Menomenee Indian tribe in northern Wisconsin threatened a veto after learning that the Department of Energy had selected their land as a possible site for the second repository (Franklin, 1986).

Even without vetoes delays grew quickly. The 1982 act instructed the president to submit a choice for the first repository to Congress by 1987, but the Department of Energy reported that political problems would help delay the recommendation until at least 1991 (GAO, 1985b:70). Furthermore, opposition was so intense to the group of sites announced in 1986 for a second disposal site in the eastern or midwestern United States that the government withdrew the list and announced it was considering cancelling the search for a second disposal site altogether (Reinhold, 1986).

Many of the factors contributing to this opposition involved doubts about the Department of Energy's credibility and concern with the interests of affected parties. The U.S. General Accounting Office (1986; 1985b) found that officials from several states were dissatisfied with the lack of opportunity to participate in the selection of sites and the development of selection criteria. The Governor of Utah insisted that he would oppose, presumably by veto, the placement of a high-level waste repository in his state unless the Department of Energy solved this problem. Other state officials doubted the federal government's concern with their interests and complained that the Department of Energy had selected the initial sites not because they were the best ones geologically but because they were either on land the federal government already owned or were places where the government anticipated only limited political opposition—criteria that would facilitate implementation but not necessarily safe disposal (GAO, 1985c:34). The National Research Council (1984) made similar criticisms and concluded that appearances of trying to exclude parties from waste management decisions exacerbated political concerns about the waste issue and threatened implementation of the government's entire plan.

The point is a familiar one. Opposition to the Department of Energy's efforts to implement the 1982 Nuclear Waste Policy Act stemmed in part from state and local suspicions that the federal government was making policy behind closed doors where political expediency, rather than sound waste management practice and the public interest, dominated the agenda. Of course there were some states and communities that simply did not want the waste at all.[9] Nevertheless, when this centralized and insulated policy-making process was coupled with a decentralized political system that provided critics with a chance to influence policy implementation, they transformed their skepticism into political obstruction that made it very difficult for the government to complete its latest plan. As of this writing, it is not clear that the situation will improve to a point where the Department of Energy will eventually succeed in its mission. These problems continue to plague the sector's health, as they have in the past.

RAMIFICATIONS FOR THE NUCLEAR SECTOR'S VIABILITY

The perpetual uncertainty surrounding the waste management program had profound implications for the nuclear sector's viability. According to the Atomic Industrial Forum, delays in reprocessing raised questions by 1975 about the comparative economic advantage of nuclear power over fossil fuel plants (*Energy User's Report,* 1975e:G-2). One of the main reasons for choosing nuclear power had been that its fuel was less expensive than coal or oil (Perry, 1979:342). However, uranium prices started rising in the early 1970s and quadrupled between 1972 and 1975 in real terms (Table 7.3). Utilities began to believe that nuclear power's fuel cost advantage was slipping away, especially since doubts were emerging that reprocessing and fuel recycling might not materialize to balance rising uranium prices (*Energy,* 1977:9). Some observers argued that the uncertainty surrounding reprocessing and, therefore, fuel recycling had itself contributed to the escalation in uranium prices because it made estimating future uranium demand almost impossible. Hence, mining companies hesitated to develop new deposits, supplies dwindled, and higher prices followed (Hogerton, 1976).

More important, absence of a working waste management facility became a major political stumbling block for utilities seeking approval of new nuclear projects. For example, the California Energy Commission announced in 1976 that it would not approve any more nuclear stations unless utilities could confidently specify fuel and waste disposal costs, a task the commission viewed as impossible without deci-

9 Jakimo and Bupp (1978) refer to this phenomenon as the "not in my backyard" syndrome and discuss it in detail.

Table 7.3. Spot-market price per pound for uranium hexafluoride, 1960–1980

Year	Price in Unadjusted Dollars	Adjusted Price[a] (1967 Dollars)
1960	$8.75	$9.18
1961	8.50	8.97
1962	8.15	8.60
1963	7.82	8.25
1964	8.00	8.40
1965	8.00	8.30
1966	8.00	8.12
1967	8.00	8.00
1968	8.00	7.80
1969	6.99	6.59
1970	6.30	5.73
1971	6.20	5.43
1972	6.25	5.30
1973	7.10	5.64
1974	15.10	9.82
1975	35.00	20.41
1976	41.00	22.48
1977	43.20	22.14
1978	43.25	20.65
1979	40.75	17.23
1980	27.00	9.83

[a]Price adjustments were made using the Department of Labor's "Producer Price Index for Industrial Commodities, Total."

SOURCES: AEC (1973b): 8, U.S. Department of Interior (1975): 1192, *Engineering and Mining Journal* (1973–81), and U.S. Department of Commerce (1982): 460.

sions on reprocessing, spent fuel storage, and ultimate waste disposal (*Energy User's Report,* 1978b:11; Smock, 1979; U.S. House, 1977a:482, 522; U.S. Senate, 1978a:327). A member of the commission blamed the decision on the government's vacillating waste policy, arguing that "federal temporizing and foot-dragging made this inevitable" (U.S. House, 1977a:151). By 1981 six states had prohibited the construction of new reactors until the federal government settled the disposal issue and two others were fighting for similar prohibitions in court (Zinberg, 1982:164). The Supreme Court supported their decisions in 1983, upholding the California ruling and arguing that it was a state's right to decide if a plant was justified on economic grounds, including the future costs of waste management.

Utilities also faced a financial dilemma. Waste management problems were beginning to hurt their ability to raise investment capital for nuclear projects contemplated or under construction. According to an executive vice-president for the Equitable Life Assurance Society, a group that had invested $50 billion in nuclear plants by 1980, it was doubtful that these financial institutions would continue to invest in nuclear power while there were not enough facilities to store spent fuel (U.S. House, 1980:117). As long as existing storage space was limited and filling up, it was not clear how long the plants would be able to operate. Utility and government representatives acknowledged that once storage was full, plants would have to shut down (e.g., Beckjord, 1978; Meyers, 1978; Smock, 1979). This made nuclear investments even riskier than before inasmuch as an abbreviated operating history meant less time for capital to earn a return. Wall Street investment houses recognized this danger by 1977—a major factor in their decisions to advise clients against investing in nuclear utilities (U.S. House, 1977a:524).

THE POLITICAL ECONOMY OF INDECISION

Despite its maneuvering, the federal government has not implemented an operating waste management program by the late 1980s. Instead, it has jumped from one technical option to another, never settling down long enough to provide a solution to the problem. As one witness explained to a congressional committee: "For twenty years the federal [government] . . . has stood as a starving donkey between bales of hay, not able to decide which one to eat. The options remain essentially untasted" (U.S. Senate, 1981b:25). While this planning fiasco may reinforce and prolong the nuclear sector's collapse, the causes run deeper than just bureaucratic bungling, mismanagement, and indecision, although these things did have important effects.

Two political factors constrained the efforts of policy makers to devise a successful solution to the waste problem. First, environmentalists, the public, lower-level governments, and officials in other federal agencies began to doubt the federal government's ability to handle the problem. Indeed, as Dorothy Zinberg (1982; 1984) has argued, government mismanagement, including the Lyons failure, leaky storage tanks, and revelations that the government suppressed a report criticizing the safety of existing storage sites, contributed to that skepticism. Undoubtedly the public's general distrust of government in the wake of the Viet Nam war and the Watergate scandal played a role as did the development of a strong environmental movement, spurred in part by the publication in 1962 of Rachel Carson's book *Silent Spring*. However, the ensuing political opposition probably would have been much less effective in influencing policy were it not for a second factor, the institutional opportunities available for engaging the policy process during implementation. Critics used these channels to try to block anything they believed might create the possibility of storing wastes in their states or communities. As a result, successive federal agencies shifted back and forth among a variety of policy options in search of a solution that would reconcile the growing tension between what was necessary for the nuclear sector and what was palatable to the public.

However, two additional institutional factors also had important, yet less direct, effects to the extent that they undermined the government's plans for a reprocessing industry. The competitive structure of the reprocessing economy and the AEC's limited capacity to control it helped prompt that industry's collapse. In turn, this failure suddenly forced federal officials to hurry with their plans for a permanent waste management system, a situation that contributed to the deterioration in public confidence, the emergence of political opposition to later policies, and the government's inability to settle on a viable waste management plan. Most observers of nuclear waste management policy in the United States tend to overlook the significance of these two constraints, perhaps because their effects were more subtle. For example, in a collection of excellent essays on the nuclear waste problem edited by E. William Colglazier (1982), the impact of the reprocessing debacle for later waste management planning was barely mentioned. As a result, the institutional analyses offered (e.g., Deese, 1982) focus only on the structure of the state, not on the structures of the economy or the state–civil society intersection, dimensions intimately connected to the waste management story. Unless the analysis is sensitive to the effects of all three institutional dimensions, it is impossible to understand fully the roots of the planning crisis. Omission of these dimensions has been particularly glaring in analyses offered by representatives from the nuclear sector, such as the Atomic Industrial Forum (1978:2), who blame waste policy failures on the interventions of antinuclear and environmental groups, which, it charges, consistently sidetracked waste management planning.

On the other hand, perhaps we could argue that the utilities, not the prevailing institutional arrangements, were the real culprits for they were the ones insisting that the economic benefits of reprocessing were worth pursuing as a preliminary step in the waste management plan. Even after reports appeared that the benefits had become marginal (e.g., *Nuclear Energy Policy Study Group*, 1977:245; Resnikoff, 1975:29), utilities and the Atomic Industrial Forum remained convinced that reprocessing and the recycling of used uranium and plutonium were desirable (*Combustion*, 1977; Hill, 1976). Were it not for this inertia, perhaps the government would have moved more conscientiously to establish a final disposal system and would have avoided many of its later problems. Hence, maybe it was simply a matter of poor judgement on the utilities' part that caused the problems of waste management planning insofar as they stemmed from an initial reliance on reprocessing. Although plausible, this argument does not preclude the importance of an institutional analysis. One must ask why the utilities insisted on reprocessing and recycling in the first place. There were two reasons. First, the plan would provide a way for them to get rid of spent fuel. Second, it would reduce their fuel costs. The promise of cheaper fuel relative to oil and coal, facilitated by reprocessing and fuel recycling, seemed to offset the disadvantage of nuclear plants' relatively high construction costs. Furthermore, as discussed in chapter 6 and the Appendix, minimizing fuel costs was a way to help increase profits once public utility commissions had established electricity rates. In short, utility support for reprocessing may seem misguided in hindsight, but there were institutional incentives for it at the time. The same was true for the AEC's support of reprocessing. During a period when the 1954 Atomic Energy Act directed the agency to encourage the nuclear sector's private commercialization, the agency decided to promote reprocessing precisely because it offered those benefits. The AEC hoped it could use them as incentives to help convince utilities to buy nuclear plants.

The story of nuclear waste policy is a fitting conclusion to the discussion of the commercial nuclear energy sector's collapse in the United States. Not only is the waste problem one that could stifle the sector's chances of recovery, but it also provides an opportunity to see how the three major institutional dimensions of the political economy that I have discussed may interconnect, how problems created by one dimension may undermine planning by bringing the effects of another dimension into play. The clearest example was the reprocessing failure, where all three dimensions—the structures of the economy, state, and state–civil society intersection—had significant effects that subverted successful planning. Furthermore, the history of waste policy illustrates the contradictions among short-term economic imperatives, democratic access to the policy process, and planning. For example, half of the reprocessing industry collapsed when two companies fled the market because it no longer seemed profitable enough for them to continue. This helped undermine the government's first waste management plan. Moreover, when a third firm, Nuclear Fuel Services, planned to expand its operations, interveners raised concerns through licensing hearings about safety issues that the company had chosen to ignore earlier in order to compete profitably. This also contributed to the company's eventual exit from the market and the further disintegration of the AEC's waste management strategy.

What would have happened with another set of institutional arrangements? Would the sector have had more success planning for the management of high-level radioactive waste? Furthermore, would the outcomes in other policy areas have been different? To answer these questions we need to compare the U.S. nuclear sector with nuclear sectors in other countries that have different institutional arrangements.

CHAPTER EIGHT

Nuclear Power in France, Sweden, and West Germany

In the nuclear sectors in France, Sweden, and West Germany the dimensions of the economy, state, and state–civil society intersection differed substantially after the mid-1960s both from the United States and from each other. So did the ensuing policies and each sector's fate. If we located these countries along continua representing our three dimensions, France would be farthest from the United States. The French policy process was entirely centralized and insulated. Policy makers controlled several important industrial monopolies through government ownership or other financial levers. As a result, they were able to take the necessary steps to ensure that the nuclear sector flourished in the 1970s and 1980s. West Germany would be closest to the United States. Policy formation was centralized and insulated, but implementation was not. Similarly, most nuclear industries were in private hands and often beyond the government's direct control. Yet they were more centralized and institutionally coordinated than industries in the United States—an advantage that enabled the West Germans to avoid some, but not all, of the U.S. planning problems, although not enough to prevent a near moratorium on reactor ordering after 1976. The Swedish case was closer to France. Except for the utilities, the nuclear industries were very centralized, and the government had some influence over them through ownership and financing. Policy implementation was centralized and insulated, but access to policy formation was more open to nuclear critics than anywhere else. This accessibility played a central role in Sweden's decision to phase out its nuclear program by 2010.

Each nation experienced intense political opposition to its commer-

136

cial nuclear programs during the 1970s and early 1980s.[1] All eventually adopted the light water reactor as the technological backbone for their nuclear sectors.[2] Each suffered an economic recession, higher interest rates, and reduced growth rates in the demand for electricity following the world oil crisis in 1973–74 (Lönnroth, 1983:7). France, Sweden, and West Germany made substantial commitments to nuclear power. Of all the countries in the world with indigenous reactor industries, these three had the largest programs by 1980 in terms of the amount of electricity per capita produced annually by nuclear power (Lönnroth, 1983:8). Finally, they were among the world leaders during the 1980s in the percentage of the nation's electricity generated by nuclear plants.[3] Because of these similarities, this chapter compares the institutional arrangements, policy outcomes, and relative vitality of these sectors without worrying too much that differences in the level of political opposition, basic technologies, national economic conditions, or size of the nuclear programs are confounding the comparisons.

This chapter offers sketches of the French, Swedish, and West German experiences for comparison with the U.S. experience. A more comprehensive treatment of the countries is well beyond the scope of this book.[4]

---

[1] Kitschelt (1986) has argued that the intensity of the antinuclear movements in the United States, Sweden, France, and West Germany was similar and can be treated as a constant when comparing the movement's policy effects in each country. He also reported that public opinion opposing nuclear power in these countries generally followed similar paths, peaking first in 1976 and, except for France, again in 1979 after the accident at Three Mile Island. See Jasper (1986b) for an excellent review of the poll data for the United States, Sweden, and France. For West Germany, see Nelkin and Pollak (1981b:107–18).

[2] Institutional arrangements influenced the reactor technology selection process in each country. However, these arrangements were quite different across the four countries and were not the only factors affecting the decisions. Others included national interests in establishing reactor manufacturing as a strong export industry, the availability of indigenous uranium supplies, and military concerns. Hence, it is doubtful that there was significant covariance between the type of institutional arrangements and the technology selected that would confound my comparisons. For good accounts of the technology selection processes in these countries, see Bupp and Derian (1978), Camilleri (1984), deLeon (1979), Kitschelt (1982), Nau (1974), and Walker and Lönnroth (1983).

[3] France ranked first in 1985 among capitalist countries, producing nearly 65 percent of its electricity with nuclear power. Sweden was third with 42 percent, West Germany was sixth with 30 percent, and the United States was eighth with 16 percent (*New York Times*, 1986).

[4] The studies by Nau (1974) and deLeon (1979) are among the best comparative work on the *initial* development and demonstration of nuclear technology. However, Lönnroth and Walker (1979) have provided the definitive comparative work on nuclear

INSTITUTIONAL PROFILES
Economic Structures

The French nuclear sector has always been one of the most centralized in the world. Electricité de France (EDF), the nationalized electric utility monopoly, was the only domestic customer for nuclear plants and provided its own architect-engineering services so that it could control the design and construction of its nuclear plants. One firm, Framatome, has manufactured all of the light water reactors purchased in France since 1973 (Masters, 1979:52–55). Although the component supply industries were not monopolies, single corporations still played dominant roles. Creusot-Loire supplied most of the heavy reactor components such as nuclear boilers. Alsthom-Atlantique, a subsidiary of Compagnie Générale d'Electricité, provided most of the turbine generating equipment. In addition, five corporations controlled uranium mining, enrichment, and fuel fabrication. Most notably, the COGEMA corporation monopolized spent fuel reprocessing. Such centralization facilitated long-range planning by eliminating almost all short- and medium-term competition throughout the sector (Lincicome, 1977; Saumon and Puiseux, 1977:159–64).

The Swedish electric utility industry was more competitive than those in France, West Germany, or the United States. Several companies competed for bulk users and distributors of electricity (Sahr, 1985:24; OTA, 1984:199). The federal government's State Power Board, the nation's largest electric utility, produced about 45 percent of Sweden's electricity annually. Privately owned utilities generated another 35 percent, while municipally owned companies, primarily the southern Swedish power company, Sydkraft, produced the rest (Lönnroth and Walker, 1979:36; Ragnarson, 1980:3). Three utilities,

---

power during the later commercial phase, the focus of this study. Yet there are two limitations to their otherwise excellent analysis. First, they established only *correlations* between institutional variables and sectoral performance. The absence of detailed historical studies for each of their eight countries prevented them from demonstrating the underlying *causal mechanisms* whereby certain institutions actually produced different outcomes. Second, they did not examine specific policy areas and the effects they had for each sector's health, an omission directly related to the first. Instead, they generalized about each sector's overall performance. Both difficulties stemmed from their methodological decision to sacrifice historical depth for sampling breadth, a decision whose limitations they acknowledged in the introduction to their study. I have tried to alleviate these problems in this project by choosing the opposite strategy, a set of detailed case studies for one country. Of course my choice entails problems associated with limited breadth, in particular the criticism that my sample is too small. This chapter is a limited attempt to compensate for that problem.

including the State Power Board, each bought nuclear plants, twelve in all (DOE, 1983c:85–90). All thirteen of the public and private utilities connected to the national power grid belonged to the Central Operating Management (CDL), an industrial association of utility companies that developed national plans for coordinating electricity production and nuclear construction (Sahr, 1985:24–30). Despite the competition, the CDL helped provide a degree of coordination in the Swedish utility industry that was often absent in the United States (Camilleri, 1984:59; Sahr, 1985:24–28). The rest of the sector was similar to France insofar as industrial centralization was concerned. The ASEA-ATOM company monopolized domestic reactor manufacturing and nuclear architect-engineering. The Uddcomb Corporation supplied heavy equipment for reactors (Camilleri, 1984:166). The Swedish Nuclear Fuel Supply Company, a wholly owned subsidiary of the nuclear utilities, provided nuclear fuel and related services (Deese, 1982:79). The Swedes never tried to develop a reprocessing industry.

The West German and the U.S. electric utility industries both had dozens of utility companies. However, the rest of the West German sector was more centralized. A single reactor manufacturer, Kraftwerk Union, dominated the industry after its creation in 1969 when Allgemeine Elektrizitäts-Gesellschaft (AEG) and Siemens, the two main West German reactor manufacturers, merged most of their nuclear operations. The main purpose of this merger, encouraged and sanctioned by the federal government, was to compete more effectively against the United States in the international market (de-Leon, 1979:205). Nevertheless, the merger did not include their respective reactor divisions, just operations like marketing, research, and development. Hence, despite the collaboration, Siemens and AEG continued to vie for domestic reactor sales until 1976 when the threat of bankruptcy stemming from construction delays and technical problems at several of its projects forced AEG to sell out to Siemens and abandon the business (Hatch, 1986:83; Mez and Watts, 1982). Since its inception, Kraftwerk Union, like Sweden's ASEA-ATOM and France's EDF, provided its own architect-engineering services. This was much different from the United States, where a dozen firms competed for the work. There was a third reactor manufacturer, Babcock-Brown Boveri, but it sold only two light water reactors domestically by 1983, barely 13 percent of the market (DOE, 1983c:84–88). Two companies, one West German and the other Austrian, supplied most of the sector's large nuclear components (Walker and Lönnroth, 1983:62). Twelve utilities owned the German Society for the Processing of Spent Fuel (DWK), a company responsible for reprocessing nuclear wastes (Deese, 1982:79).

Economic arrangements in the French, Swedish, and West German nuclear sectors posed vivid contrasts to those in the United States. The European countries had more institutional opportunities to coordinate sectoral activities and facilitate long-term planning by virtue of their more centralized, often monopolistic, reactor manufacturing, architect-engineering, reprocessing, and component supply industries. Only among the West German utilities did an industry begin to approach the level of decentralization found in the United States.

State Structures

A centralized, insulated policy apparatus facilitated consistent nuclear policy formation in France from the outset in the 1940s (e.g., Bupp, 1980a:32; Bupp and Derian, 1978; deLeon, 1979; Scheinman, 1965). An elite group of administrators, called the PEON Commission (Commission Consultative pour la Production d'Electricité d'Origine Nucléaire), from EDF, the Atomic Energy Commission (CEA), the nuclear industries, and a few other government departments reviewed the nuclear program annually, established reactor ordering goals, and coordinated all facets of nuclear policy. EDF played a particularly dominant role on the PEON Commission, successfully promoting nuclear power (Masters, 1979:51–52). Participation by the ministries of finance and industry helped tie nuclear policy to the government's overall energy and industrial objectives. Although the Mitterrand regime disbanded the PEON Commission after coming to power in 1981, a small cadre of administrators retained control of nuclear policy making through the mid-1980s (Walker and Lönnroth, 1983:54). Citizens, environmentalists, and antinuclear groups had virtually no access to this policy-making forum.[5]

The same was true for policy implementation, particularly during licensing. The CEA did not have to publish safety studies for each proposed plant as the NRC did in the United States. Furthermore, although the law required public inquiries during licensing, they did not involve hearings or other opportunities for critics, such as state and local officials, to present oral objections, ask questions, or request information. Instead, the federal government's local representative

[5] The French state is noted for its insulated planning (e.g., Cohen, 1977; Green, 1983; Shonfield, 1965). However, see Hayward (1982) for important qualifications.

simply collected the public's written comments about the license application, reviewed them, and made his licensing recommendation to the federal authorities. Because they were bureaucratic appointees of the central government, not independent political actors, the officials did not challenge national nuclear policy (Barkenbus, 1984). It is not surprising, then, that the government never rejected a licensing request despite vigorous opposition from citizens. Other than the inquiry there was little formal communication between federal and lower-level government officials (NRC, 1982c:23).

The courts bolstered the federal government's hegemony. Critics could try to appeal licensing decisions through the courts, but judges rarely permitted such challenges. When they were allowed, they usually failed. For example, the Conseil d'Etat rejected all eighty-nine petitions in 1979 by various ecological and antinuclear groups to stop construction of the Super-Phenix breeder reactor (Deese, 1982:89). Licenses had the status of government decrees and were practically immune from legal action unless the court found that federal officials violated proper licensing procedures. Objections to environmental, safety, economic, or other substantive concerns were not sufficient grounds for granting a hearing (Nelkin and Pollak, 1980b; 1981b:155–67; Pelzer and Bischof, 1977:59). Judges were also inclined to reject appeals because they believed that government officials had already made their decisions in the public interest, as the administration defined it—a judicial philosophy antithetical to that found in the United States, where the courts were primarily concerned with upholding the rights of individual citizens (Barkenbus, 1984:44; Jasper, 1986a).

About the only way critics could hope to influence nuclear policy was to elect their peers to office. Yet this was a difficult strategy to pursue for several reasons. First, all the major political parties supported the government's nuclear expansion, making it difficult for opponents to gain any leverage through the party system (Hatch, 1986:154). Second, even if activists could win office, many observers felt that the National Assembly, France's parliament, was incapable of exerting significant control over nuclear policy. Administrators limited parliamentary debate by withholding planning information until the last minute and monopolized the technical expertise necessary for politicians to understand and criticize nuclear policy (Bauer et al., 1976:37; Touraine et al., 1983:63). Indeed, it was not until 1981 that the National Assembly ever voted on a nuclear policy issue. Overall, French political institutions provided federal officials an ideal opportunity to form and implement nuclear policy while virtually ignoring public opinion and opposition (e.g., Barkenbus, 1984; Kitschelt, 1986).

The formation of Swedish nuclear policy was also initially a closed process, but became much more open with the politicization of energy issues after the mid-1970s. Until then, to the extent that energy planning occurred at all, the Ministry of Industry supervised and coordinated it, usually without much input from citizens. For example, when the ministry convinced various government agencies, energy corporations, and other industrial actors to support a national energy conservation policy after the 1973–74 world oil crisis, environmentalists charged that the government had excluded them from the negotiations (Sahr, 1985:52–67). Furthermore, Parliament was responsible for granting preliminary approval of all nuclear projects, an arrangement that gave citizens at least indirect access to policy formation through their representatives, but the Social Democrats, staunch advocates of nuclear power, dominated Parliament until 1976. Until then approval of the administration's nuclear plans was nearly automatic. Hence, when the utility trade association proposed a program in the late 1960s to expand electricity production by building eleven nuclear plants during the following decade, Parliament approved the plan unanimously (Bupp and Derian, 1978:137; Lönnroth, 1977:257). However, the institutional framework existed for opposition groups to gain access to the policy formation process, if they wanted to, long before Parliament considered legislation. One way was the common practice of appointing ad hoc government commissions with representatives and expert staffs with various perspectives on an issue to help ministries prepare legislative proposals. Hundreds of commissions operated during the 1970s as a means of developing consensus on specific policy issues and for legitimizing the policy-making process. Some commissions were probably used to co-opt and disarm political opposition (e.g., Premfors, 1983), but both commission members and experts were free to dissent and have their comments printed as part of the final report. The so-called remiss procedure provided another systematic opportunity for public participation by which the government solicited written comments on every commission report from all concerned public agencies, interest groups, and citizens. Officials then analyzed the comments and reported them as part of the legislative bill.[6]

---

[6] See Premfors (1983) for further discussion of government commissions and the remiss procedure. These kinds of democratic, consensus building procedures were typical in Sweden (e.g., Childs, 1980; Liljestrom, 1978; Lundmark, 1983; Ruin, 1982).

On the other hand, implementation of Swedish nuclear policy remained administratively centralized, and it minimized public participation even after nuclear power became a hot political issue. The Swedish Nuclear Power Inspectorate was responsible for regulating most aspects of the sector, including plant safety and waste disposal. The agency had tremendous institutional autonomy because the ministries could not give it direct orders (Deese, 1982:84). In contrast to the United States, the inspectorate licensed all nuclear installations without holding public hearings. Citizens could not appeal the final decision through the courts unless they persuaded a judge that the utility had violated some other law, such as a building or zoning code (Kitschelt, 1986; Pelzer and Bischof, 1977). An alternative was to appeal licensing and other policy decisions to the Ombudsman, an all-purpose public representative. However, the Ombudsman could only investigate a case to ensure that the law had been followed and could only make nonbinding recommendations to the administration and courts (Pelzer and Bischof, 1977).[7] Similarly, citizens had little recourse through local government, whose only substantive opportunity to affect licensing rested on its ability to veto the use of land for industrial purposes within its jurisdiction (NRC, 1982c:56). This has not happened yet for a nuclear plant, but is a possibility, although one that Parliament could overturn by passing special legislation preempting local authority. Parliament has overturned laws affecting the construction of roads, railways, and government buildings (Deese, 1982:84–85).

The structure of the West German nuclear policy process was opposite to that of Sweden. Policy formation was relatively centralized in two administrative agencies, the Ministry for Atomic Questions, established in 1955 to devise and coordinate a strategy for commercializing nuclear energy, and the German Atom Commission, founded in 1956 to advise the ministry. Eventually the government abolished the commission and blended the ministry's functions into the Ministry of Education and Science (deLeon, 1979). The Ministry of the Interior assumed overall responsibility for regulatory policy. Although the organizations changed, policy formation was administratively insulated from both legislative control and the public (Dyson, 1982; Nelkin and Pollak, 1981b:19–20). Notably, the West German Parliament played only a minor role; it was not required to approve nuclear projects as was the Swedish Parliament and lacked a dominant force comparable to the congressional Joint Committee on

---

7 For a general discussion of the Ombudsman's role, see Childs (1980:38).

Atomic Energy in the United States. Politicians, scientists, and industrialists from the private sector favoring nuclear power dominated these policy-making bodies in West Germany, primarily because conservative Christian Democratic governments were in power during the 1950s and 1960s, and because there was little military interest in nuclear weapons (Keck, 1981:19–24).[8]

Policy implementation, particularly with respect to regulatory policy, was more decentralized and accessible to the public. First, although the federal government made most of the laws and regulations under which licensing occurred, regional governments (*Länder*) approved sites, granted construction permits, and issued operating licenses within their jurisdictions (Meyer-Abich and Dickler, 1982:230). They had to abide by federal regulations, but were free to develop additional guidelines as they saw fit. When a utility requested a license it was the *Länder's* responsibility, not the federal government's, to evaluate the safety aspects of the application. For technical help the *Länder* hired one of seven private, nonprofit, consulting groups called Technical Inspection Agencies. Second, each phase of the licensing process was subject to both public intervention through formal hearings in the *Länder* and approval by the Ministry of the Interior (NRC, 1982c:92–110). However, the hearings resembled France's public inquiries more than the licensing hearings in the United States. They included only local citizens, not national organizations, provided no opportunities for cross-examining witnesses, and generally lasted only a day or two (Nelkin and Pollak, 1981b:34; Rüdig, 1986). However, to the extent that *Länder* regimes were beholden to their constituents, particularly at election time, the potential for politically charged, unstable, and fragmented licensing always existed. Third, the judicial system compounded the problem. Under German law there were three layers of administrative and appeals courts offering citizens opportunities to question the technical, safety, and environmental aspects of nuclear plants (Camilleri, 1984:101; Falk, 1982:216). Furthermore, in contrast to France the German courts were more concerned with upholding the interests

[8] Nau (1974:68–75) and deLeon (1979) review this history in detail. The emphasis on private development with minimal government involvement is characteristic of other West German economic sectors (e.g., Shonfield, 1965; Streeck, 1984). However, Dyson (1982) reminds us that there are exceptions. See Deubner (1979) for an interesting discussion of the important role the West German coal, chemical, electric utility, and electrical equipment industries played during the 1950s in encouraging the development of commercial nuclear technology, especially in cooperation with other European countries through the Euratom program, an international joint project designed to facilitate the growth of nuclear power.

144

and rights of individuals than with backing government policy. As a result, opponents of nuclear power had an impressive assortment of institutional opportunities to penetrate the policy process through the courts and disrupt, delay, and prevent policy implementation in general and licensing in particular (Camilleri, 1984:101; Kitschelt, 1986; Nelkin and Pollak, 1980b). For these reasons the NRC (1982c:120) reported that the West German licensing system was the only one in the world more complex and cumbersome than its own. Others agreed and added that this made sectoral coordination and planning extraordinarily difficult for the West Germans (Lönnroth, 1983:21).

Compared to the U.S. policy process, the French process was more centralized and insulated during both policy formation and implementation. The Swedish policy process was also more closed to the public during policy implementation than was the U.S. process, especially with respect to licensing and the courts, although the system was a bit more accessible than the French system, for there were a few mechanisms like the Ombudsman that offered opportunities for appeal. However, policy formation in Sweden offered more access to the public than any of the other countries, including the United States, given the frequent use of commissions and remiss procedures. West Germany most closely resembled the United States on these dimensions. In both countries nuclear policy formation tended to include only those who wanted to promote nuclear energy, and policy implementation was fragmented, decentralized, and accessible to nuclear critics.

Structure of the State–Civil Society Intersection

The government gained extensive control over the nuclear sector in France with a variety of powerful policy tools. State ownership was very important. For example, by deciding in 1975 to purchase reactors only from Framatome, EDF deliberately restructured the reactor manufacturing industry and gave Framatome a monopoly (Lucas, 1979:83–88). The CEA acquired a 30 percent share in Framatome the same year, thereby providing the government with a second means of control within the reactor industry (Masters, 1979:55). The government's ability to control the sector through ownership increased substantially in 1981 when the Mitterrand government nationalized Compagnie Générale d'Electricité, a company with controlling shares in Alsthom-Atlantique, the turbine supplier. The government also nationalized Paribas, a firm with controlling interest in Creusot-Loire, the reactor component manufacturer. Because Creusot-Loire owned controlling interest in Framatome, the French government achieved even greater leverage over the reactor industry both from within, through the CEA's original ownership in Framatome, and from above, through the nationalization of Framatome's grandparent company, Paribas (Walker and Lönnroth, 1983:55). In addition, the CEA established and owned Compagnie Générale des Matières Nucléaires (COGEMA), the corporation that operated the government's reprocessing facilities. Through COGEMA the CEA held controlling shares in Eurodif, the international uranium enrichment consortium, and lesser shares throughout the fuel fabrication industry (Glaize, 1977; Lucas, 1979:34).[9]

The government also controlled much of the banking system that supplied the nation's finance capital, a second powerful policy tool (Zysman, 1983). As a result officials, particularly at the Ministry of Finance, provided credit, preferential interest rates, loans, and loan guarantees to those industries it saw as vital to the nuclear sector's future (Lönnroth, 1983:19). They also helped direct the capital formation and investment activities of EDF and the CEA. Hence, the government had several sources of financial leverage with which to participate directly in the decisions of nuclear energy firms.[10] Ownership prerogatives and financial clout provided the government a tremendous capacity to help the sector absorb short-term expenses while developing a long-term growth strategy. Planning bodies like the PEON Commission and the Ministry of Finance further enhanced those possibilities (Walker and Lönnroth, 1983:54).

Policy makers had several institutional opportunities for controlling the nuclear sector in Sweden, but fewer than they had in France. For example, the federal government owned the State Power Board, one of the most important actors in the development of Swedish energy policy through the mid-1970s (Sahr, 1985:28). However, with private investors or municipal governments owning the other utilities—more than half of the nation's generating capacity—the State Power Board

[9] The government reorganized the CEA in 1970 and again in 1975 to transform it from a technical agency with research and development objectives to an economic institution with commercial ones. The reorganizations were explicit attempts to create an instrument that policy makers could use to promote commercialization and economic growth throughout the nuclear sector. It was during this period that the CEA obtained authority to purchase holdings in private firms as a means to that end (Lucas, 1979:chap. 2). For a fascinating comparison of the CEA's earlier research and development activities and its later economic interventions, compare Scheinman's (1965) description of the CEA with Lucas's (1979).

[10] See Lucas (1979:chaps. 3–4) for details about the government's financial capacities in this regard.

did not wield the exclusive influence over the rest of the sector that EDF did in France. Nevertheless, the State Power Board did provide a strong voice in the sector through both its purchasing power and its joint ownership with other utilities in the Swedish Nuclear Fuel Supply Company (Deese, 1982:79). The government also owned 75 percent of Uddcomb, the heavy equipment supplier, and half of ASEA-ATOM until 1982 when it sold out to its partner, the Swedish General Electric Company (Sahr, 1985:24–26). The government's quest for ownership in the sector stemmed from its concern that Swedish private enterprise, small by international standards, would not be able to bear all the financial risks associated with developing and commercializing nuclear power (Lönnroth and Walker, 1979:11).

Because the government did not dominate the Swedish financial sector, it did not have many opportunities for favoring nuclear related industries with special credit and loans. However, the Ministry of Industry controlled the State Power Board's budget and could use its leverage to control the utility's investment strategy (Sahr, 1985:28). The federal government also managed three general pension funds worth roughly $20 billion and distributed $300 million from them by 1976 as loans for various reactor construction projects in an effort to grease the wheels of nuclear progress (Childs, 1980:63). Nevertheless, the private and municipal utilities relied on the bond market for underwriting much of their nuclear construction (Lönnroth and Walker, 1979:36). Except for the State Power Board, the government had only very indirect control over the utilities' ability to generate capital internally. The competitive market, not government regulation, was responsible for determining electricity rates. Yet because the State Power Board was the only one allowed to build long-distance transmission lines, it always had the opportunity to compete with any utility, if it wished. This additional silent threat of competition helped the government indirectly control electricity rates (Lönnroth, 1977:274–75).

There was much less government intervention in the West German nuclear sector. The government played primarily a distant, regulatory role, allowing the market and private groups to coordinate most sectoral activity. The federal government did not own shares in corporations in the various nuclear industries. With two exceptions, ownership was entirely in private hands. First, the *Länder* and, to an extent, municipal governments often owned controlling shares in utilities, and private investors held the rest. This was especially typical of the big utilities like Rheinisch-Westphälische Elektrizitätswerke (RWE), the nation's largest (deLeon, 1979:161; Keck, 1981:21). Second, twelve utilities, some with similar mixed ownership, owned DWK, the reprocessing corporation.

Nor did the government have much control over the flow of investment capital in the sector. The primary sources of external financing for utilities building nuclear plants were the capital markets and three large private banks: Deutsche, Dresdner, and Commerz (Nelkin and Pollak, 1981b:17; Walker and Lönnroth, 1983:62). In fact, the federal government was forbidden from directly financing nuclear plant construction (deLeon, 1979:74). On the other hand, policy makers did have some control over internal utility capital formation. Where the *Länder* held shares in the utilities, as they did in many with nuclear plants, government officials helped company personnel formulate initial electricity rate requests. Rate making was usually a smooth process, for the *Länder* also had responsibility for approving the requests later. However, the *Länder* did not otherwise participate in utility business policy regardless of their share holdings (Keck, 1981:21).

The West German government did try to facilitate private development, but it did so indirectly rather than by imposing its will coercively on the sector as the government did in France (Keck, 1981:41). One of its most important tools was the provision of technical support. In conjunction with the *Länder,* universities, and private firms, the federal government subsidized the construction of a vast network of research laboratories, much as the U.S. government did. Government support gradually increased to a point where it covered almost the entire nuclear research effort by the early 1970s (Keck, 1981:25; Rycroft and Brenner, 1981:106). In addition, the administration provided subsidies, tax breaks, loan guarantees, and guarantees against operating losses to private groups during the sector's early development.

The lack of federal control over sectoral activity and the primary reliance on private interests acting through the market did not mean that there was no chance for farsighted nuclear planning in West Germany. To the contrary, there was an intricate web of control that permeated the sector and provided a degree of cohesion absent for the most part in the United States.[11] High-ranking officials from corporations, banks, utilities, government, and research institutes collaborated on supervisory boards and in other forums. Interlocking

---

[11] It was primarily after the accident at Three Mile Island in 1979 that the U.S. nuclear sector began forming private organizations to govern important sectoral activities. For an elaboration, see Campbell (1986).

directorates involving many of these actors reinforced that network, facilitated an exchange of information, and provided an important element of sectoral coordination (Walker and Lönnroth, 1983:62). The presence in this network of large banks willing to provide the long-term financial support the sector needed, coupled with the *Länder's* willingness to share risk through partial ownership in the utilities, made it easier for the sector to tolerate short-term commercial risks (Lönnroth, 1983:20; OTA, 1984:200). Hence, the federal and *Länder* governments were only a small part of a larger coalition of industrial interests that developed the sector's strategy, an institutional pattern typical of German industries accustomed to taking strategic, long-term views of technological developments and markets.[12]

In contrast to the United States, where political control over the nuclear sector was primarily regulatory, both the French and Swedish governments enjoyed extensive public ownership and had potentially greater financial leverage over nuclear activities, except as far as utility rate regulation was concerned. Public utility commissions regulated electricity rates in the United States; there was no formal rate regulation in Sweden. The West German case was closest to the United States on these dimensions; with the exception of limited stock holdings in the utilities, there was no public ownership and about the same amount of government control over external financing and utility rate making.

The key institutional arrangements of the French, Swedish, West German, and U.S. nuclear sectors during the late 1970s are summarized in Table 8.1. In light of the discussion in chapter 2, it appears that all of the European countries offered more institutional opportunities for coherent sectoral planning than were available to policy makers in the United States, where important nuclear industries were more competitively structured, where policy formation was centralized, fragmented, and closed, but where implementation was decentralized, fragmented, and open, and where policy makers had less direct leverage over sectoral activity. However, to see whether institutional variations helped policy makers in these European countries plan more effectively and, if so, to see what effects that planning had on the viability of their nuclear programs, we need to compare the outcomes in the key policy areas.

---

[12] See Shonfield (1965) and Zysman (1983) for discussions of the central role banks have played in German economic planning. See Esser, Fach, and Dyson (1983) for a good illustration about how networks of private corporations coordinate German industrial policy.

Table 8.1. Institutional features of the French, Swedish, West German, and U.S. nuclear energy sectors during the late 1970s

| | Economy | State | | State–Civil Society Intersection | |
		Policy Formation	Policy Implementation	State Ownership	State Financial Control
France	RM: Monopoly U: Monopoly AE: Monopoly R: Monopoly	Centralized Unified[a] Closed	Centralized Unified Closed	High	I: High E: High
Sweden	RM: Monopoly U: Competitive AE: Monopoly R: None	Centralized Unified Open	Centralized Unified Closed	Moderate	I: Low E: Moderate
West Germany	RM: Competitive U: Regional monopolies AE: Monopoly R: Monopoly	Centralized Unified Closed	Decentralized Fragmented Open	Moderate-Low	I: Moderate E: Low

United States	RM: Competitive
	U: Regional
	  monopolies
	AE: Competitive
	R: Competitive
	  (until 1977)
		Centralized
		Fragmented
		Closed
			Decentralized
			Fragmented
			Open
				Low	I: Moderate
					E: Low

NOTE: RM = reactor manufacturing; U = electric utility industry; AE = architect-engineering; R = reprocessing; I = internal utility capital formation; E = external utility capital formation.

[a] "Unified" and "fragmented" refer to the degree to which the policy process is spread across different policy forums within a level of government. For example, policy formation was relatively unified within the AEC. However, it was more fragmented after the NRC and the Energy Research and Development Administration replaced it in 1975.

STANDARDIZATION

The United States nuclear sector sought standardized reactor designs as one way to speed up plant licensing, reduce long construction times, and better control the costs of nuclear plants. However, shortsighted competition in the reactor manufacturing industry and a legal framework guarding against antitrust violations undermined much of that effort. In contrast, the French program was the most standardized in the world; this standardization, many observers agree, contributed to its prolonged vitality (e.g., Lucas, 1979:89; Masters, 1979; Raber, 1976; Tanguy, 1980; Walker and Lönnroth, 1983). Where the United States adopted several sizes of both the boiling and pressurized water reactor, the French built just two sizes of the pressurized version.

There were two institutional keys to the French success. One was the insulated position of CEA officials that allowed them to ignore the demands of antinuclear groups for improving reactor safety. CEA officials were able to minimize new regulatory requirements that would have undermined standardization by requiring expensive and lengthy modifications to plants, either during or after construction (NRC, 1982c:32).[13] Second, EDF was the only domestic customer for nuclear plants, and, therefore, it could force Framatome to produce a standardized product. Government planners decided to accelerate the French nuclear program in 1970 after an ordering hiatus during which they abandoned a French concept in favor of the American pressurized water reactor.[14] Officials at EDF began ordering a few plants each year, but launched a more ambitious program following the world oil crisis in 1973–74, ordering sixteen identical 900-megawatt plants with staggered construction starts. Two years later they ordered another ten, plus eight identical 1,350-megawatt plants. By the late 1970s the French were beginning construction on four or five standardized plants annually (Alexander, 1984).

EDF's strategy paid off. Large orders for standardized plants guaranteed Framatome enough long-term business to justify building new and expensive mass production facilities. As a result, the manufac-

[13] Standardization has its price and has raised concerns about reactor safety in France. Safety problems have developed in French plants that probably would have led to their closing for repairs or modifications in most other countries, but not in France. To the extent that such problems are characteristic of the standardized design, they could recur throughout a set of identical plants (Cohen, 1982:38).

[14] The decision to change reactor designs involved intense political conflict within the French administrative bureaucracy. See Bupp and Derian (1978:chap. 3) for an account of this history.

Table 8.2. Comparative costs and lead times of commercial nuclear plants

	Average Cost per Kilowatt Hour (Dollars)	Average Lead Time (Years)
France	1,231	6–7
Sweden	2,000	7–8
West Germany	2,077	8–10
United States	2,250	10–12

SOURCE: Adapted from NRC (1982c): 116–18.

turer achieved significant economies of scale in production, which helped reduce the costs of nuclear plants (Lucas, 1979:88–89; Tanguy, 1980). By some estimates standardization cut the average cost of a French nuclear plant by 20 to 30 percent (NRC, 1982c:120). The low cost of nuclear power reflected the savings. By 1982 the average cost per kilowatt hour of nuclear generated electricity in France was roughly half that of the United States, West Germany, and Sweden— countries that did not standardize their programs (Table 8.2).

However, standardization also helped the French reduce plant costs in other ways. It let builders begin projects with a finished set of plans, thereby enabling them to avoid construction delays caused by incomplete designs (OTA, 1984:67). It also allowed Framatome and its component suppliers to stockpile parts and avoid supply shortages during construction (Tanguy, 1980). All of this helped minimize lead times, the time elapsed from the decision to build until the plant began operating, an important factor influencing project costs. By 1982 the average lead time on most French nuclear projects was only six or seven years, significantly shorter than in Sweden, West Germany, and especially the United States (Table 8.2). I am not arguing that standardization was the only thing that kept French lead times and project costs relatively low.[15] Instead, the point is that the French successfully standardized their program and reaped the associated rewards because they did not face the institutional barriers that undermined the effort in the United States.

In Sweden, ASEA-ATOM, the lone domestic manufacturer, built only boiling water reactors, thereby presenting utilities an opportu-

[15] See Lester (1978) for an excellent comparative analysis of the institutional factors influencing nuclear plant lead times. See Lucas (1979:89) for a discussion about how the CEA's joint ownership of Framatome helped keep costs down by giving the government enough institutional leverage to convince the company to minimize profits on domestic sales and make up the difference on exports.

nity to standardize at least the sector's basic reactor concept. Yet the standardization never happened. To the extent that institutional arrangements were responsible, the chief stumbling block was a fragmented utility industry. Because three utilities bought nuclear plants, the possibility for standardization through coordinated ordering was more remote than in France, where only one was involved. Furthermore, the Swedish utility association had orchestrated a general plan for the industry to build several plants, but did not help coordinate specific ordering afterward. So although all the participating utilities purchased boiling water reactors from ASEA-ATOM by 1984, the State Power Board bought three additional pressurized reactors from Westinghouse in the United States. Furthermore, in an effort to achieve economies of scale the utilities insisted on building progressively larger plants ranging from 440 to 1,060 megawatts (Camilleri, 1984:60; DOE, 1983c:85–90).

The State Power Board's purchase of two different reactor types helps put the institutional argument into perspective. The board had the institutional *capacity* to standardize at least its own reactor program, but it chose not to do so. The same could have happened in France, despite EDF's monopoly over the utility industry, if policy makers there had not been committed to standardization. The presence of either centralized producers or buyers may increase the *possibilities* for standardization, or any other kind of planning; the possibilities will be realized only if policy makers want to take advantage of them, as they did in France. However, this does not imply that institutional arrangements are any less important than decision makers' preferences. After all, in the United States, where the institutional limits to planning were especially narrow, utility and government policy makers tried, but failed, to implement a standardization policy—one that was more modest than France's and, therefore, presumably easier to achieve, other things being equal. On the other hand, the presence of three independent utilities in Sweden made it institutionally difficult to standardize plants, but not impossible. Were it not for the State Power Board's purchases from Westinghouse, the utilities would have standardized the reactor concept, although in a rather haphazard fashion.

Sweden resembled the United States to the extent that it had a fragmented utility industry, but West Germany bore an even closer resemblance in that it also had a somewhat competitive reactor manufacturing industry. Initially AEG sold boiling water reactors, and Siemens offered pressurized models. The German Atom Commission encouraged the competition between these firms by providing research funds for both designs in the mid-1960s, just as its counterpart in the United States had done years earlier.[16] However, even after their consolidation, Kraftwerk Union continued to offer both types. Furthermore, Babcock-Brown Boveri entered the market in 1971, selling its version of the pressurized water reactor—presumably with the encouragement of German utilities concerned with preventing a monopoly by Kraftwerk Union. Apparently, utilities bought different types of reactors from these companies at least in part to help keep prices down by encouraging competition (Keck, 1981:44). RWE, for example, ordered a reactor from Babcock-Brown Boveri precisely to keep Kraftwerk Union in line (Nau, 1974:151). In addition, the utilities demanded progressively larger reactors to achieve economies of scale in generating capacity. As a result, reactor sizes doubled in West Germany from 630 to 1,300 megawatts between 1967 and 1975 (Keck, 1981:41–44; Pringle and Spigelman, 1983:352).

There were also political barriers to standardization, although of a different nature from those in the United States, where antitrust law was so important. The German Atomic Energy Law required reactor manufacturers to incorporate the latest safety improvements into their plants. As a result, designs were in constant flux and subject to frequent modification, a common problem in the United States (NRC, 1982c:106). However, these two cases were identical in one important respect. Because the law prohibited the federal government in both countries from owning nuclear corporations or directly financing nuclear projects, policy makers lacked the institutional tools to force the sector to standardize. Hence, West Germany's plants varied considerably (Walker and Lönnroth, 1983:62–65).

The Germans believed that the absence of standardization contributed to both licensing delays and escalating plant costs (Kitschelt, 1982:286), and they made serious attempts to overcome some of these institutional problems. For example, the German Atom Forum, the nuclear sector's trade association, pressed the government for licensing changes, including a standardization program designed to speed up the licensing process. Both federal and *Länder* officials began considering the plan in 1981. Kraftwerk Union suggested that the government allow five or six plants of common design to be licensed as a convoy and then built over a ten-year period, a plan reminiscent of the strategies proposed in the United States. The Ministry of the

[16] Keck (1981), deLeon (1979), and Nau (1974) discuss the West German promotional history. Similar histories abound for the United States. For a sampling, see Allen (1977), Bupp and Derian (1978), Del Sesto (1979), Dawson (1976), and Hertsgaard (1983).

Interior accepted the idea in 1982 and authorized construction of three standardized units. It allowed them to move through licensing simultaneously in different *Länder* with the understanding that approval of any of them would automatically constitute approval of the rest (Camilleri, 1984:140; Hatch, 1986:135; OTA, 1984:194–97). However, some observers felt that the plan would ultimately founder on the requirement that manufacturers incorporate the latest safety features into their designs—an institutional condition that would provide opportunities for antinuclear groups to delay licensing and construction through the courts (Falk, 1982:216; NRC, 1982c:106).

What can we learn from these comparisons? The institutional barriers that undermined standardization in the United States, such as a competitive reactor manufacturing industry, a government incapable of coercing the sector to action, and a fragmented utility industry, also undermined standardization elsewhere. At first glance, it might appear that the presence or absence of a unified utility industry was the most important institutional feature. After all, the only country that successfully standardized its program, France, was also the only one with a single utility company. However, the French government created EDF and later used the utility to foster Framatome's reactor manufacturing monopoly and to demand a standardized product. It was the government's capacity and desire to coordinate economic activity, in large part by eliminating competition, that prevented the imperatives of short-term profitability within the reactor manufacturing industry from contradicting and undermining the long-range planning required for standardization. If policy makers, industrialists, and utility executives in the United States had wanted to create either a manufacturing monopoly or some sort of collusive reactor-ordering scheme to achieve that goal, antitrust law would surely have prohibited it. Although some of the institutional mechanisms to achieve standardization, such as substantial government ownership, were present in Sweden, policy makers chose not to use them for that purpose. In West Germany, the institutional configuration was quite similar to that in the United States. The short-term imperatives of a competitive reactor manufacturing industry prevented the development of a single reactor concept. Not only did the fragmented utility industry fail to develop a unified ordering scheme to overcome the problem as EDF did in France, but in some cases utilities actually encouraged such competition. Furthermore, West German policy makers had no way to impose standardization on the sector. The best they could do was to offer licensing advantages as incentives to promote such planning, and even then they did so only at the request of the private sector. Perhaps this was why the West Germans' standardization plan was so similar to that in the United States. It remains to be seen whether it will be any more successful.

POLITICS AND THE REGULATORY PROCESS

Antinuclear opposition in France developed in the early 1970s for many of the same reasons it did in the United States. At first, concern developed about the dangers nuclear plants posed to public safety, health, and the environment. As EDF embarked on its massive ordering campaign, critics began questioning their lack of substantive democratic participation in the policy process (Hatch, 1986:148; Touraine et al., 1983). They charged that siting and licensing inquiries were merely symbolic formalities lacking any real influence (Fagnani and Moatti, 1982) and that the personnel EDF appointed to run them were biased and unqualified. This may have been true. For example, although major opposition developed over an inquiry in 1977, the commissioner in charge granted final approval even after admitting that he lacked the technical expertise necessary to make an objective decision. Critics also complained that regional assemblies, established in 1972 to help EDF select reactor sites, were a charade, for they depended on EDF for the information used in making their decisions (Nelkin and Pollak, 1981b:29–31).

Dissent among nuclear experts received much publicity and fueled the conflict (Nelkin and Pollak, 1981b:59). Four hundred scientists from various prestigious institutions signed a petition in early 1975 condemning both the nuclear program and the closed policy-making process. Small groups of scientists, some from EDF, but most working for the CEA and belonging to the Confédération Française Démocratique du Travail (CFDT), one of France's largest trade unions, began providing technical advice and information to antinuclear groups. Later these and other experts formed scientific public interest organizations like the Groupe de Scientifiques pour l'Information sur l'Energie Nucléaire, similar to the Union of Concerned Scientists in the United States, that continued to consult with antinuclear activists. To an extent, this resembled the internal legitimation crisis that catapulted the antinuclear movement to new heights in the United States during the mid-1970s. However, the French antinuclear movement was well underway before government and EDF staff members began cooperating with nuclear critics (Nelkin and Pollak, 1981b:89–91).

Civil disobedience and mass demonstrations were commonplace.

Beginning in 1975 protests at Gironde, Fessenheim, Flamanville, and other reactor sites often involved bloody confrontations between thousands of activists and police. These demonstrations lost much of their appeal after police killed a protestor at Creys-Malville in 1977, although antinuclear groups still staged large demonstrations at Plogoff in 1980 and the La Hague reprocessing facility in 1982. Moreover, the CFDT circulated a petition in 1980 calling for more democratic decision making in nuclear policy, including a national referendum on the issues, the development of regional energy plans, and a moratorium on further construction until policy makers reviewed the nuclear plan (Fagnani and Moatti, 1982). Reflecting these concerns, public support for nuclear power dropped from 74 percent of those surveyed in 1974 to 47 percent by 1978 (Hatch, 1986:148). Yet despite these developments, the movement did not have much effect on either nuclear policy or on the sector's development because activists still did not have access to the policy process (Zinberg, 1982:181). EDF changed plant sites a few times in response to opposition, but never actually stopped projects. Although licensing did slow down a bit, attempts to halt licensing failed (Hatch, 1986:150–59). The antinuclear movement's relative impotence in this regard is suggested in Table 8.3. Average construction delays, which increased from about one to seven months between 1974 and 1980, were rather modest compared to Sweden, West Germany, and the United States, where activists were more successful in penetrating the policy process. Annual ordering rates for nuclear plants remained constant throughout the 1970s in France, another indication that critics did not alter the basic policy course (Table 8.4).

Disenchanted with demonstrations and fed up with administrative procedures, critics turned to electoral politics. This was perhaps the most realistic channel of access available to them (Barkenbus, 1984:44), but it was no panacea. Ecologists and antinuclear activists formed their own local and regional parties for the 1977 elections and captured as much as 10 percent of the vote around Paris and near some nuclear sites (Rüdig, 1986). However, during the national elections the following year, none of the ecologist candidates lasted past the first round of balloting. The major parties were all committed to nuclear power and provided little support for the environmentalists, although the degree of commitment varied according to internal party politics. The Socialist party's support for nuclear power was the most tentative, with one wing of the CFDT union, a major socialist constituent, providing some of the harshest criticism of the government's nuclear policies. However, another wing countered with the

Table 8.3. Average construction delays of all nuclear power plants under construction or in commercial service (in months)

	1974	1977	1980	1984
France	0.7	3.6	7.1	11.3
Sweden	2.7	4.9	15.9	19.8
West Germany	6.1	13.8	30.6	42.4
United States	20.0	35.9	49.4	53.1

Note: Delays for each plant are the number of months behind the construction schedule expected when the plant order was given. For each country, delays were calculated only for plants already in operation or under construction and still scheduled to be completed. Plants whose construction had not yet begun or plants mothballed while under construction were not included.
SOURCE: Herbert Kitschelt, "Political Opportunity Structures and Political Protest: Antinuclear Movements in Four Democracies," *British Journal of Political Science* 16, 1 (1986): 80. Reprinted by permission of the author and of Cambridge University Press.

Table 8.4. Domestic nuclear plant ordering rates per year (in gigawatts per year)

	1970–74	1975–79
France	3.4	3.4
Sweden	0.5	0.2
West Germany	1.8	1.0
United States	21.6	2.4

SOURCE: Adapted from Lönnroth and Walker (1979): 28.

argument that the nuclear program was an important source of jobs. In any case, there was enough opposition to nuclear power among the socialists two years later for their presidential candidate, François Mitterrand, to promise voters at least a reconsideration of nuclear policy if elected, a pledge that helped him win both the largest share of the ecology vote and the election in 1981 (Hatch, 1986:154–57; Walker and Lönnroth, 1983:58).[17]

Once in office the new government ordered EDF to hold its public inquiries earlier to avoid charges that the proceedings merely provided automatic approval for decisions already made elsewhere. The socialists also established regional energy agencies as the CFDT requested and increased the involvement of local authorities in nuclear installation procedures (Fagnani and Moatti, 1982). Mitterrand stopped construction on the controversial Plogoff plant in 1981 and

[17] See Hatch (1986), Nelkin and Pollak (1981b), and Rüdig (1986) for detailed analyses of the electoral struggles and party politics involved with the nuclear issue.

suspended work on five others until Parliament could discuss and vote on nuclear policy. However, because the ecologists and antinuclear forces still did not dominate any of the major parties, a large majority of the Parliament voted that October to support the government's nuclear program. Mitterrand reduced his predecessor's 1980 plan; he decided to build six plants rather than nine in 1982–83, four rather than six in 1983–84, and two in 1985–86. Nevertheless, the basic thrust of the program remained unchanged. The socialists were committed to nuclear power as a means of stimulating economic growth, jobs, energy independence, and France's stature as a world leader in nuclear technology (Walker and Lönnroth, 1983:59–61). These cuts would have been even shallower were it not for a temporary excess of generating capacity due to a recession (Hatch, 1986:170; Rüdig, 1986).

Some observers believe that many of these changes were an attempt to move the policy process in a more corporatist, consensus-oriented direction (e.g., Fagnani and Moatti, 1982). If so, preliminary indications were that it may have worked. According to polls, public support for nuclear power increased under Mitterrand from 56 to 65 percent between 1981 and 1982 (Jasper, 1986b:13). Opposition to specific plants decreased. For example, local and regional officials originally opposed building a nuclear plant at the Golfech site. However, after the socialists came to power the government arranged negotiations between the officials and EDF to iron out their differences, a task accomplished when EDF convinced local leaders to support the new plant by offering to minimize ecological damage, use local construction workers on 60 percent of the project, channel over one billion francs of the project's budget into local companies, and pay the regional council six million francs annually during the plant's lifetime (Fagnani and Moatti, 1982).[18] Nevertheless, despite attempts to generate consensus and infuse parts of the policy process with a little more democracy, nuclear policy remained far more insulated from nuclear opponents than it was in the United States (Barkenbus, 1984; Hatch, 1986:162). As a result, French nuclear policy emerged from the conflict relatively unscathed.

In stark contrast, antinuclear groups actually reversed nuclear policy in Sweden by gaining access to the policy formation process. During the early 1970s opposition to nuclear power in Sweden

[18] In fact, this was really nothing new. EDF had often granted fiscal favors like lower electricity rates and school subsidies to encourage the support of local officials in the past. For examples, see Kitschelt (1986:75), Nelkin and Pollak (1981b:26), Touraine et al. (1983:60–63), and the U.S. Office of Technology Assessment (1984:198).

focused on environmental hazards and more general concerns about urban development (Nelkin and Pollak, 1977:341; Rycroft and Brenner, 1981; Zinberg, 1982:178). However, it was sporadic until the Center party, led by Thorbjörn Fälldin, began criticizing the ruling Social Democratic party's plans for expanding the nation's nuclear generating capacity. In addition to Fälldin's steadfast opposition to the technology, the Center party used the issue to gain political clout in the government by criticizing nuclear energy as an evil of centralized bureaucratic power. They proposed in 1973 that Parliament not approve, without further study, any nuclear plants beyond the eleven currently operating, under construction, or planned. Parliament defeated the resolution, but formed a royal commission to report on nuclear safety and waste issues by 1974. Parliament agreed not to make any other decisions on new nuclear plants until it could examine the results of the study. This signalled a major shift in control over nuclear policy from the administrative bureaucracy to Parliament, the beginning of a trend toward democratizing nuclear policy formation, and an indication that the legislature was no longer willing to approve automatically the bureaucracy's nuclear plans as it had until then. According to Måns Lönnroth (1977:259), an influential member of the Social Democratic party during the period, this was clearly a public questioning and partial rejection of the legitimacy of the decision-making process, a conflict between established technocratic and ascendent democratic policy paradigms. In large part as a result of the Center party's criticism, the Social Democrats lost their parliamentary majority in the 1973 elections, leaving a precarious balance of political power that would soon tip decisively in favor of the nuclear critics.

In the wake of the OPEC embargo, the Social Democrats moved to regain control over what was now a heated policy debate. Believing that an informed public would support their position, they called for the formation of small study groups around the country to educate people and provide an opportunity to discuss the issues.[19] Over eighty thousand people in eight thousand groups filled out questionnaires by 1975 that reported a strong preference for energy conservation. However, to the Social Democratic party's chagrin, the discussions did little to generate more support for the nuclear program. The effects of the study groups are difficult to judge; it appears that those who were either firmly opposed to, or in favor of, nuclear

[19] The government has convened study circles only a few times in Sweden's history (Swedish Institute, 1973). The closest example the United States has to study circles is the caucus system that some states, such as Iowa, use to select candidates during the presidential primaries.

power before the groups convened remained so afterward. There was a slight increase among those who were undecided (Nelkin and Pollak, 1977:344; Zinberg, 1982:177).

Although the Social Democrats pushed a bill through Parliament in 1975 calling for conservation policies and authorizing two more nuclear plants, the situation continued to deteriorate. Mass demonstrations became more frequent. Protests at the Barsebeck site drew over ten thousand people in 1976 and 1977 (Kitschelt, 1986). Polls indicated that by 1976 the balance of public opinion was roughly 50 percent against nuclear power, 30 percent favoring it, and the rest unsure (Jasper, 1986b:14). Furthermore, the Social Democrat and Communist party coalition lost control of Parliament in the 1976 elections. The Social Democrats were out of power for the first time in over forty years, a clear indication that voters were dissatisfied with the party's support for nuclear energy. The Center party formed a new government with its Liberal and Conservative partners. During the campaign Fälldin had promised to phase out Sweden's five operating reactors within ten years, to suspend work on the five under construction, and to cancel the three being planned. In partial fulfillment of those promises, the Center party proposed the Nuclear Power Stipulation Act, a bill Parliament passed in 1977 suspending all new licensing for nuclear plants until utilities could prove that they would have access to adequate waste reprocessing and/or permanent waste management programs. The utilities responded by signing reprocessing contracts later that year with COGEMA, the French reprocessor, and by helping establish a nuclear fuel safety project to investigate the possibilities for burying high-level radioactive waste in Sweden. The project proceeded quickly and by 1978 most of the scientists involved believed that the geological problems of waste disposal could be solved. As a result, when it appeared that the Stipulation Act would not prevent two new reactors from receiving their licenses that year, the Center party tried blocking them by adding new licensing requirements. This so antagonized the party's ruling partners, both supporters of nuclear power, that the coalition fell apart and a Liberal minority cabinet was formed (Sahr, 1985:chap. 4).

By this point two governments had fallen prey to the energy debate, and all the major parties were convinced by 1978 that the political risks associated with the issue were too high. As a result, with the support of both Social Democratic and Center party leaders, the Liberal government submitted a bill to Parliament in early 1979 calling for an end to further nuclear expansion within the foreseeable future beyond those reactors currently in the pipeline. Then the accident at Three Mile Island occurred in the United States. Shortly thereafter the Social Democrats suggested holding a national advisory referendum on nuclear power to resolve the issue, something Fälldin had long advocated but Social Democrats opposed. Hoping to remove the issue from the agenda of the upcoming 1979 elections, the other parties agreed to hold it the following year and abide by the outcome. This would be only the fourth national refendum held in Sweden since the turn of the century. There were several reasons for the Social Democrats' change of heart. First, energy conservation was succeeding, and electricity demand projections indicated Sweden might not need nuclear power to meet its future energy needs. Second, the accident at Three Mile Island a month earlier raised new doubts about the technology's safety (Linde, 1983; Zinberg, 1982). Finally, a grassroots movement concerned that nuclear power could lead to a centralized, technocratic form of society had developed within the party, pushing leaders to support a referendum. The vote was close. A 39 percent plurality chose to eliminate nuclear power in Sweden gradually by building no more than the twelve plants currently operating, under construction, or planned, and by redoubling the conservation effort. Parliament approved a plan two months later to begin phasing out nuclear plants by 1997 and to finish by 2010.[20]

In contrast to France and especially the United States, scientists and other experts critical of nuclear power played a relatively minor role in stimulating Swedish antinuclear activity. Many experts with different points of view were already involved in the policy formation process, a standard feature of Swedish policy making in general.[21] For example, after the 1976 elections the three bourgeois parties formed a commission on energy to examine various alternatives for Swedish energy policy, including phasing out nuclear power by 1985. Although many experts were involved and there was great disagreement within the commission, the final report recommended a continued, yet scaled-down, expansion of nuclear power, a position that did not satisfy antinuclear groups. Nevertheless, the government had consulted the experts and given their opinions serious consideration. The government also sought their input through the remiss procedures on legislative proposals and the utility waste management study

[20] For excellent histories of the electoral struggles around the nuclear issue, see Sahr (1985), Childs (1980:92–120), and Bupp and Derian (1978:137–44).
[21] Weir and Skocpol (1985:129) note that the integration of experts with different points of view into the policy formation process has also been important in building consensus and long-range planning in other policy areas in Sweden.

(Kitschelt, 1984; Sahr, 1985:91–95). Furthermore, Swedish law afforded citizens virtually unlimited access to government information, even more than did the Freedom of Information Act in the United States (Sahr, 1985:162). As a result, the sorts of scandalous revelations and internal legitimation crises that created so many problems for policy makers in the United States never occurred in Sweden. There was simply no need for scientists and other experts to expose a policy process that already operated in full public view and to which they had ready access.

Implementation of the referendum decision proceeded smoothly. The nuclear industries seemed to accept the outcome and by 1983 were concentrating more on fuel services and other functions than on building new reactors (Linde, 1983). Despite the Social Democrats' return to power in 1982, it was doubtful that they would try to reverse the policy, for they had invested a tremendous amount of political capital in this decision (Sahr, 1985:135). To do so would have jeopardized their electoral support unless they held another referendum, something quite unlikely since energy issues had fallen from the electoral agenda after the referendum and no party wanted to revive them (Linde, 1983). Most important, because citizens had tremendous input during policy formation, it was unlikely that they would try to block implementation (Sahr, 1985:169–71).

In West Germany public participation in the policy process occurred during implementation, not formation, and dealt the sector severe blows, much as it did in the United States. There was only limited opposition to nuclear power in West Germany before 1974, but by the end of the decade over one thousand citizen action groups had organized nearly one million people in protest against the technology's commercialization (Camilleri, 1984:88). Again, safety, environmental, and waste disposal concerns were at issue first; complaints that there were no opportunities for really influencing policy developed later (Dyson, 1982:26). Critics charged that licensing hearings were exercises in symbolic politics rather than meaningful opportunities to influence policy during implementation, particularly in view of the fact that the *Länder* had never denied a license (Rüdig, 1986). In one case they complained that the official in charge of the licensing procedure was also the acting vice-chairman of the utility's board of directors. In another, officials acknowledged that secret negotiations with the applicants had already been underway for a year prior to application for the construction permit. The low tolerance among civil servants for public participation in these forums reinforced the critics' perceptions (Nelkin and Pollak, 1981b:34–36).

Eventually political conflicts marked by mass protests emerged. The *Länder's* approval of a construction permit in 1975 for nuclear plants at Whyl triggered the first. An estimated 35,000 people showed up and occupied the construction site for almost a year. They claimed that the public hearings held during licensing were a farce. Other demonstrations, sometimes violent, followed at Brokdorf, Kalkar, Grohnde, and Gorleben. Some 250,000 people participated in seven similar demonstrations between 1975 and April 1979. Demonstrations in Bonn during the fall of 1979 and again at Brokdorf in 1981 each drew over 100,000 people (Hatch, 1986; Kitschelt, 1986). National polls found that opposition to nuclear power had increased to 57 percent by 1981 (Hatch, 1986:137).

As in Sweden, scientific opposition to nuclear power did not have a catalytic effect on the antinuclear movement. First, there was no centralized group of scientists working full time in conjunction with antinuclear groups to change policy as the Union of Concerned Scientists did in the United States. Instead, scientists openly critical of nuclear power were scattered throughout the German academic system in universities at Bremen, Heidelberg, and elsewhere. Second, dissent among German scientists did not develop within government agencies as it had in the United States and France, but from outside (Nelkin and Pollak, 1981b:93–98). Hence, although dissenters did provide activists with technical ammunition for carrying out their attack on the sector, the legitimacy of the policy system did not suffer the kind of blow from within that it had in the United States—a blow that precipitated a qualitative escalation in antinuclear activity on both legal and civil-disobedience fronts.

Demonstrations in West Germany focused attention on nuclear power, but the courts provided critics a more effective point of access to policy implementation. For example, activists convinced judges to suspend construction permits at Whyl after questioning reactor safety and at Brokdorf because there was no clear plan for radioactive waste management. Legal action froze several projects by 1979, although higher courts reversed many of these rulings later. Three of the eleven plants under construction then had lost their construction permits and four more had stopped because of actual or threatened suits (Kitschelt, 1986; Rüdig, 1986). In turn, construction delays skyrocketed from about six to thirty months between 1974 and 1980 (see Table 8.3). As a result, average lead times approached ten years, close to those in the United States (see Table 8.2). These delays contributed to nuclear plant cost escalation. Some projects in the latter stages of construction, but delayed in the courts, lost millions of dollars a month (Camilleri, 1984:125; Falk, 1982:216–19). Some observers argued that the courts constrained nuclear power's commercialization more in West Germany than anywhere else in the world (Rycroft and Brenner, 1981:72).

Activists also tried electoral politics. However, none of the major parties took strong antinuclear positions at the national level. The conservative Christian Democratic Union and Christian Social Union both supported nuclear power. The critics' chances looked brighter with the Social Democratic and Free Democratic parties, which initially favored a moratorium on new nuclear plants until the government could license a site for disposing radioactive waste. However, momentum for the moratorium stalled in 1977 when the Federation of German Trade Unions objected that the policy would threaten jobs in nuclear construction. Leaders in both parties urged members, already divided over nuclear power, not to let the issue destroy their delicate ruling coalition (Kitschelt, 1986; Nelkin and Pollak, 1981b:45). In an attempt to appease all sides, the government announced a revised national energy plan in December 1977 giving nuclear power a lower priority and establishing a licensing policy similar to Sweden's Stipulation Act. New nuclear projects would not receive initial construction permits and those under construction would not get licenses until their operators could assure adequate waste disposal either at home or abroad (Hatch, 1986:chap. 4).

Yet this was much less than the permanent moratorium many nuclear critics sought. As a result, activists began forming Green parties in the *Länder* for the 1978 elections. The Greens won enough votes in Lower Saxony and Hamburg to tip the balance of power in both coalition governments that spring, although not enough actually to win seats for themselves. Equally important, their presence altered the terrain of political debate and the positions of some parties at the *Länder* level, infusing both with greater concern for environmental and nuclear issues. The Greens' regional clout was perhaps most obvious when the Minister-President of Lower Saxony refused to grant a construction permit for the Gorleben reprocessing and waste management complex in 1979 after thousands of demonstrators opposed it. Fearing a backlash in the next election, he explained that although the project was feasible and safe, it would have been political suicide to approve it.[22] Green power continued to grow. The Greens

[22] For more detailed discussions of the politics involved, see Nelkin and Pollak (1981b; 1980a), Hatch (1986), and Falk (1982).

won seats in most *Länder* governments and in the national Parliament during the 1980s (Hatch, 1986:chap. 5).

The point is that implementation politics made it more difficult to build nuclear plants, something utilities wanted to do because imported oil and domestic coal were expensive. However, they recognized that the political situation made licensing difficult and increased plant costs (Lönnroth and Walker, 1979:63–68). As a result, they ordered only one plant between 1976 and 1986. With no new orders on the horizon, there was a virtual de facto moratorium on new nuclear projects in West Germany (Hatch, 1986:139).

In all four countries conflicts developed over nuclear power that transcended concerns about safety and the environment. Eventually nuclear critics complained that a technocratic approach to policy focusing on the sector's growth must give way to a democratic approach favoring greater public access to the policy process. However, when they tried to act on their objections, the outcomes were quite different depending on the institutional arrangements involved. In France, the system was so closed and insulated that the antinuclear movement had very little substantive effect on either policy or the sector's health. In the United States and West Germany nuclear critics used accessible implementation arenas to disrupt policy enough to help facilitate de facto ordering moratoria. Sweden experienced an ordering moratorium too, but there was an important difference. The Swedes arrived at a moratorium through orderly planning, not in a reactive, ad hoc manner. Institutions encouraged negotiation and consensus building during the early stages of policy formation. The other nations did not.[23] The lesson is that although many Swedes did not agree with the ultimate outcome, they were willing to live with it because it had been achieved democratically. In the other countries where the technocratic approach remained dominant, activists continued to fight policy tooth and nail precisely because they had not

[23] Others have drawn similar conclusions in different policy contexts. For example, Weir and Skocpol (1985) argued that the prolonged commitment among Swedish policy makers to "social Keynesianism" stemmed in large part from their working within an administratively centralized, yet accessible, policy system that encouraged consensus building among a wide variety of interest group representatives and policy experts during the initial stages of policy formation. In contrast, policy formation was more fragmented in the United States and included a less representative cross-section of interests—conditions that both undermined social bargaining and limited economic planning. Similarly, Vogel (1986:271) found that the absence of compromise and consultation during the formation of environmental policy helped account for the relative instability of policy in the United States compared with Britain.

been party to its initial creation. Hence, although it may be that interests in economic accumulation and political accountability, expressed through the technocratic and democratic policy paradigms, respectively, routinely contradict each other in advanced capitalist democracies, as Dickson (1984) and Nelkin (1984) argue, institutional variations in the policy process significantly modify the effects of that confrontation. In the nuclear sector, the institutions determined the manner in which the expression of that contradiction affected the policy process and plans for further nuclear development.

In particular, differences in the institutional structure of electoral politics were important. In the United States, because there were only two major parties and a winner-take-all electoral process, regimes did not hinge on fragile coalitions as they often did in the European countries with multiparty, parliamentary systems. The probability that antinuclear groups could force a change in government by shifting their electoral support was much smaller in the United States than in Europe. As a result, nuclear critics spent much less time playing party and electoral politics than their European counterparts. Indeed, the range of institutional opportunities played a major role in influencing the strategies of political opposition in each country. Of course, despite the relative similarities among the French, Swedish, and West German electoral systems, antinuclear groups had quite different experiences. In Sweden and to an extent in West Germany they achieved significant victories. In France they did not. Although institutional opportunities for action may be present, participants do not always capitalize on them if, as in France, the prevailing political conditions do not permit action.

CAPITAL FORMATION

Direct government involvement in the financial affairs of EDF stabilized the utility's capital formation processes and enabled it to avoid the capital shortages that crippled the United States nuclear sector. First, the Ministry of Finance regulated EDF's ability to generate capital internally by dictating the rates the utility charged its customers (Lucas, 1979:136). Second, the ministry controlled EDF's access to external sources of finance capital by subsidizing some of EDF's projects, providing loans, and approving all financing the utility did through the private capital markets (Lucas, 1979:chap. 4). However, EDF's relationship with the ministry was reciprocal. While the ministry used its financial leverage to ensure that EDF conformed to the intent of national energy policy, the utility held important positions on the PEON Commission, which had established this policy in the first place, and therefore enjoyed considerable latitude in charting its own course (Lucas, 1979:chap. 5).

Policy makers in the United States have noted that these institutional arrangements were very important in helping the French sustain their commitment to nuclear power (U.S. Senate, 1981a:4). The government kept EDF's electricity rates low to promote electricity consumption until 1968. The policy worked, but created internal cash flow shortages that would have prohibited the construction of new generating capacity to meet demand unless the utility could raise the necessary capital elsewhere. The Ministry of Finance intervened on EDF's behalf by arranging government loans until 1965 and direct subsidies afterward. Eventually, the ministry allowed EDF to raise its rates between 1968 and 1973, thereby relieving the internal capital formation dilemma and permitting the utility to reduce its dependence on other forms of external public financing without affecting the nuclear program. However, with the beginning of the nuclear expansion in 1974, the requirements for investment capital soared. Government subsidies and credit increased in response. In some cases the government suspended the interest on EDF's loans to help keep the costs of nuclear projects under control (Camilleri, 1984:146). In others, officials let EDF increase its indebtedness in the capital markets at home and especially abroad (Lucas, 1979:chap. 4). As a result, the amount of finance capital the utility raised externally climbed between 1973 and 1977 from 40 to 70 percent of its annual capital formation effort (Camilleri, 1984:147). The need for capital increased substantially with the nuclear expansion, and, in bold contrast to the United States, institutional arrangements helped EDF raise adequate funds through a combination of state and private financing packages.

Citizens had no formal role in rate making because the government made the decisions in insulated political arenas removed from public pressures. However, EDF could not build nuclear plants at will, nor was it immune from financial trouble. For example, the utility had to reduce its nuclear orders slightly in 1976 because the Ministry of Finance wanted to limit the general level of public investment throughout the economy. By refusing to grant EDF the full rate increase it requested, the government limited the utility's ability to generate enough capital internally to purchase all the reactors it wanted that year (Hatch, 1986:153). It is likely that the government's desire to trim nuclear spending stemmed in part from the realization that the massive long-term investments tied up in the nuclear program were helping to fuel both inflation and a national capital short-age (Cohen et al., 1982:51). More recently, electricity consumption fell short of projected annual growth rates in 1980 and 1981 and left EDF with a serious revenue shortage. EDF lost eight billion francs in 1982 as a result of the shortage and high interest charges on its nuclear program. While it remains to be seen what effect this will have, some observers feel that this financial performance, the worst in thirty years for EDF, may undercut the nuclear program's growth by 1990 (Walker and Lönnroth, 1983:58).

The Swedish case is interesting because although the government had less comprehensive control over internal capital formation throughout the utility industry than did the governments of either France or the United States, capital shortages jeopardizing nuclear power did not materialize. In Sweden there was no formal rate regula-tion at any level of government. Instead, the ability of both the State Power Board and the municipal utilities to set their own rates and compete with each other and private electricity producers for bulk users and distributors was the government's chief regulatory tool in this regard—one that offered moderate control over rates as the public utilities produced about 65 percent of Sweden's electricity. Although this control was fragmented, the potential for competition, especially from the State Power Board, did help keep rates down (Lönnroth, 1977:275; Sahr, 1985:24–25). Just as important, Sweden did not have a rate-making system that encouraged capital intensive investments like nuclear projects. If anything, there were incentives to exercise investment *restraint,* for in the presence of competition and the absence of rate regulation, there were no guarantees that earnings would cover investments. This was much different from the United States, where rate-making formulae ensured that utilities would earn a profit on their capital expenditures, at least until consumers rebelled against rate increases.[24]

Such fiscal restraint kept the Swedish utilities financially healthy and undoubtedly helped them avoid problems in raising money through the capital markets. So did the government's participation in external capital formation, for policy makers helped utilities raise the funds necessary to sustain their nuclear ambitions. The Ministry of

---

[24] See chapter 6 and the Appendix for details of the regulatory incentives for capital investment in the U.S. electric utility industry. This argument does not imply that deregulation of electricity rates would produce the same results in the United States. After all, the utility industry is not competitive in the United States as it is in Sweden, so the effects of deregulation might be quite different, perhaps leading to price increases rather than price restraint.

Industry and Parliament approved the State Power Board's budget and financed part of its nuclear construction from federal coffers. With the State Power Board owning seven of Sweden's twelve nuclear plants, the federal government was able to ensure financing for at least a significant portion of the nuclear program. Furthermore, while the rest of the utility industry raised most of its finance capital through revenues and the bond market, the government provided some loans for nuclear construction from its pension funds (Lönn-roth and Walker, 1979:36).

This is not to suggest that the Swedish nuclear program was free from all financial concerns. Both private and public participants worried during the mid-1970s that because the technology was so capital intensive a massive nuclear program could provoke capital shortages in other industrial sectors. This concern helped convince nuclear power firms, participants in other energy sectors, and industry in general that energy conservation, especially a reduction in electricity consumption, was good policy after the 1973–74 world oil crisis (Sahr, 1985:63). To the extent that an interest in conservation helped create support for the nuclear program's reduction later, financial worries may have contributed to the sector's decline, although in a very indirect way. More to the point, even if this was the case, the institutional arrangements governing utility capital formation in Sweden did not choke off funds from nuclear projects already underway as they did in the United States.

At first glance the West German case seems to be an anomaly. The institutional structure of utility capital formation there was very similar to that in the United States, yet capital shortages did not threaten the West German nuclear program. In both countries there was electricity rate regulation and utilities relied on private sources for most of the capital needed to build nuclear plants. However, there was enough variation within these common parameters to produce quite different outcomes. For example, although a German utility established its own electricity rates subject to approval by the *Länder* and federal government (Lönnroth, 1983:18; OTA, 1984:198), the *Länder* was intimately familiar with the company's financial condition and revenue needs by virtue of its stock holdings and its representation on the board of directors. These channels of influence let *Länder* officials play an active role in determining the initial rate request long before the utility sought formal approval. By the time the utility actually made its request, the company and the *Länder* had retreated to the corporate board room and settled whatever differences they may have had. As a result and in contrast to the United States, rate approval was not a problem in West Germany, something that bolstered the utility industry's financial condition (Camilleri, 1984:138; Keck, 1981:21; Lönnroth, 1983:18).

Private capital markets provided about 60 percent of the funds required for the nation's nuclear projects (Camilleri, 1984:138). However, unlike in the United States, capital markets in West Germany were not subject to short-term competitive impulses. The *Länder* governments were willing to bear some of the financial risks through ownership and by financing portions of the projects (OTA, 1984:198). In addition, the federal government offered to reimburse utilities for some of the costs associated with modifying nuclear plants when regulators or the courts required it (NRC, 1982c:106). Finally, big banks also owned portions of the utilities and participated in their management. These features helped ensure investors that their interests would be protected and that nuclear projects would be well managed financially. The healthy financial condition of the utilities, attributable in part to the ease with which rates were set, must also have contributed to investor confidence. All of this helped cultivate the long-term perspective in financial circles necessary to sustain nuclear projects (Lönnroth, 1983:18–20; Lönnroth and Walker, 1979:34–37). This was especially important because project lead times were almost as long in West Germany by the early 1980s as they were in the United States (see Table 8.2) and because costs for West German nuclear plants tripled between 1972 and 1981 (Mez and Watts, 1982).

Two common institutional features stand out as having helped provide the financial stability and long-term investment horizons in France, Sweden, and West Germany necessary for a vigorous nuclear program—features conspicuously absent for the most part from the United States. First, in all three countries the government played a critical role in reducing financial risks to investors in a variety of ways, most notably through ownership, direct financing, or both. The West Germans relied on public funding perhaps less than the other two, but they had the additional advantage of large banks infusing financial planning with a degree of farsightedness and patience uncharacteristic of the United States, but something typical of West Germany's financial system (e.g., Zysman, 1983). In short, there was a variety of institutional mechanisms at work in these countries that helped transcend whatever problems the contradiction between short-term profitability, especially in the financial markets, and long-range investment planning might have posed to the nuclear sector. Second, the general public was not privy to rate making to the extent that it was in the United States, where public utility commissions routinely held open hearings on rates. Hence, it was less likely that obstructionist politics would develop to undermine the utility's internal capital formation process enough to jeopardize planned or ongoing nuclear projects.

HIGH-LEVEL RADIOACTIVE WASTE DISPOSAL

The contrast between the French and the U.S. experiences with high-level waste management is the sharpest. The Atomic Energy Act forced the U.S. Atomic Energy Commission to rely on the private sector for commercial reprocessing, whereas there were no such limits in France. So, using the Purex technology developed in the United States, the CEA built its own facilities at La Hague, established COGEMA to run them, and began serving all of the nation's commercial reprocessing needs in 1966 (Lucas, 1979:34). COGEMA's reprocessing costs skyrocketed tenfold and the operation lost money consistently throughout the 1970s. Nevertheless, the CEA remained dedicated to reprocessing as an intermediary step in their waste management system, kept it running, and absorbed much of the loss (Bupp, 1980a:38; Deese, 1982:69; Rippon, 1978:62). Observers have concluded that without the government's ability to pursue the long-range plan at the expense of short-term profit considerations, the industry would have failed, much as its counterpart did in the United States (Fagnani and Moatti, 1982:15). However, this is not to say that the government threw fiscal caution entirely to the wind. The CEA and COGEMA agreed to reprocess wastes from other countries if these customers were willing to help defray the losses by paying a fixed percentage of the operating costs at La Hague. In addition, several countries also agreed to help pay for a second, much larger, and presumably more efficient, reprocessing plant later (Cohen, 1982:38–39; Deese, 1982:69).

Nor did public criticism of the La Hague plant convince the government to abandon reprocessing. The facility suffered a variety of accidents, some severe, and never came close to operating at full capacity (Barlett and Steele, 1985:111; Nelkin and Pollak, 1981b:83–85). Antinuclear and environmental groups objected to reprocessing for many of the same reasons they did in the United States, but also because the CEA was planning to reprocess wastes from other countries. Members of the CFDT trade union who worked at La Hague shut the plant down in 1976 for several months in protest over what they considered to be dangerous working conditions (Camilleri,

1984:211; Deese, 1982:69). Nevertheless, except for these job actions inside the plant, the closed and insulated nature of the policy process generally neutralized the opposition and ensured that reprocessing would continue.

The French government also assumed responsibility for disposing of the sector's high-level waste after reprocessing. For years, unless destined for recycling as fresh reactor fuel, the French sealed wastes in containers and dumped them into the ocean, a policy long banned in the United States (Barlett and Steele, 1985:111). However, the government has been building interim storage facilities and plans to solidify reprocessed wastes for burial on the mainland (U.S. Senate, 1981a). COGEMA has run a prototype solidification plant at Marcoule since 1978 as a step in that direction (Camilleri, 1984:217; Fagnani and Moatti, 1982). There has been little opposition to this phase of the waste management plan. It is doubtful that activists could have much effect, given their limited access to the policy process. In any case, waste management never became an impediment to the nuclear sector's development in France.

The Swedish experience falls between France and the United States in terms of both the government's ability to develop effective policy and the issue's influence on the viability of the nuclear sector. As noted earlier, the waste issue generated political turmoil as nuclear critics convinced Parliament to pass the Nuclear Power Stipulation Act in 1977, which temporarily suspended licensing. Although the conditions of the act appeared to have been met soon thereafter, final responsibility for approving permanent waste disposal sites rested with the Swedish Nuclear Power Inspectorate. When a site was suggested, leaders in Parliament hoped for a clear-cut ruling from the inspectorate, one that would make the legislature's decision about whether to resume licensing equally straightforward. The inspectorate decided in 1979 that the site in question was not geologically sound. However, it also argued that the decision did not imply there were no acceptable sites in Sweden, just that this particular one was bad. By using such ambiguities to salvage political neutrality, the agency turned the controversial final decision on the Stipulation Act back to Parliament and left the door open for plant licensing if legislators decided to allow it (Sahr, 1985:100–101). In an attempt to dodge the political bullet, the legislature elected to defer its decision until after the national referendum. When the referendum was over, the government approved fuel loading for all the reactors that were ready, and licensing proceeded accordingly.

As it turned out, the waste issue was not a major impediment to the sector's development in Sweden, only a temporary delay. So far, it appears that the Swedish plan for interim storage and final disposal has proceeded without much difficulty. First, although there has been local opposition to the development of permanent waste disposal facilities at some of the proposed sites (Linde, 1983), the institutional opportunities to block development once the federal government picks a site are limited, for citizens do not have much access to licensing or the courts in these matters (Deese, 1982:84–85). As noted earlier, municipal authorities can deny permission to use their land, but Parliament can override that decision with special legislation. Second, and perhaps more important, the nuclear waste issue has become a relatively moot political point since the referendum. Critics no longer need it to help them stop the nuclear program.

West German officials ran into many of the same problems with waste management policy that their counterparts did in the United States—and for many of the same institutional reasons. The parallels with reprocessing were the most striking. Because federal law provided that private corporations would develop most aspects of the nuclear sector, a consortium of utilities, not the government, planned to build reprocessing facilities, but later balked after deciding that the venture would not be profitable. Counting on the project's successful completion, the federal government had procrastinated in developing a final waste management program and was caught off guard when reprocessing failed to develop as planned (Hatch, 1986:89–93; Pringle and Spigelman, 1981:405). However, Chancellor Schmidt warned in 1976 that he would suspend reactor licensing until the government issued a construction permit for a reprocessing facility and made preliminary decisions on a final waste disposal site—a shrewd attempt to accelerate solutions to the waste problem and move the sector's development forward while appeasing those factions within the Social Democratic and Free Democratic parties opposed to nuclear power (Deese, 1982:79; Hatch, 1986:89; Rüdig, 1986). Several administrative courts supported Schmidt by blocking licenses for nuclear plants until operaters could provide convincing plans for waste management. The government formalized this policy in 1979 when it adopted the Federal-State Declaration of Principles, which instructed regulators not to license additional nuclear plants without those plans (Meyer-Abich and Dickler, 1982:236). Several observers agreed that these rulings were among the most serious stumbling blocks to the West German nuclear program (e.g., Dyson, 1982:29; Meyer-Abich and Dickler, 1982; Rüdig, 1986).

The sector moved quickly to overcome the obstacle. The federal government identified a site for a reprocessing and waste management complex in 1977 at Gorleben in Lower Saxony, began geological studies there, and received preliminary approval from the *Länder* to develop permanent disposal facilities. The reprocessing consortium applied to the *Länder* for a construction permit and signed contracts with the French for reprocessing services until the Gorleben complex was finished. By 1978 it appeared that the sector had met all the prerequisites for renewed licensing (Hatch, 1986:112). However, antinuclear groups struck again. The *Länder* held public hearings in 1979 as part of its construction permit review for the complex, but local authorities refused to grant it, fearing electoral retaliation by the Greens during the next election. Frantic negotiations ensued between the federal and *Länder* governments in search of a solution. They agreed to build temporary storage facilities for used fuel away from reactor sites and two smaller reprocessing plants in separate locations. They also decided to permit utilities to expand on-site storage pools and to continue planning for permanent disposal at Gorleben (Deese, 1982:78; Rüdig, 1986). Construction began on the temporary storage facilities and the consortium filed applications for construction permits on the reprocessing plants in 1983. Nevertheless, political opposition persisted. Antinuclear groups raised objections in the courts that delayed permission for expanding on-site storage capacity in several cases (Meyer-Abich and Dickler, 1982). The *Länder* government in Hesse abandoned plans for a reprocessing plant, apparently succumbing to intense political pressure similar to that surrounding the Gorleben project earlier (Hatch, 1986:137).

Whenever private actors were responsible for providing the initial step in waste management, as they were in West Germany and the United States, planning was extremely difficult because short-term profitability considerations tended to outweigh the more long-range, sectoral interest in resolving waste problems. This occurred in the reprocessing industry regardless of whether there was competition. It would seem, then, that although competition may exacerbate the develoment of a short-term profitability calculus within an industry, this calculus is always present and potentially disruptive of planning as long as the private sector is fundamentally in charge. In France, where the government assumed full responsibility for reprocessing, concerns about profits were easily transcended and the service was readily available. However, what makes the West German case particularly interesting is that although reprocessing was in private hands, the government eventually played a very strong role in forcing the industry to overcome its short-sighted view. Schmidt's warning, later codified in the Declaration of Principles, convinced the utility consortium to proceed with reprocessing despite concerns that it might not be profitable. Of course the utilities' ownership in the reprocessing firm infused the industry with a broader sectoral perspective than in the United States, where the sector was less integrated in this way. After all, it was the utility industry, among others, that wanted to develop nuclear power and that stood to lose if the absence of waste management plans blocked the sector's development. In any case, the United States government was unwilling to force reprocessors into adopting the farsighted view. Jimmy Carter decided to ban reprocessing, not encourage it. Indeed, the decisions of administrative and other political elites *were* important in explaining these different policy outcomes. On the other hand, pressure from the federal government could not guarantee that the West German reprocessing plan would succeed. There were too many *institutional* opportunities for nuclear critics to obstruct implementation, just as there were in the United States. Similarly, even if policy makers in the United States had not forbidden reprocessing, serious political obstacles would have remained, threatening the industry's survival and disrupting further waste management planning. In other words, variations in the relationship between the state and private sector were important in this policy area, but so were differences in the institutional features of the policy process itself, that is, in the structure of the state. This is perhaps clearest when contrasting pairs of cases. In France and Sweden, the policy process was relatively insulated, particularly during implementation, and waste management planning seems to have proceeded without serious problems. In the United States and West Germany, political groups had the opportunity to dirsrupt policy at every turn and chose to do so.

Alternative Explanations

Institutional differences were clearly important among the French, Swedish, West German, and U.S. nuclear sectors, but could other factors account for the variations in policy and sectoral performance? For example, perhaps those countries with fewer domestic energy resources had greater incentives to develop nuclear power in order to achieve some degree of independence from foreign energy imports, particularly after the rapid escalation in world oil prices during the latter half of the 1970s. France depended on imported oil for 75 percent of its total energy requirement in 1973, Sweden for 70 percent, West Germany for 42 percent, and the United States for 10 percent (Ikenberry, 1986:108; Sahr, 1985:16). The decline of France's coal industry exacerbated its import dependence (Saumon and Puiseux, 1977). Similarly, Sweden had exploited about as much of its hydropower as possible, had virtually no known gas reserves, but was rich in domestic uranium, with about 80 percent of Western Europe's deposits (Nelkin and Pollak, 1977:341; Sahr, 1985:74). In contrast, West Germany enjoyed vast supplies of domestic coal, which supplied nearly 38 percent of the nation's energy needs in 1970 (Meyer-Abich and Dickler, 1982:226). The United States was rich not only in coal but also in uranium, oil, and natural gas, although according to some estimates the latter two resources were seriously depleted by the early 1970s (Vietor, 1984:194).

If dependence on imported oil and the availability of indigenous energy alternatives somehow determined the strength of a nation's commitment to nuclear power and, therefore, the steadfastness of its nuclear program, we would expect France and Sweden, countries heavily dependent on oil imports and relatively poor in domestic alternatives, to have pursued nuclear power more aggressively than either West Germany or the United States. In fact, after the 1973–74 world oil crisis, all four countries planned to expand their nuclear programs, regardless of the availability of indigenous energy supplies. France's program was quite successful, judging from the continuous ordering pattern EDF pursued through the 1980s. As we might expect, the nuclear programs in both the United States and West Germany stalled and suffered de facto moratoria on nuclear orders. However, Sweden developed a plan to phase out nuclear power systematically over a thirty-year period, a result contrary to the oil dependency and resource scarcity thesis.[25]

We might also argue that shifts in the demand for electricity were an important underlying cause for the variation in the nuclear sector's viability across countries. Yet, as suggested earlier in chapter 6, the decline in electricity demand growth rates does not seem to be a fully adequate explanation for the decline of the nuclear sector in the United States. Nor is it sufficient to explain what happened elsewhere. A decline in electricity demand growth rates and overcapacity in the electric utility industry were common problems in all of these countries during the latter half of the 1970s (Lönnroth, 1983:7). Yet the

---

[25] This supports John Ikenberry's (1986:119–20) contention that variation in energy reserves was not the critical factor determining the responses of most countries to the mid-1970s oil crisis.

national responses toward nuclear power were quite different. The French kept ordering nuclear plants while utilities in West Germany and the United States did not. However, despite substantially reduced rates predicted through the end of the century (Meyer-Abich and Dickler, 1982:244–45) the Germans began trying to send a convoy of plants through the licensing process in the early 1980s, an indication that they would build more plants if they could, regardless of the electricity demand trends. On the other hand, the Swedes designed policies to expand electricity consumption to save oil while they phased out nuclear power (Sahr, 1985:125).

In short, although dependence on imported oil, relative supplies of indigenous energy reserves, and shifts in electricity demand growth rates may have had some influence on the nuclear power programs in some countries, these factors alone do not provide a sufficient explanation of the fate of each country's sector. A more powerful explanation for these outcomes requires an analysis of the institutional arrangements of each nuclear sector's political economy. Otherwise it is virtually impossible to explain either policy outcomes or the relative health of each program.

REFLECTIONS

In fact, it appears that several different institutional arrangements facilitated planning in the nuclear sector during commercialization. The French and to an extent the Swedes planned effectively, although toward quite different ends. Even the West Germans accomplished a degree of planning, at least financially, that permitted them to avoid the capital formation problems that emerged in the United States. In comparison, the United States was at a distinct institutional disadvantage in planning. Its nuclear sector suffered accordingly.

What is perhaps most striking about these comparisons is the relationship between centralized state involvement and planning. In most cases the private sector was either unable or unwilling to transcend short-term commercial interests in favor of long-range, sectoral goals without some sort of push from the central government. The French accomplished their planning agenda in large measure because a few federal agencies assumed firm control over sectoral activity. Policy failures in the United States were often associated with the absence of such intervention. In Sweden, centralized state apparatuses helped rationalize capital formation and reactor manufacturing. The West German sector, almost as privatized as the U.S. sector, did not follow through on waste reprocessing until the federal government decided to make licensing contingent upon progress in reprocessing. However, there were a few cases in which centralized state agencies did *not* plan effectively. The absence of standardized reactor ordering in the Swedish State Power Board's program is an example. Yet the evidence presented here and in previous chapters suggests that it was very difficult for private actors *alone* to plan at the sectoral level with much success, especially when they were competitively arranged. The example that comes closest to undermining this argument is capital formation in the West German sector, where capital flows were well planned but where the federal government's only role was its willingness to absorb some of the costs associated with modifying plant designs. Nevertheless, such pledges seemed to help bolster investor confidence and encourage a more farsighted planning perspective. Of course, so did the coordinating role of a centralized banking system. Although firm conclusions are risky in the absence of more cases, we can at least hypothesize that the central state's forceful participation is a necessary, though not sufficient, condition for successful long-term planning in the nuclear sector.[26]

However, even when there *was* planning, it did not automatically ensure the sector's continued health and viability. After all, the Swedes planned effectively, but set out to dismantle their program. What, then, are the critical institutional conditions required for the kind of planning necessary to sustain the commercialization of a complex technology as potentially dangerous and unforgiving as nuclear power?[27] Judging from the countries discussed here, it seems that the principle requirement is a policy system relatively impervious to the demands of citizens concerned with the perceived dangers. Re-

[26] This thesis and the evidence from which it is derived contradict the recommendations of those who have suggested that governments reduce their involvement in the sector and provide only operating subsidies and regulatory direction once commercialization begins (e.g., deLeon, 1979:235). However, their recommendations were based on data collected before many significant events discussed here came to light. Furthermore, we must be careful not to draw policy recommendations for the current situation from studies done of stages in the technology's history prior to commercialization. For example, although several researchers have argued that competition among reactor manufacturers was beneficial to initial reactor development and demonstration (e.g., Burn, 1967; Dawson, 1976; deLeon, 1979:246–47), it would be misleading to infer that competition would also benefit the sector after it had achieved commercialization. After all, competition posed serious barriers to both reprocessing and effective standardization in the United States.

[27] By *unforgiving* I mean that nuclear power is a technology involving complex, tightly integrated organizational and technical interactions. These characteristics make the technology unforgiving in the sense that if something goes wrong, not only is it very difficult to regain control of the system, but given the nature of the radioactive materials, the consequences can be disastrous. See Perrow (1984) for a fascinating discussion of these problems.

gardless of whether access came during policy formation (Sweden) or implementation (West Germany and the United States), citizens acting on these fears jeopardized the sector's longevity when given the chance. Only where critics were denied substantial input (France) did the sector continue to thrive. Whether such restrictions ought to be a policy goal is another very sensitive question, one perhaps best left to the public to decide.

In another context, David Vogel (1986:253) has suggested that at least in the United States the public is generally not worried so much with the dangers of technology per se, as with its perception that business is inherently irresponsible in managing technology and that the government is either unable or unwilling to do anything about it. In other words, citizens may recognize that corporate interests contradict their own and that government often sides with business. There is some truth to this for other countries as well, at least with respect to the nuclear sector. Måns Lönnroth and his colleagues (1980:163–64) have argued that in Western societies nuclear power became a symbol of wider concern about the lack of democratic control over industrial systems in general. Indeed, concerns about these contradictory interests and doubts about the ability of both public and private institutions to safely manage nuclear technology contributed substantially to the nuclear controversy in all the countries examined here. However, despite Vogel's generalization, there *was* concern over the inherent danger of this particular technology. Since the reactor accidents at both Three Mile Island in the United States and Chernobyl in the Soviet Union, it is probably safe to assume that mistrust of the technology will not diminish for the time being, particularly insofar as these accidents revealed that both politically open and closed governments, and both capitalist and state-socialist economies, are susceptible to nuclear accidents. Given this mistrust of the technology itself, if the only way to sustain the sector's expansion is to restrict dramatically citizen involvement in the policy process, then it is ironic that policy makers in the United States and elsewhere opened up new channels of political access for nuclear critics in the hopes of easing opposition and facilitating the continued development of nuclear power. It may be that at least with respect to this technology in the West, formal democratic institutions and prolonged commercial success are fundamentally incompatible.

Part III

INSTITUTIONS AND CONTRADICTIONS

CHAPTER NINE

Institutional Mediation
and the State's
Relative Autonomy

The policy cases examined in the preceding chapters show that to understand industrial planning and performance in the U.S. nuclear energy sector we need more than just an analysis of elite decision making, pluralist politics, and the dynamics of supply and demand. We must also pay close attention to the political and economic institutions that set limits, imposed constraints, and conditioned policy outcomes in the public and private spheres. However, the evidence offers additional insights into the different *types* of effects institutions had on the sector. Institutional arrangements undermined planning and contributed to the sector's decline in two conceptually distinct ways, which are best explained by comparing the four policy areas of standardization, reactor safety, finance, and high-level waste management.

Competition within the private reactor manufacturing and the architect-engineering industries, combined with the fragmented nature of the electric utility industry, undermined attempts to standardize nuclear plants, even though almost everyone recognized the long-term benefits a standardization plan could bring to the sector. Furthermore, federal regulators did not have the institutional capacity to overcome these impediments and force the corporations to standardize. Given the limited range of policy tools at their disposal, regulators could only use indirect and, as it turned out, rather ineffective incentives, such as the promise of faster licensing, to try coaxing the sector to adopt the plan. Similarly, competition both within the reactor manufacturing industry and between the industry and conventional power plant manufacturers for a share of the generating plant market established the technical preconditions, including rapid increases in reactor sizes and more metropolitan siting, for a massive legitimation crisis over reactor safety policy. Furthermore, high-ranking officials at the AEC, trying not to stifle the sector's development, refused to suspend licensing while the agency conducted further safety research. In their protests, members of the regulatory staff exposed a contradiction between the public's interest in reactor safety and the nuclear sector's interests in profit and growth, a contradiction inscribed within the AEC's legislative mandate and evident in the internal agency conflict over democratic and technocratic policy paradigms. A more aggressive antinuclear movement resulted.

Institutional arrangements *directly* facilitated the development of the two contradictions that neo-Marxists argue are common to all advanced capitalist democracies (discussed in chapter 2). In the standardization case, competition encouraged the development of a contradiction between individual corporate interests in short-term profit and long-term sectoral planning. For example, the desire to offer larger and presumably more efficient reactors in order to attract utility customers made the collective goal of standardization virtually impossible to achieve. In the reactor safety policy case, corporate interests in short-term profit contradicted the general public interest, a concern that people would be safe from the dangers of reactor accidents. Furthermore, the institutional structure of the regulatory apparatus, closed during policy formation to citizen, but not corporate, input on safety issues, heightened the public's perception that the government was favoring corporate interests over their own. Institutional arrangements undermined smooth planning and helped create other problems, including licensing delays, regulatory changes, and escalating plant costs, which were symptomatic of the more fundamental contradictions rooted deep within the sector's institutional structure.

However, institutions also *indirectly* influenced the impact these symptoms had on the sector later. First, the structure of the state, the political side of the state–civil society intersection, provided many opportunities for antinuclear groups to obstruct the policy process during implementation. This exacerbated the licensing, regulatory, and plant cost problems, and ultimately increased the demand for finance capital. In turn, the structure of capital formation, part of the economic side of the state–civil society intersection, transformed demands for capital into a financial crisis. As a result, utility planners began cancelling or deferring new nuclear projects, a trend that accelerated when the growth in demand for electricity slowed after 1974.

Institutional arrangements were therefore responsible for a double determination. On the one hand, they directly contributed to the *initial manifestation* of contradictory tendencies that surfaced as critical policy problems. On the other hand, they also mediated the *impact* these problems had later on planning within the sector. Hence, institutional arrangements were responsible for both primary and secondary determinations. Both types of effects were present in the radioactive waste management policy case. Competition within the reprocessing industry *directly* crippled the first stage in the government's waste management plan by driving several reprocessors out of business and by leaving the industry with a technology eventually requiring very expensive modifications that delayed reprocessing for years. Competitive pressure also convinced some reprecessors to try saving money by cutting safety corners, decisions that generated public concern about the safety of reprocessing. Eventually, access to key policy arenas provided opportunities for activists to convince the Carter administration to ban reprocessing indefinitely, thereby destroying what was left of the industry. As a result, the short-term imperatives of competition contradicted and directly subverted the sector's more distant interest in establishing a viable waste management plan. When the government tried to respond with alternatives, institutional opportunities *indirectly* facilitated obstructionist politics and additional policy failures. By 1986 the absence of an effective waste management plan had exacerbated earlier financial and regulatory problems and further jeopardized whatever chances the sector might have had of recovering from its collapse.

People from the agencies and industries in the sector have offered analyses and policy prescriptions critical of these institutional arrangements. For example, representatives from the Atomic Industrial Forum and the American Nuclear Energy Council have told me that the sector ought to increase construction efficiency and reduce plant costs by establishing a single, super architect-engineering firm to handle all the nation's new nuclear projects. Indeed, such an arrangement would be similar to the French and Swedish cases where the national utility or the lone domestic reactor manufacturer, respectively, assumed the responsibility. Victor Gilinsky, former commissioner of the NRC, has advocated the organization of regional operating companies to manage and operate nuclear plants for several utilities in an effort to eliminate problems associated with both inadequate financing and utility inexperience in handling the technology (NRC, 1983). When asked why standardization failed to materialize in the United States, NRC officials told me that excessive competition was to blame. Representatives from the Electric Power Research Institute (Levenson and Zebroski, 1977), a utility research organization, and from the reprocessing industry (Dickeman, 1977) have argued that different institutional arrangements, such as a joint government-industry partnership, would have saved the reprocessing industry by providing government help in absorbing the costs of regulatory changes and licensing delays otherwise born entirely by the private corporations involved. This suggestion is reminiscent of the West German reprocessing consortium to the extent that both government and the private sector shared the financial risks.

Overall, not only do these people recognize that different institutional arrangements might have been more conducive to planning, but they also echo the findings of much of the institutional literature on political economy reviewed in chapter 2. Both argue that greater industrial centralization and more direct involvement by the federal government may be more conducive to planning than the competitive, highly privatized arrangements typical of the U.S. nuclear sector—a position that highlights the analytic approach used here.

Generalizing the Argument: Aircraft and Pharmaceuticals

Can this analysis be applied to industrial planning and performance in other sectors of the U.S. economy? The question of generalization is tricky because the nuclear sector is idiosyncratic. It is extremely capital intensive, has very long project lead times, and requires an extremely complex technology. Also, it presents extraordinary risks that could result in catastrophic damage to public health and the environment if an accident occurred. For these reasons not only is planning more important in this sector than in most others, but the effects institutional variations have on planning may be magnified. Nevertheless, there are some U.S. industrial sectors, such as commercial aircraft manufacturing and pharmaceuticals, that share many of the nuclear sector's idiosyncrasies.

Complex aviation technologies, including special construction materials, electronics, navigation equipment, and propulsion systems make aircraft very expensive to develop and build, especially since the advent of the jet engine. For example, the Boeing corporation expects to spend over $1 billion developing its 767 commercial jetliner. Of course commercial aircraft are also potentially dangerous because of the unforgiving nature of the technology when something goes wrong.[1] Finally, a great deal of expensive, long-range planning is required for aircraft manufacturers to survive in domestic and world markets which tend to reward firms offering the most technologically advanced products. Yet the planning and expense involved have not hindered the sector's development. Manufacturers in the United States have dominated both markets over the last several decades (Mowery and Rosenberg, 1982:110–13). Why have they been so successful?

In contrast to the nuclear sector, where the federal government gradually reduced its financial participation, various government agencies continue to absorb many of the aircraft sector's financial risks. This support has been important in overcoming a potential contradiction between short-term profit and the more farsighted planning required for continued technological innovation. The National Advisory Committee on Aeronautics (NACA), later the National Aeronautics and Space Administration (NASA), and the military assumed an increasing share of the sector's development costs. The government's annual contribution to research and development rose from $9 billion to $15 billion during the 1960s (Knight et al., 1976:48).[2] Apparently it was money well spent. NACA and NASA provided much of the applied research that led to major breakthroughs in aerodynamics pivotal to the sector's dynamism (Eads and Nelson, 1971). In addition manufacturers originally developed many technical innovations for the Department of Defense that they used later in designing new commercial aircraft, including the DC-3, DC-8, DC-10, the Lockheed L-1011, and the Boeing 747 jumbo jet (Hollingsworth and Lindberg, 1985:242). Significantly, the government funded most of the long-term research and development because it was financially too risky for the private capital and credit markets to bear. The private sector invested in product improvement and cost reduction efforts—short-term objectives involving less economic risk (Eads and Nelson, 1971:415; Knight, et al., 1976:48).[3] Furthermore,

---

[1] Perrow (1984:chap. 5) argues that although the level of risk associated with flying jet aircraft is lower than that for using nuclear power plants, the organization of their technologies is similar and, as a result, they share many of the same unforgiving characteristics. See chapter 8, note 27 for further discussion about "unforgiving" technologies.

[2] Most of the increase was from the military. Defense spending for aircraft research and development accounted for 65 percent of all aircraft research and development between 1945 and 1969. The private sector provided about 20 percent (Mowery and Rosenberg, 1982:133).

[3] There is other evidence that the government's financial support is critical to the

the sector benefited enormously from extensive military and space procurement programs that allowed private aircraft manufacturers to risk low bids for commercial sales with the assurance that lucrative and steady government contracts would partially defray whatever losses they might incur (Mowery and Rosenberg, 1982:14). Lower aircraft prices undoubtedly contributed to the sector's success by helping to keep airlines interested in buying new designs, particularly in the United States, where they competed more on the basis of service than on ticket prices because the Civil Aeronautics Board controlled air fares until deregulation in 1978.[4]

Competition among aircraft manufacturers also encouraged a contradiction between corporate interests in short-term profit and the public's interest in safe aircraft technology, although for institutional reasons the contradiction did not appear to undermine the sector's viability. Four manufacturers, Boeing, McDonnell Douglas, Lockheed, and General Dynamics, dominated the domestic market for jetliners since 1973 in competition based on price and speed of delivery. Occasionally, the competition became so intense that they neglected design problems that resulted in several fatal crashes (Mowery and Rosenberg, 1982:117). The problems with the McDonnell Douglas DC-10 were perhaps the most notorious and well publicized during the late 1970s and early 1980s (Perrow, 1984:137–41). Consumer groups like the Aviation Consumer Action Project pressed for safety improvements, but they seem to have had considerably less effect on the aircraft sector than their antinuclear counterparts did on the nuclear sector. The Federal Aviation Administration's (FAA) apparent unwillingness to impose new safety requirements on manufacturers unless the changes also increased aircraft efficiency and airline profits, led some to speculate that policy making in the agency may have been more accessible to industry representatives than to the public (Perrow, 1984:chap. 5). If this was so, then it seems that when manufacturers had to choose between immediate profits and the public's safety, not only did the pressures of competition convince them to

---

aircraft sector. When the NASA and Defense Department budgets for aerospace research temporarily declined in the early 1970s, airframe manufacturers, such as Boeing, began to diversify into a variety of other commercial activities, some not directly related to aircraft manufacturing (Knight et al., 1976:47).

[4] The parallel with the French nuclear sector is interesting. In both cases the government helped stimulate and sustain sectoral development not only by directly subsidizing research and development but also by creating steady demand for the finished product through procurement, a policy combination that worked well. See Nelson (1982) for a discussion of the significance of government procurement as a policy prerequisite for economic health in the aircraft and other high-tech industrial sectors.

pursue the former over the latter, but the institutional structure of the FAA also prevented the resulting political conflict from having much substantive effect either on regulatory policy or the sector overall.

Similar problems developed in the U.S. pharmaceutical sector, but with different results. Like the nuclear sector, the pharmaceutical sector was capital intensive and required long product development lead times. Pharmaceutical companies spent an average of $54 million on research and development costs for each new drug introduced in 1976 and often waited more than a decade for the Food and Drug Administration (FDA) to grant marketing approval (Grabowski and Vernon, 1982). Some said the wait was justified because the introduction of an unsafe drug into the market could pose serious threats to public health. Nevertheless, although the pharmaceutical industry had been one of the most profitable manufacturing industries in the United States since World War II, it began slipping in the mid-1970s because of lower rates of product development, a condition that reflected the sector's unwillingness to plan for the introduction of fundamentally new drugs (Knight, et al., 1976:68).

The sector was competitively organized. Twelve to fifteen research-intensive multinational corporations based in the United States accounted for most of the new drugs introduced to the domestic market. They dominated the market and competed primarily on the basis of product innovation because patent laws permitted firms with new products exclusive marketing rights for seventeen years. There were also several smaller domestic companies developing drugs on a more limited scale and others manufacturing generic versions of products whose patents had expired. Apparently, the competitive and financial incentives to develop and market new products in a hurry led to a series of tragedies that created enough public pressure to gradually increase both the federal government's regulatory control over the sector and citizens' access to the policy process. The death of over one hundred people from the elixir sulfanilamide after the Massengill company rushed it to market without adequate safety testing led to passage of the Food, Drug, and Cosmetics Act in 1938, legislation that gave the FDA authority to force manufacturers to demonstrate a drug's safety before marketing. A similar tragedy in Europe twenty-three years later involving the discovery of severe birth defects from thalidomide, a sedative administered to pregnant women, led to another public outcry in the United States for tougher regulation. As a result, Congress passed stringent amendments to the act in 1962. Consumers gained greater formal access to the FDA review process by being allowed to participate in an elaborate system of advisory committees, and the agency assumed a more cautious approach to the approval of new drugs (Grabowski and Vernon, 1982:350; Quirk, 1980). In short, market competition facilitated the urge to realize short-term profits at the expense of public safety, a contradiction that precipitated scandals and then more rigorous regulation, much as happened during the AEC's reactor safety crisis in the mid-1970s.[5]

It is not clear that the opportunity for more direct consumer participation on advisory committees had a greater substantive effect on FDA policy than the development of more aggressive congressional oversight on the public's behalf (Friedman, 1978). Nevertheless, researchers have found that these new opportunities for democratic pressure on regulatory policy contributed to the FDA's more conservative posture. In turn, because pharmaceutical companies had to test new drugs more carefully, the time required to develop and begin marketing them doubled after the early 1960s. Given the finite lifetime of a drug's patent, the reduced time a manufacturer could market its drug exclusively cut into the company's profits. The expense of conducting enough research to convince the FDA that the drug was safe compounded the financial problems by increasing development costs from about $2 million per drug just before the new legislation to $24 million by 1976. Yet despite the increased time and money involved, the FDA's rate of rejection jumped from roughly 66 to 90 percent of the drugs submitted for approval during that period because the agency was being more cautious (e.g., Grabowski and Vernon, 1982:314–15; Seidman, 1977; Wardell and Lasagna, 1975).

Because of the higher costs and financial risks, pharmaceutical companies began spending less effort on developing new products (Quirk, 1980:229). The average number of new drugs introduced to market each year dropped from about fifty in the late 1950s to seventeen during the 1970s largely because the economic incentives for development had deteriorated (Grabowski and Vernon, 1982:314). Pharmaceutical companies began diversifying into other medically related areas, such as hospital equipment, and, in an effort to circumvent patent barriers, started investing more in the development of substitute drugs with only very minor chemical differences from those their competitors were already selling. Representatives from some pharmaceutical companies worried that this downturn in

5 Parallels between the political struggles surrounding the FDA and AEC are interesting. For example, experts inside the FDA supplied consumer groups with information and tips about potentially controversial issues and thereby fueled public criticism about agency policy (Quirk, 1980:213) much as experts inside the AEC did both during and after the reactor safety crisis.

innovation would eventually threaten the sector's general health. To the extent that its future hinged on innovation, the imperatives of short-term corporate profitability, coupled with a set of political institutions accessible to citizens concerned with safety, threatened the sector's long-term interest. Of course these problems would have been less severe if the federal government was willing to help subsidize rising costs. However, it was not prepared to do that. Except for the hundreds of millions of dollars budgeted for cancer research each year, the National Institutes of Health did not provide the sector with much money for developing new drugs (Knight et al., 1976:61–68).

Although we can use these brief sketches of the aircraft and pharmaceutical sectors only with great circumspection, they suggest that the analytical framework I have used may apply to various industrial sectors. Two basic contradictions emerged in the sectors although the different institutional arrangements in each dramatically influenced the outcomes. First, corporate interests in short-term profits, encouraged by competitive pressures, compromised public safety and generated political activity as a result. However, only in the pharmaceutical and nuclear sectors were there relatively accessible policy processes through which the public could express its concerns in ways that influenced policy. As a result, in these two sectors, but apparently not in the aircraft sector, product lead times and costs increased to a point where they began undermining long-term planning with detrimental effects. Second, in all three cases either corporate or investor interests in securing immediate profits appeared to threaten plans for riskier, long-term investment strategies necessary for each sector's prolonged health. Yet once again only in the nuclear energy and pharmaceutical sectors did these contradictory interests actually disrupt planning. The key was that in the aircraft sector the federal government was committed to providing much of the long-term financing that neither the manufacturers nor the capital markets would hazard. Without government help when long-term financing became riskier and more difficult to obtain, nuclear construction declined and pharmaceutical innovation began to stall.

This is not to say that because the pharmaceutical sector shared some common institutional characteristics with the nuclear sector that it was also bound to suffer a total collapse. I am only arguing that planning became more of a problem. By 1986 the pharmaceutical sector was still profitable despite these difficulties but primarily because the big companies enjoyed patent rights, an important institutional factor that enabled them to keep prices high. In addition some companies merged with each other to defray production costs; a few

191

new drugs were bringing huge profits; and favorable exchange rates were facilitating exports (Cutaia, 1987). In short, while institutions undermined planning in both the pharmaceutical and the nuclear sectors, the impact was far more disruptive in the latter. This underscores the important point that in addition to institutions and planning there are always other factors, often historically contingent, that affect sectoral performance.

THEORETICAL IMPLICATIONS FOR POLITICAL ECONOMY

In addition to offering a framework for analyzing policy and, to an extent, industrial performance, this study has theoretical implications for theories of the state and political economy. Neo-Marxists have argued that the state tries, but is often unable, to manage problems that plague capitalist democracies, including those stemming from the contradictory tendencies among short-term capital accumulation, democratic politics, and planning (e.g., Habermas, 1973; O'Connor, 1973; Offe, 1975a; Poulantzas, 1978:173; Wright, 1978). Why is the state unable to plan and manage more effectively? There are limits to the kinds of things policy makers can do to deal with capitalism's problems. Political struggles among different classes and interest groups over policy (Esping-Anderson et al., 1976), threats of capital flight in response to policy proposals that business perceives as threatening to its interests (Block, 1977), an inability of the state to enter production directly (Offe and Ronge, 1975), and the need to maintain political legitimacy (O'Connor, 1973; Wolfe, 1977) are examples of the kinds of limits neo-Marxists see as constraining the range of policy options available to state officials—limits that prevent the state from enjoying the autonomy it needs to save capitalism from itself. In short, although the capitalist state has some leeway to develop different policy options, it must always operate within these limits and can never attain more than just *relative* autonomy from them.[6]

However, the concept of the state's relative autonomy has problems of its own. In particular it is not clear from this literature why some states (and specific apparatuses within a state) have more policy flexibility and can help plan capitalist activity more effectively than others. As noted in chapter 2 this is because the concept is so abstract in the sense that it lacks much institutional content.[7] Institutionalist

[6] For references to the debates about the capitalist state's relative autonomy, see chapter 2, note 2.

[7] For an elaboration of this argument see chapter 2, note 3. It appears that some neo-Marxists using the concept for their own analytic purposes have sensed its emptiness.

state theory helps fill that gap at a more concrete level by offering a typology of capitalisms, that is, liberal, corporatist, statist, that actually spans a continuum ranging from systems in which the state's autonomy is rather limited (liberal) to those in which it is much greater (statist).

Thus we can think about the state's relative autonomy at two conceptually distinct levels of analysis. At the more abstract level we can talk about all those situations where the general imperatives of capital accumulation and democratic politics limit the state's activities. This abstract level of analysis is analytically useful because it alerts us to the possibility that in most historical situations of capitalism the state does not enjoy complete autonomy. In most situations its officials cannot completely disregard external constraints and do whatever they want to plan political and economic activity throughout the rest of society. However, the concept needs more precision if we are to specify anything more than just the outermost limits to state policy. We can achieve that precision if we develop a set of concepts, such as those employed in this study, at a less abstract level of analysis.

On the one hand, state officials experience variation in the degree to which they formulate policy goals autonomously from the constraints and demands imposed by business, consumers, and other politically organized groups and classes in society. Such variation stems in large measure from the degree to which the policy process is organizationally centralized, unified, and differentially insulated from the demands of these groups. On the other hand, there are also variations in the degree to which state officials may autonomously impose their will on society depending on the degree to which external groups are institutionally involved in implementation but also on the assortment of policy tools at the government's disposal, such as control over capital formation. As the U.S. nuclear energy case illustrates, the institutional structure of the economy also limits the degree to which state planners may achieve their goals. Of course both sets of limits, freedom from external political demands and freedom to manipulate activity in civil society, are interrelated in complex ways, with

---

For example, Poulantzas (1973a:287–89) initially argued that the capitalist state's relative autonomy depended on its ability to rise above and mediate class struggles, to play different classes and class fractions against each other. Yet despite his ground-breaking analysis, he did not thoroughly explain how the state actually gained its manipulatory leverage; he refers only to "the play of its institutions," precisely the content that requires further specification. In another context Friedland et al. (1977) offered a fascinating analysis of the state from a neo-Marxist position that addresses the problem of institutional content. However, their focus was on the structure of the state, only one of the three major dimensions of the political economy addressed in this study.

political struggles over both the structure of state apparatuses and the nature of policy tools available playing very important preliminary roles. These variations help explain why state officials generally have more relative autonomy in statist systems, like France, and less in liberal systems, like the United States. Corporatist arrangements, like those often found in Sweden and West Germany, fall somewhere in the middle, particularly to the extent that the policy process is institutionally removed from a wide range of external social constraints. Indeed, at this more specific level of analysis it is more accurate to talk about the degree to which the state is *institutionally* autonomous because this language directs attention to the institutional variations in historical situations; the more abstract concept of relative autonomy glosses over those details.[8] Hence, institutionalism offers neo-Marxist state theory a way to help answer (and ask) the question Why do some states plan or manage capitalism better than others?

The case of nuclear power in the United States suggests that when capitalism is marked by a less institutionally autonomous state with little freedom from external constraints and limited capacities for intervention, it will probably have great difficulty planning. Of course institutions alone do not determine whether there will be planning, or, as noted earlier, whether planning will actually achieve a policy goal like economic growth. As John Zysman (1977:199) found in his study of French industrial policy, institutional variations only establish the range of possibilities available to policy makers. A complementary political explanation will always be necessary. Hence, it remains an open empirical question whether state officials in a specific historical situation will effectively take advantage of whatever institutional autonomy they may possess.

This is not to say that a purely institutionalist perspective can supercede entirely neo-Marxist theories about political economy or the state. I have tried to show that the two approaches operate at different levels of analysis in complementary ways. Institutionalism opens neo-Marxism to the concrete variations in political and economic arrangements that influence policy outcomes, and neo-Marxist theory provides institutionalism with insights into the underlying structural contradictions common to all advanced capitalist democracies, contradictions that may materialize as policy problems depend-

[8] Of course it is misleading to talk about the institutional autonomy of "the state" at all. Sensitivity to these sorts of institutional variations forces us to realize that states are composed of many different apparatuses and that each one's institutional autonomy may vary dramatically from each other, in different policy areas, and over time (e.g., Skocpol, 1985:17; Skowronek, 1982; Vogel, 1986:268).

ing on institutional arrangements. As this study has demonstrated, a blending of these perspectives, rather than a rejection of one in favor of the other, can enhance our understanding of political economy.[9] Such a blending can also help put in perspective the insights offered by the more traditional pluralist, elite, and economic approaches to political economy.[10]

QUESTIONS OF DEMOCRACY AND RECOVERY

It is reasonable to wonder what the implications of this analysis are for nuclear power in the United States. Is the prognosis good or bad? This study suggests that the answer hinges in large part on what, if anything, happens to the sector's institutional structure. On the one hand, if the institutional arrangements remain basically the same, it seems unlikely that much else will change. Most likely, political opposition will persist, management mistakes will continue, the costs of construction will remain exorbitant, and utility companies will continue to balk at building new nuclear plants. On the other hand, if structural changes occur, so might the sector's political and economic viability; at least two different scenarios quickly come to mind. If policy makers and others choose to restructure the sector in ways similar to the French model, then construction time, licensing delays, and costs could decline to a point where the sector begins to rise from the ashes, albeit at the expense of some public participation in the policy process. However, if, following the Swedish experience, we try to overcome current policy stalemates by opening up the policy process and increasing democratic participation, particularly during policy formation, it is feasible that nuclear critics could put an *official* end to the technology's future in this country. Of course there are undoubtedly other institutional options available that could have different impacts on the sector's health. Whether any of these changes are likely in the United States remains an open question well beyond the scope of this study.

Whatever surprises the future may hold, all of these policy options involve a more fundamental question—one that has received considerable attention during the 1980s in the general debates about eco-

---

[9] Bob Jessop (1982:chap. 5) provides an excellent theoretical argument for this kind of paradigmatic synthesis.
[10] Robert Alford and Roger Friedland (1985) offer one of the most comprehensive theoretical attempts at this kind of synthesis.

nomic policy. If some form of government or government-sponsored planning is required to sustain this or any other sector commercially, whose interests will be served by that planning?[11] Similarly, to what extent will different institutional forms of planning, for example, closed versus open, private versus public, or centralized versus decentralized, systematically benefit one group rather than another? These questions cut straight to the heart of our preferences not only for or against nuclear power but for democracy itself. As we have seen, there are institutional alternatives that reduce citizen participation in the policy process and create opportunities for the interests of technocrats or the business community to prevail, at the expense of environmentalists, antinuclear groups, and others in society. Other options increase public participation in ways that have the opposite effect. So although it is impossible to offer a definitive prognosis for the nuclear sector in the United States, one thing is clear: our policy choices (including the decision to do nothing) should involve more than just an assessment of nuclear power's technical and economic value relative to other energy sources. They should also include consideration of the technology's impact on our democratic practices.

[11] For discussions of this issue with respect to economic policy in general, see, for example, Bowles, Gordon, and Weisskopf (1983) and Dolbeare (1984).

Public Utility Commission
Rate Regulation

The public utility commission is charged with the responsibility of determining revenue requirements—the total funds to be collected from electricity consumers—for each utility under its jurisdiction. Generally, this is done by calculating the utility's rate base—its total capital investment—and multiplying it by the rate of return that the commission decides to allow. Operating costs, such as fuel, labor, management, and taxes, are added to the product. The general formula is represented below and is discussed in detail by Gormley (1983:chap. 1) and Berlin et al. (1974:chap. 4).

$$
\begin{array}{c}
\text{Revenue} \\
\text{Requirements}
\end{array}
=
\left[
\begin{array}{c}
\text{Rate} \\
\text{Base}
\end{array}
\times
\begin{array}{c}
\text{Allowable Rate} \\
\text{of Return}
\end{array}
\right]
+
\begin{array}{c}
\text{Estimated} \\
\text{Operating} \\
\text{Costs}
\end{array}
$$

The idea is that the rate of return should allow income sufficient to provide a fair or reasonable return to investors and to cover interest on accumulated debt. The rate of return in effect determines the utility's profit rate. The commission also develops a rate structure of prices for various types of customers, for example, business and residential, that will provide the utility with enough revenue to meet its needs. The commission faces a quandary. To what extent should it minimize the rate of return to protect the consumer's interest in low prices and to what extent should it maximize the rate of return to protect the utility's interest in keeping profits and retained earnings high? The commission must always walk a fine line between public and private interests during this decision-making process.

Consumers often resist efforts to increase the rate of return, and regulators usually do not grant the full increase utilities request. If the rate of return is unsatisfactory, the utility has two options to increase its gross revenues. First, it can try to expand the size of its rate base. A larger rate base increases the utility's total revenue requirements as calculated by the formula and leads to higher electricity rates allowed by the public utility commission. Averch and Johnson (1962) and Westfield (1965) have discussed this strategy in depth. Second, because estimated operating costs also influence revenue requirements, the utility can also reduce costs below the estimate. The reduction also increases profitability and retained earnings. Therefore, any additions to the utility's physical plant that would increase the rate base and/or reduce operating costs would be desirable from the utility's profit-maximization perspective.

References

Advisory Commission on Intergovernmental Relations. 1981. "Alternative Perspectives on Federalism." Pp. 1–25 in *The Condition of Contemporary Federalism: Conflicting Theories and Collapsing Constraints*. A-78. Washington, D.C.

——. 1980. "The Questions of Federalism." Pp. 3–34 in *A Crisis of Confidence and Competence*. A-77. Washington, D.C.

Alexander, Charles P. 1984. "From Paris to Peking, Fission Is Still in Fashion." *Time* 123(7)44–45.

Alexander, Tom. 1981. "The Surge to Deregulate Electricity." *Fortune* 104(1)98–105.

Alford, Robert. 1975. "Paradigms of Relations between State and Society." Pp. 145–60 in Leon Lindberg, Robert Alford, Colin Crouch, and Claus Offe, eds., *Stress and Contradiction in Modern Capitalism*. Lexington, Mass.: Lexington Books.

Alford, Robert, and Roger Friedland. 1985. *Powers of Theory: Capitalism, the State, and Democracy*. New York: Cambridge University Press.

Allen, Wendy. 1977. *Nuclear Reactors for Generating Electricity: U.S. Development from 1946 to 1963*. Santa Monica, Calif.: Rand Corporation.

Allison, Graham. 1971. *Essence of Decision: Explaining the Cuban Missile Crisis*. Boston: Little, Brown.

Arnold, W. H., and D. R. Grain. 1972. "Standardization of the Nuclear Steam Supply System." *Proceedings of the American Power Conference* 34:207–15.

Arthur D. Little, Inc. 1968. "Competition in the Nuclear Power Industry, Part 1, Overview: Summary and Government Policy Implications." Report to the U.S. Atomic Energy Commission and U.S. Department of Justice, contract no. AT (30-1)-3853. Washington, D.C.: U.S. Atomic Energy Commission.

Atomic Industrial Forum. 1982. "State Nuclear Moratoria, 1982." Unpublished report. Public Affairs and Information Program. Washington, D.C.

——. 1978. *Licensing, Design, and Construction Problems: Priorities for Solution*. Washington, D.C.

Averch, Harvey, and Leland Johnson. 1962. "Behavior of the Firm under Regulatory Constraint." *American Economic Review* 52(5)1052–69.

Bachrach, Peter, and Morton Baratz. 1962. "Two Faces of Power." *American Political Science Review* 57(4)947–52.

Baran, Paul, and Paul Sweezy. 1966. *Monopoly Capital: An Essay on the American Economic and Social Order.* New York: Monthly Review Press.

Bardach, Eugene. 1977. *The Implementation Game: What Happens after a Bill Becomes a Law.* Cambridge: MIT Press.

Barfield, Claude. 1973. "Broad Campaign against Nuclear Power Begins with Nader Suit on Reactor Safety." *National Journal* 9(5)850–51.

Barkan, Steven. 1979. "Strategic, Tactical, and Organizational Dilemmas of the Protest Movement against Nuclear Power." *Social Problems* 27(1)19–37.

Barkenbus, Jack. 1984. "Nuclear Power and Government Structure: The Divergent Paths of the United States and France." *Social Science Quarterly* 65(1)37–47.

Barlett, Donald, and James Steele. 1985. *Forevermore: Nuclear Waste in America.* New York: W. W. Norton.

Battelle Memorial Institute. 1978. *An Analysis of Federal Incentives Used to Stimulate Energy Production.* Richland, Wash.: Pacific Northwest Laboratory.

Bauer, Etienne, Louis Puiseux, and Pierre-Frederic Teniere-Buchot. 1976. "Nuclear Energy: A Fateful Choice for France." *Bulletin of the Atomic Scientists* 32(1)37–41.

Beckjord, Eric. 1978. "The Federal Perspective on Spent Fuel Policy." Pp. 16–18 in *American Nuclear Society Executive Conference on Spent Fuel Policy and Its Implications, April 2–5, 1978.* LaGrange Park, Ill.: American Nuclear Society.

Berlin, Edward, Charles Cicchetti, and William Gillen. 1974. *Perspective on Power: A Study of the Regulation and Pricing of Electric Power.* Cambridge, Mass.: Ballinger.

Block, Fred. 1980. "Beyond Relative Autonomy: State Managers as Historical Subjects." Pp. 227–42 in Ralph Miliband and John Saville, eds., *The Socialist Register.* London: Merlin Press.

——. 1977. "The Ruling Class Does Not Rule: Notes on the Marxist Theory of the State." *Socialist Review* 7(3)6–28.

Bluestone, Barry, and Bennett Harrison. 1982. *The Deindustrialization of America: Plant Closings, Community Abandonment, and the Dismantling of Basic Industry.* New York: Basic Books.

Bowles, Samuel, and Herbert Gintis. 1986. *Democracy and Capitalism: Property, Community, and the Contradictions of Modern Social Thought.* New York: Basic Books.

Bowles, Samuel, David Gordon, and Thomas Weisskopf. 1983. *Beyond the Wasteland: A Democratic Alternative to Economic Decline.* New York: Anchor Press.

Brand, David. 1975. "Nuclear Safety Debate Rages over Reliability of Emergency System." *Wall Street Journal* July 9:1.

Bright, G. O. 1973. "Light Water Reactor Safety." *Nuclear Safety* 12(5)433–38.

Bright, G. O., C. Cooper, H. Bradburn, G. Brockett, C. Gilmore, C. More. 1965. *A Review of the Generalized Reactivity Accident for Water-Cooled and Moderated, UO$_2$ Fuelled Power Reactors.* PTR-738. Idaho Falls, Idaho: Phillips Petroleum Company.

Brittan, Samuel. 1975. "The Economic Contradictions of Democracy." *British Journal of Political Science* 5(2)129–59.

Bupp, Irvin C. 1981. "Forward." Pp. i–iii in Charles Komanoff, *Power Plant Cost Escalation.* New York: Van Nostrand Reinhold.

———. 1980a. "The French Nuclear Harvest: Abundant Energy or Bitter Fruit?" *Technology Review* 83(2)30–35.

———. 1980b. "The Actual Growth and Probable Future of the Worldwide Nuclear Industry." *International Organization* 35(1)59–76.

———. 1979. "Nuclear Stalemate." Pp. 127–66 in Robert Stobaugh and Daniel Yergin, eds., *Energy Future: Report of the Energy Project at the Harvard Business School.* New York: Ballantine.

Bupp, Irvin C., and Jean-Claude Derian. 1978. *Light Water: How the Nuclear Dream Dissolved.* New York: Basic Books.

Bupp, Irvin C., Jean-Claude Derian, Marie-Paule Donsimoni, and Robert Treitel. 1975. "The Economics of Nuclear Power." *Technology Review* 77(4)14–25.

Burn, Duncan. 1978. *Nuclear Power and the Energy Crisis: Politics and the Atomic Industry.* New York: New York University Press.

———. 1967. *The Political Economy of Nuclear Energy.* London: The Institute of Economic Affairs.

Business Week. 1973. "Entering the Age of Off-the-Shelf Reactors." May 26:89–90.

Business Week Team. 1982. *The Reindustrialization of America.* New York: McGraw-Hill.

Caldwell, Lynton, Lynton Hayes, and Isabel MacWhirter. 1976. *Citizens and the Environment: Case Studies in Popular Action.* Bloomington, Ind.: Indiana University Press.

Camilleri, Joseph. 1984. *The State and Nuclear Power: Conflict and Control in the Western World.* Brighton, U.K.: Wheatsheaf.

Campbell, John L. 1987. "Legitimation Meltdown: Weberian and Neo-Marxist Interpretations of Legitimation Crisis in Advanced Capitalist Society." Pp. 133–58 in Maurice Zeitlin, ed., *Political Power and Social Theory,* Vol. 6. Greenwich, Conn.: JAI Press.

———. 1986. "Crisis and the Transformation of Governance Mechanisms: Public vs. Private Government in Nuclear Energy." Paper presented at the annual meetings of the American Sociological Association, New York.

———. 1982. "The Antinuclear Movement in the United States." Pp. 291–96 in Robert Wolensky and Edward Miller, eds., *The Small City and Regional Community,* Vol. 5. Stevens Point, Wis.: University of Wisconsin–Stevens Point Press.

Carnoy, Martin. 1984. *The State and Political Theory.* Princeton: Princeton University Press.

Carson, Rachel. 1962. *Silent Spring.* Boston: Houghton Mifflin.

Catalano, Lee. 1982. "Utilities Cancel 17 Powerplants." *Power* 126(3)35.

Caves, Richard E. 1980. "Industrial Organization, Corporate Strategy, and Structure." *Journal of Economic Literature* 18(1)64–92.

Chandler, Alfred D. 1977. *The Visible Hand: The Managerial Revolution in American Business.* Cambridge: Harvard University Press.

Chandler, Alfred D., and Herman Daems, eds. 1980. *Managerial Hierarchies: The Rise of the Modern Industrial Enterprise.* Cambridge: Harvard University Press.

Chemical and Engineering News. 1973. "Quicker Startup of Nuclear Plants Sought." 51(48)7–8.

Childs, Marquis. 1980. *Sweden: The Middle Way.* New Haven: Yale University Press.

Clarke, Lee. 1985. "The Origins of Nuclear Power: A Case of Institutional Conflict." *Social Problems* 32:474–87.

Cochran, Thomas, and Arthur Tamplin. 1978. "Nuclear Waste: Too Much too Soon." Paper presented before the U.S. Senate, Committee on Environment and Public Works, Subcommittee on Nuclear Regulation. *Hearings on Nuclear Waste Management.* No. 95-H58. 95th Cong. 2d sess.

Cohen, Bernard. 1979. "The Situation at West Valley." *Public Utilities Fortnightly* 104(7)26–32.

Cohen, Joshua, and Joel Rogers. 1983. *On Democracy: Toward a Transformation of American Society.* New York: Penguin.

Cohen, Linda. 1979a. "Essays on the Economics of Licensing Nuclear Power Plants." Unpublished Ph.D. dissertation, California Institute of Technology.

———. 1979b. "Costs and Benefits of Nuclear Regulatory Commission Procedures." Paper presented at the Symposium on Regulatory Policy, Chicago, Ill.

Cohen, Stephen S. 1982. "Informed Bewilderment: French Economic Strategy and the Crisis." Pp. 21–48 in Stephen Cohen and Peter Gourevitch, eds., *France in a Troubled World Economy.* London: Butterworth Scientific.

———. 1977. *Modern Capitalist Planning: The French Model.* Berkeley: University of California Press.

Cohen, Stephen S., James Galbraith, and John Zysman. 1982. "Rehabbing the Labyrinth: The Financial System and Industrial Policy in France." Pp. 49–75 in S. Cohen and P. Gourevitch, eds., *France in a Troubled World Economy.* London: Butterworth Scientific.

Colglazier, E. William, ed. 1982. *The Politics of Nuclear Waste.* New York: Pergamon Press.

Combustion. 1977. "Completing the Nuclear Fuel Cycle." 48(12)34–39.

Commerce Today. 1974. "Standardized Plants to Speed Move toward Nuclear Power." 4(10)13–15.

Cook, James. 1985. "Nuclear Follies." *Forbes* 135(3)82–100.

Corrigan, Richard. 1979. "Nuclear Investment: Risks and Returns." *National Journal* 11(17)679.

Cottrell, William. 1974. "The ECCS Rule-making Hearing." *Nuclear Safety* 15(1)30–55.

Council of State Governments. 1977. *The States and Electric Utility Regulation.* Lexington, Ky.: Council of State Governments.

Crouch, Colin. 1979. "The State, Capital, and Liberal Democracy." Pp. 13–54 in Colin Crouch, ed., *State and Economy in Contemporary Capitalism.* New York: St. Martin's.

Crozier, Michel, Samuel Huntington, and Joji Watanuki. 1975. *The Crisis of Democracy.* New York: New York University Press.

Cutaia, Jane H. 1987. "For Drugmakers, These Will Be the Good Old Days." *Business Week* January 12:94.

Dawson, Frank G. 1976. *Nuclear Power: Development and Management of a Technology.* Seattle: University of Washington.

Deddens, J. C. 1981. "The Future of Nuclear Power in the U.S." *Mechanical Engineering* 103(2)26–31.

Deese, David A. 1982. "A Cross-national Perspective on the Politics of Nuclear Waste." Pp. 63–97 in E. William Colglazier, ed., *The Politics of Nuclear Waste.* New York: Pergamon Press.

deLeon, Peter. 1979. *Development and Diffusion of the Nuclear Power Reactor: A Comparative Analysis.* Cambridge, Mass.: Ballinger.

Dellaire, Gene. 1981. "Are America's Utilities Sorry They Went Nuclear?" *Civil Engineering* 51(1)37–41.

Del Sesto, Stephen L. 1979. *Science, Politics, and Controversy: Civilian Nuclear Power in the United States, 1946–1974.* Boulder, Colo.: Westview Press.

Deubner, Christian. 1979. "The Expansion of West German Capital and the Founding of Euratom." *International Organization* 33(2)203–28.

Dickeman, R. L. 1977. "Nuclear Fuel Reprocessing from a Commercial Point of View." *Proceedings of the American Power Conference* 39:87–93.

Dickson, David. 1984. *The New Politics of Science.* New York: Pantheon.

Dieckamp, Herman. 1979. "Utility Views on the Nuclear Industry." Pp. 242–53 in *American Nuclear Society Executive Conference on Economic Viability of the Nuclear Industry, October, 1978.* LaGrange Park, Ill.: American Nuclear Society.

Dolbeare, Kenneth. 1984. *Democracy at Risk: The Politics of Economic Renewal.* Chatham, N.J.: Chatham House.

Domhoff, G. William. 1983. *Who Rules America Now? A View For the '80s.* Englewood Cliffs, N.J.: Prentice-Hall.

———. 1978a. *The Powers That Be: Processes of Ruling Class Domination in America.* New York: Vintage.

———. 1978b. *Who Really Rules? New Haven and Community Power Reexamined.* Santa Monica, Calif.: Goodyear.

Domhoff, G. William, and Hoyt Ballard, eds. 1968. *C. Wright Mills and the Power Elite.* Boston: Beacon.

Dyson, Kenneth. 1983. "The Cultural, Ideological, and Structural Context." Pp. 26–66 in Kenneth Dyson and Stephen Wilks, eds., *Industrial Crisis: A Comparative Study of the State and Industry.* Oxford: Martin Robertson.

——. 1982. "West Germany: The Search for a Rationalist Consensus." Pp. 17–46 in Jeremy Richardson, ed., *Policy Styles in Western Europe*. London: George Allen and Unwin.

Dyson, Kenneth, and Stephen Wilks, eds. 1983. *Industrial Crisis: A Comparative Study of the State and Industry*. Oxford: Martin Robertson.

Eads, George, and Richard Nelson. 1971. "Governmental Support of Advanced Civilian Technology: Power Reactors and the Supersonic Transport." *Public Policy* 19(3)405–27.

Ebbin, Stephen, and Raphael Kasper. 1974. *Citizen Groups and the Nuclear Power Controversy*. Cambridge: MIT Press.

Edlund, M. C. 1963. "Economics of Recycled Fuels." *Proceedings of the American Power Conference* 15:128–33.

Edmonds, Martin. 1983. "Crisis Management in the United States." Pp. 67–102 in Kenneth Dyson and Stephen Wilks, eds., *Industrial Crisis: A Comparative Study of the State and Industry*. Oxford: Martin Robertson.

Eichner, Alfred S. 1983. "Why Economics Is Not Yet a Science." Pp. 205–41 in Alfred Eichner, ed., *Why Economics Is Not Yet a Science*. Armonk, N.Y.: M. E. Sharpe.

Electric Light and Power. 1982. "PUC's Move to Halt Pebble Springs, Limerick Nukes." 60(6)1, 16.

——. 1978. "Nuclear Standardization—What Has It Accomplished?" 56(12)21–22.

Emshwiller, John. 1973. "AEC's Safety Plans for Nuclear Reactors Assailed by Critics." *Wall Street Journal* November 6:1.

Energy. 1977. "Nuclear Wastes: End Project or Just the End?" 2(2)9–11.

Energy User's Reports. 1982. No. 396. March 12. Washington, D.C.: Bureau of National Affairs.

——. 1978a. No. 271. November 19. Washington, D.C.: Bureau of National Affairs.

——. 1978b. No. 263. August 24. Washington, D.C.: Bureau of National Affairs.

——. 1978c. No. 239. March 9. Washington, D.C.: Bureau of National Affairs.

——. 1976a. No. 162. September 16. Washington, D.C.: Bureau of National Affairs.

——. 1976b. No. 148. June 10. Washington, D.C.: Bureau of National Affairs.

——. 1976c. No. 133. February 26. Washington, D.C.: Bureau of National Affairs.

——. 1975a. No. 119. November 20. Washington, D.C.: Bureau of National Affairs.

——. 1975b. No. 90. May 1. Washington, D.C.: Bureau of National Affairs.

——. 1975c. No. 89. April 24. Washington, D.C.: Bureau of National Affairs.

——. 1975d. No. 88. April 17. Washington, D.C.: Bureau of National Affairs.

——. 1975e. No. 78. February 6. Washington, D.C.: Bureau of National Affairs.

——. 1974a. No. 65. November 7. Washington, D.C.: Bureau of National Affairs.

——. 1974b. No. 61. October 10. Washington, D.C.: Bureau of National Affairs.

——. 1974c. No. 52. August 8. Washington, D.C.: Bureau of National Affairs.

——. 1974d. No. 47. July 4. Washington, D.C.: Bureau of National Affairs.

——. 1974e. No. 32. March 21. Washington, D.C.: Bureau of National Affairs.

——. 1974f. No. 31. March 14. Washington, D.C.: Bureau of National Affairs.

Engineering and Mining Journal. 1973–81. 174–182(3).

Esping-Anderson, Gosta, Roger Friedland, and Erik Olin Wright. 1976. "Modes of Class Struggle and the Capitalist State." *Kapitalistate* 4–5:186–220.

Esser, Josef, Wolfgang Fach, and Kenneth Dyson. 1983. " 'Social Market' and Modernization Policy: West Germany." Pp. 102–27 in Kenneth Dyson and Stephen Wilks, eds., *Industrial Crisis: A Comparative Study of State and Industry.* Oxford: Martin Robertson.

Fagnani, Jeanne, and Jean-Paul Moatti. 1982. "France: The Socialist Government's Energy Policy and the Decline of the Anti-nuclear Movement." Paper presented at the European Consortium for Political Research Nuclear Energy Policy Workshop. International Institute for Environment and Society, Science Center, Berlin.

Falk, Jim. 1982. *Global Fission: The Battle Over Nuclear Power.* New York: Oxford University Press.

Falkin, Norman. 1975. "A Utility Experience with the Replication Option of Standardization." *Transactions of the American Nuclear Society* 21:361.

Forbes, Ian, Daniel Ford, Henry Kendall, and James MacKenzie. 1972. "Cooling Water." *Environment* 14(1)40–47.

——. 1971. "Nuclear Reactor Safety: An Evaluation of New Evidence." *Nuclear News* 14(9)32–40.

Ford, Daniel. 1982. *Cult of the Atom: The Secret Papers of the Atomic Energy Commission.* New York: Simon and Schuster.

Ford, Daniel, and Henry Kendall. 1975. "Nuclear Misinformation." *Environment* 17(5)17–20, 25–27.

——. 1972. "Nuclear Safety." *Environment* 14(7)2–9.

Ford, Daniel, Henry Kendall, and James MacKenzie. 1972. "A Critique of the AEC's Interim Criteria for Emergency Core Cooling Systems." *Nuclear News* 15(1)28–35.

Foth, Joseph H. 1930. *Trade Associations: Their Services to Industry.* New York: Ronald Press.

Franklin, Ben A. 1986. "Indians Angry That U.S. Put Lands on Nuclear Waste Dump List." *New York Times* April 18:14.

Freeman, Leslie. 1981. *Nuclear Witnesses: Insiders Speak Out.* New York: W. W. Norton.

Frewing, J. L., and J. T. Owens. 1979. "Experience with Local/State Interventions for Reracking Trojan Spent Fuel Pool." *Transactions of the American Nuclear Society* 32:678.

Friedland, Roger, Frances Fox Piven, and Robert Alford. 1977. "Political Conflict, Urban Structure, and Fiscal Crisis." *International Journal of Urban and Regional Research* 1(3)447–71.

Friedman, Robert. 1978. "Representation in Regulatory Decision Making: Scientific, Industrial, and Consumer Inputs to the FDA." *Public Administration Review* 38 (May/June)205–14.

Galbraith, John Kenneth. 1971. *The New Industrial State.* New York: Mentor.

Gandara, Arturo. 1977. *Electric Utility Decisionmaking and the Nuclear Option.* Santa Monica: Calif.: Rand Corporation.

Gartman, Warren. 1968. "How to Buy a Reactor." *Power Engineering* 72(6)47–49.

Gilinsky, Victor. 1978. "Plutonium Proliferation and the Price of Reprocessing." *Foreign Affairs* 57(2)374–86.

Gillette, Robert. 1974. "Nuclear Fuel Reprocessing: G.E.'s Balky Plant Poses Shortage." *Science* 185(4153)770–71.

———. 1972a. "Nuclear Safety (IV): Barriers to Communication." *Science* 177(4054)1080–82.

———. 1972b. "Nuclear Safety (III): Critics Charge Conflict of Interest." *Science* 177(4053)970–75.

———. 1972c. "Nuclear Safety (II): The Years of Delay." *Science* 177(4052)867–71.

Glaize, G. 1977. "The Reorganization of the French Commissariat a l'Énergie Atomique." *Nuclear Law Bulletin* 19(May)43–52.

Golay, Michael. 1981. "How Prometheus Came to Be Bound: Nuclear Regulation in America." *Technology Review* 83(7)28–39.

Goldthorpe, John, ed. 1984. *Order and Conflict in Contemporary Capitalism: Studies in the Political Economy of Western European Nations.* Oxford: Clarendon Press.

Goodman, Robert. 1979. *The Last Entrepreneurs: America's Regional Wars For Jobs and Dollars.* Boston: South End Press.

Gordon, Emanuel. 1978. "Comments on Spent Fuel Storage Costs, Prices, Schedules, and Pool Capacities." Pp. 239–42 in *American Nuclear Society Executive Conference on Spent Fuel Policy and Its Implications, April 2–5.* LaGrange Park, Ill.: American Nuclear Society.

Gormley, William. 1983. *The Politics of Public Utility Regulation.* Pittsburgh: University of Pittsburgh Press.

Grabowski, Henry, and John Vernon. 1982. "The Pharmaceutical Industry." Pp. 283–360 in Richard Nelson, ed., *Government and Technical Progress: A Cross-Industry Analysis.* New York: Pergamon.

Green, Diana. 1983. "Strategic Management and the State: France." Pp. 161–92 in Kenneth Dyson and Stephen Wilks, ed., *Industrial Crisis: A Comparative Study of the State and Industry.* Oxford: Martin Robertson.

Green, Harold, and Alan Rosenthal. 1963. *Government of the Atom: The Integration of Powers.* New York: Atherton.

Greenhouse, Linda. 1983. "High Court Rules a State May Ban New Atomic Plant." *New York Times* April 21:1.

Greenwood, Ted. 1982. "Nuclear Waste Management in the United States." Pp. 1–62 in E. William Colglazier, ed., *The Politics of Nuclear Waste*. New York: Pergamon Press.

Gyorgy, Anna, and friends. 1979. *No Nukes: Everyone's Guide to Nuclear Power*. Boston: South End Press.

Habermas, Jürgen. 1973. *Legitimation Crisis*. Boston: Beacon Press.

Hage, Jerald, and Remi Clignet. 1982. "Coordination Styles and Economic Growth." *Annals of the American Academy of Political and Social Science* 459:77–92.

Hamilton, J. R. 1975. "Babcock-205/A Standard 205 Fuel Assembly NSSS." *Proceedings of the American Power Conference* 38:226–36.

Hatch, Michael T. 1986. *Politics and Nuclear Power: Energy Policy in Western Europe*. Lexington: University of Kentucky Press.

Hayward, Jack. 1982. "Mobilizing Private Interests in the Service of Public Ambitions: The Salient Element in the Dual French Policy Style?" Pp. 111–40 in Jeremy Richardson, ed., *Policy Styles in Western Europe*. London: George Allen and Unwin.

Heltemes, C. J. 1979. "NRC Perspective on Standardization." *Transactions of the American Nuclear Society* 32:603–4.

Hendrie, J. M. 1976. "Safety of Nuclear Power." Pp. 663–83 in J. M. Hollander and M. K. Simmons, eds., *Annual Review of Energy*, Vol. 1. Palo Alto, Calif.: Annual Reviews Inc.

Hertsgaard, Mark. 1983. *Nuclear Inc.: The Men and Money Behind Nuclear Energy*. New York: Pantheon.

Hill, Robert. 1976. "Reconciling Foreign and Domestic Nuclear Energy Policies." *Public Utilities Fortnightly* 98(11)13–15.

Hitch, Charles J. 1982. "Utilities in Trouble." *Public Utilities Fortnightly* 109(3)18–20.

Hogerton, John. 1979. "The Crossroads of Nuclear Energy." *Mining Congress Journal* 65(12)30–32.

——. 1976. "Uranium Supply in the United States: A Current Assessment." *Nuclear News* 19(8)73–76.

Hollingsworth, J. Rogers. 1982. "The Political and Structural Basis for Economic Performance." *Annals of the American Academy of Political and Social Science* 459:28–45.

Hollingsworth, J. Rogers, and Leon N. Lindberg. 1985. "The Governance of the American Economy: The Role of Markets, Clans, Hierarchies, and Associative Behavior." Pp. 221–54 in Wolfgang Streeck and Philippe C. Schmitter, eds., *Private Interest Government: Beyond Market and State*. Beverly Hills, Calif.: Sage.

Hollis, Martin, and Edwin Nell. 1975. *Rational Economic Man*. London: Cambridge University Press.

Howard, J. Edward. 1978. "Spent Fuel Management Policy and Utility Needs." Pp. 4–15 in *American Nuclear Society Conference on Spent Fuel Policy and Its Implications, April 2–5*. LaGrange Park, Ill.: American Nuclear Society.

Hunter, Floyd. 1953. *Community Power Structure*. Chapel Hill: University of North Carolina Press.

Ikenberry, G. John. 1986. "The Irony of State Strength: Comparative Responses to the Oil Shocks in the 1970s." *International Organization* 40(1)105–37.

Interagency Review Group on Nuclear Waste Management. 1979. *Report to the President by the Interagency Review Group on Nuclear Waste Management.* TID-29442. Washington, D.C.: GPO.

Itteilag, Richard L., and James Pavle. 1985. "Nuclear Plants' Anticipated Costs and Their Impact on Future Electric Rates." *Public Utilities Fortnightly* 115(6)35–40.

Jacobs, Sanford. 1974. "Money Raising Problems Cause Utilities to Cut Spending for New Electric Plants." *Wall Street Journal* July 19:30.

Jakimo, Alan, and Irvin C. Bupp. 1978. "Nuclear Waste Disposal: Not in My Backyard." *Technology Review* 80(5)64–72.

Jasper, James. 1986a. "From Social Organization to Policy Styles: Risk Attitudes in the Nuclear Debate." Paper presented at the conference Évaluer et Maîtriser les Risques: La Société Face au Risque Majeur; Chantilly, France.

———. 1986b. "High Technology and Public Opinion in Comparative Perspective." Paper presented at the American Sociological Association meetings, New York.

Jessop, Bob. 1982. *The Capitalist State: Marxist Theories and Methods.* New York: New York University Press.

———. 1978. "Capitalism and Democracy: The Best Possible Shell?" Pp. 10–51 in Gary Littlejohn, Barry Smart, John Wakeford, and Nira Yuval-Davis, eds., *Power and the State.* London: Croom Helm.

Joskow, Paul. 1979. "Problems and Prospects for Nuclear Energy in the United States." Pp. 231–54 in Gregory Daneke, ed., *Energy Economics and the Environment.* Lexington, Mass.: Lexington Books.

Katzenstein, Peter. 1978a. *Between Power and Plenty.* Madison: University of Wisconsin Press.

———. 1978b. "Conclusion: Domestic Structures and Strategies of Foreign Economic Policy." Pp. 295–336 in Peter Katzenstein, ed., *Between Power and Plenty.* Madison: University of Wisconsin Press.

Keck, Otto. 1981. *Policy Making in a Nuclear Program: The Case of the West German Fast Breeder Reactor.* Lexington, Mass.: Lexington Books.

Keith, Dennis, and Donald Karner. 1978. "Replication: Experience in Licensing a Replicate Plant at the Same Site." *Proceedings of the American Power Conference* 40:157–61.

Kelman, Steven. 1981. *Regulating America, Regulating Sweden: A Comparative Study of Occupational Safety and Health Policy.* Cambridge: MIT Press.

Kemeny, John. 1980. "Saving American Democracy: The Lessons of Three Mile Island." *Technology Review* 83(7)65–75.

Kennedy, William, Brian Schultz, and Anthony Morse. 1976. "Nuclear Power Plant Standardization—Reference Plant Design." *Transactions of the American Nuclear Society* 23:423–33.

Kitschelt, Herbert. 1986. "Political Opportunity Structures and Political Protest: Anti-nuclear Movements in Four Democracies." *British Journal of Political Science* 16(1)57–85.

———. 1984. "Resolving Policy Conflict through Expert Advice: Corporatist Intermediation, Government Commissions, and the Conflict about Long-Term Energy Strategies." Paper presented at the annual meeting of the American Political Science Association, Washington, D.C.

———. 1982. "Structures and Sequences of Nuclear Policy-Making: Suggestions for a Comparative Perspective." Pp. 271–308 in Maurice Zeitlin, ed. *Political Power and Social Theory*, Vol. 3. Greenwich, Conn.: JAI Press.

Knight, Kenneth, George Kozmetsky, and Helen Baca. 1976. *Industry Views of the Role of the Government in Industrial Innovation.* Austin: Graduate School of Business, University of Texas.

Komanoff, Charles. 1981. *Power Plant Cost Escalation: Nuclear and Coal Capital Costs, Regulation, and Economics.* New York: Van Nostrand Reinhold.

Kouts, Herbert. 1975. "The Future of Reactor Safety Research." *Bulletin of the Atomic Scientists* 31(7)32–37.

Krasner, Stephen. 1978. "United States Commercial and Monetary Policy: Unraveling the Paradox of External Strength and Internal Weakness." Pp. 51–88 in Peter Katzenstein, ed., *Between Power and Plenty.* Madison: University of Wisconsin Press.

Kurth, James. 1979. "The Political Consequences of the Product Cycle: Industrial History and Political Outcomes." *International Organization* 33(1)1–34.

Laclau, Ernesto. 1977. *Politics and Ideology in Marxist Theory.* London: New Left Books.

Lanouette, William. 1979. "Nuclear Power—An Uncertain Future Grows Dimmer Still." *National Journal* 11(17)676–86.

Large, Arlen. 1982. "Ailing Industry: Ills of Nuclear Power Aren't Likely to End with Faster Licensing." *Wall Street Journal* August 30:1.

Lawrence, Michael. 1978. "The Department of Energy's Spent Fuel Storage Program." *Transactions of the American Nuclear Society* 28:312–13.

Lawrence, Paul, and Davis Dyer. 1983. *Renewing American Industry.* New York: Free Press.

Lawson, C. G. 1968. *Emergency Core Cooling Systems for Light Water Cooled Power Reactors.* ORNL-NSIC-24. Oak Ridge, Tenn.: Oak Ridge National Laboratory.

Lester, Richard K. 1978. *Nuclear Power Plant Lead-Times.* New York and London: The Rockefeller Foundation and the Royal Institute of International Affairs.

Lester, Richard K., and David J. Rose. 1977. "The Nuclear Wastes at West Valley, New York." *Technology Review* 76(6)20–29.

Lester, William. 1970. "Information Requirements and Their Impact on Nuclear Power Plant Design and Construction." *Proceedings of the American Power Conference* 32:267–75.

Levenson, M., and E. Zebroski. 1977. "Overview of the Fuel Cycle, 1977–1981." *Proceedings of the American Power Conference* 39:67–86.

Lewis, Richard. 1972. *The Nuclear Power Rebellion.* New York: Viking.

Liberman, Joseph. 1966. "The AEC Program for Reactor Safety." *Proceedings of the American Power Conference* 28:307–17.

Liljestrom, Rita. 1978. "Sweden." Pp. 19–48 in Sheila Kamerman and Alfred Kahn, eds., *Family Policy: Government and Families in Fourteen Countries.* New York: Columbia University Press.

Lincicome, Robert A. 1977. "France Stakes Its Future on Nuclear Power." *Electric Light and Power* 55(1)11–12.

Lindberg, Leon. 1982a. "The Problems of Economic Theory in Explaining Economic Performance." *Annals of the American Academy of Political and Social Science* 459:14–27.

———. 1982b. "Economists as Policy Intellectuals and Economics as a Policy Profession: Reflections on the Retreat from Keynesianism and from the Interventionist State." Paper presented at the 12th World Congress of the International Political Science Association, Rio de Janeiro, Brazil.

Lindberg, Leon, and Charles Maier. 1985. *The Politics of Inflation and Economic Stagnation.* Washington, D.C.: Brookings Institution.

Lindblom, Charles. 1977. *Politics and Markets.* New York: Basic Books.

Linde, Claes. 1983. "Where Did All the Worries Go? The Present Status of the Swedish Nuclear Policy." Paper presented at the European Consortium for Political Research Nuclear Energy Policy Workshop. International Institute for Environment and Society, Science Center, Berlin.

Lönnroth, Måns. 1983. "Nuclear Energy in Western Europe." Paper presented at the East-West Center conference on Nuclear Electric Power in the Asia-Pacific Region, Honolulu.

———. 1977. "Swedish Energy Policy: Technology in the Political Process." Pp. 255–83 in Leon Lindberg, ed., *The Energy Syndrome.* Lexington, Mass.: Lexington Books.

Lönnroth, Måns, and William Walker. 1979. *The Viability of the Civil Nuclear Industry.* New York and London: The Rockefeller Foundation and the Royal Institute for International Affairs.

Lönnroth, Måns, Peter Steen, and Thomas B. Johansson. 1980. *Energy in Transition: A Report on Energy Policy and Future Options.* Berkeley: University of California Press.

Lucas, N. J. D. 1979. *Energy in France: Planning, Politics, and Policy.* London: Europa Publications.

Lukes, Steven. 1974. *Power: A Radical View.* New York: MacMillan.

Lundmark, Kjell. 1983. "Welfare State and Employment Policy: Sweden." Pp. 220–44 in Kenneth Dyson and Stephen Wilks, eds., *Industrial Crisis: A Comparative Study of the State and Industry.* Oxford: Martin Robertson.

Lundqvist, Lennart J. 1980. *The Hare and the Tortoise: Clean Air Policies in the United States and Sweden.* Ann Arbor: University of Michigan Press.

MacMillan, J. H., and T. O. Johnson. 1974. "Once Through Performance at 3800 MWT—The Babcock-241 Standardized Nuclear Steam System." *Proceedings of the American Power Conference* 36:117–24.

Mandel, Ernest. 1975. *Late Capitalism.* London: New Left Books.

Mann, Marvin. 1966. "The Government's Role and Current Policies." *Proceedings of the American Power Conference* 28:293–96.

Marx, Karl. 1967. *Capital: A Critique of Political Economy,* Vol. 1 (1867). New York: International Publishers.

Masters, Richard. 1979. "Progress Report on France." *Nuclear Engineering International* 24(282)47–62.

Mayntz, Renate. 1975. "Legitimacy and the Directive Capacity of the Political System." Pp. 261–74 in Leon Lindberg, Robert Alford, Colin Crouch, and Claus Offe, eds., *Stress and Contradiction in Modern Capitalism.* Lexington, Mass.: Lexington Books.

Mazuzan, George, and Roger Trask. 1979. *An Outline History of Nuclear Regulation and Licensing, 1946–1979.* Unpublished manuscript. Historical Office, Office of the Secretary, U.S. Nuclear Regulatory Commission, Washington, D.C.

Melber, B., S. Nealey, J. Hammersla, and W. Rankin. 1977. *Nuclear Power and the Public: Analysis of Collected Survey Research.* PNL-2430. Report prepared for the U.S. Department of Energy. Seattle, Wash.: Battelle Human Affairs Research Center.

Messing, Mark. 1978. *Reasons for Delay in Powerplant Licensing and Construction: An Initial Review of Data Available on Powerplants Brought on Line from 1967 through 1976.* Washington, D.C.: Environmental Policy Institute.

Metz, William D. 1977. "Reprocessing: How Necessary Is It for the Near Term?" *Science* 196(4285)43–45.

Metzger, Peter. 1972. *The Atomic Establishment.* New York: Simon and Schuster.

Meyer-Abich, Klaus-Michael, and Robert Dickler. 1982. "Energy Issues and Policies in the Federal Republic of Germany." Pp. 221–59 in J. M. Hollander, ed., *Annual Review of Energy,* Vol. 7. Palo Alto, Calif.: Annual Reviews.

Meyers, Desaix. 1977. *The Nuclear Power Debate: Moral, Economic, Technical, and Political Issues.* New York: Praeger.

Meyers, Sheldon. 1978. "Regulatory Aspects of Spent Fuel Storage Facilities." Pp. 136–38 in *American Nuclear Society Executive Conference on Spent Fuel Policy and Its Implications, April 2–5.* LaGrange Park, Ill.: American Nuclear Society.

Mez, Lutz, and Nicholas Watts. 1982. "Comparative Research on Nuclear Energy Policy: The State of the Art—West Germany." Paper presented at the European Consortium for Political Research Nuclear Energy Policy Workshop. International Institute for Environment and Society, Science Center, Berlin.

Miliband, Ralph. 1977. *Marxism and Politics.* New York: Oxford University Press.

——. 1973a. "Poulantzas and the Capitalist State." *New Left Review* 82:83–92.

——. 1973b. "Reply to Nicos Poulantzas." Pp. 253–62 in Robin Blackburn, ed., *Ideology in Social Science.* New York: Vintage.

——. 1969. *The State in Capitalist Society.* New York: Basic Books.

Milius, Peter. 1975. "Major Battle Is Brewing on A-Plants." *Washington Post,* June 23: A4.

Mills, C. Wright. 1956. *The Power Elite.* New York: Oxford University Press.

Mitchell, Robert Cameron. 1982. "Public Response to a Major Failure of a Controversial Technology." Pp. 21–38 in David Sills, C. P. Wolf, and Vivien B. Shelanski, eds., *Accident at Three Mile Island: The Human Dimensions.* Boulder, Colo.: Westview.

———. 1981. "From Elite Quarrel to Mass Movement." *Society* 18(5)76–84.

Mitchell, William. 1978. "The Anatomy of Public Failure: A Public Choice Perspective." Paper presented at the Institute for Economic Research, Los Angeles.

Mizruchi, Mark, and Thomas Koenig. 1986. "Economic Sources of Corporate Political Consensus: An Examination of Interindustry Relations." *American Sociological Review* 51(4)482–91.

Montgomery, W. David, and James Quirk. 1978. "Cost Escalation in Nuclear Power." EQL memo number 21. Pasadena, Calif.: Environmental Quality Laboratory, California Institute of Technology.

Morgan Guarantee Survey. 1980. "The Future of Nuclear Power." Pp. 8–15 in *Morgan Guarantee Survey,* June. New York: Morgan Guarantee Trust.

———. 1968. "The New Look in Electric Power Generation." Pp. 3–9 in *Morgan Guarantee Survey,* August. New York: Morgan Guarantee Trust.

Mowery, David, and Nathan Rosenberg. 1982. "The Commercial Aircraft Industry." Pp. 101–61 in Richard Nelson, ed., *Government and Technical Progress: A Cross-Industry Analysis.* New York: Pergamon.

Nader, Ralph, and John Abbotts. 1979. *The Menace of Atomic Energy.* New York: W. W. Norton.

Nappi, Rebecca. 1985. "Poll: Tri-Cities Alone Support N-Waste Dump." Spokane (Wash.) *Spokesman-Review* February 24:1.

National Research Council. 1984. *Social and Economic Aspects of Radioactive Waste Disposal: Considerations for Institutional Management.* Washington, D.C.: National Academy Press.

Nau, Henry R. 1974. *National Politics and International Technology: Nuclear Reactor Development in Western Europe.* Baltimore: Johns Hopkins University Press.

Naylor, Emmett H. 1921. *Trade Associations: Their Organization and Management.* New York: Ronald Press.

Naymark, Sherman. 1978. "Nuclear Option: An Uncertain Future." *Consulting Engineer* 50(4)106–10.

Neese, R. J. 1982. *The Effect of Nuclear Ownership on Utility Bond Ratings and Yields.* PNL-4175. Report prepared for the U.S. Department of Energy. Richland, Wash.: Pacific Northwest Laboratory.

Nelkin, Dorothy. 1984. "Science, Technology, and Political Conflict: Analyzing the Issues." Pp. 9–24 in Dorothy Nelkin, ed., *Controversy: Politics of Technical Decisions.* 2d ed. Beverly Hills, Calif.: Sage.

Nelkin, Dorothy, and Susan Fallows. 1978. "The Evolution of the Nuclear

Debate: The Role of Public Participation." Pp. 275–312 in J. Hollander, M. Simmons, D. Wood, eds., *Annual Review of Energy*, Vol. 3. Palo Alto, Calif.: Annual Reviews.

Nelkin, Dorothy, and Michael Pollak. 1981a. "Nuclear Protest and National Policy." *Society* 18(5)34–38.

——. 1981b. *The Atom Besieged: Extraparliamentary Dissent in France and Germany.* Cambridge: MIT Press.

——. 1980a. "Political Parties and the Nuclear Energy Debate in France and Germany." *Comparative Politics* 12(2)127–42.

——. 1980b. "Citizens Appeal to the French and German Courts." *Bulletin of the Atomic Scientists* 36(5)36–42.

——. 1977. "The Politics of Participation and the Nuclear Debate in Sweden, The Netherlands, and Austria." *Public Policy* 25(3)333–57.

Nelson, Richard. 1982. "Government Stimulus of Technological Progress: Lessons from American History." Pp. 451–82 in Richard Nelson, ed., *Government and Technical Progress: A Cross-Industry Analysis.* New York: Pergamon.

New York Times. 1986. "Plugged In." August 31 (Section 4)1.

Noble, David F. 1977. *America by Design: Science, Technology, and the Rise of Corporate Capitalism.* New York: Oxford.

Nuclear Energy Policy Study Group. 1977. *Nuclear Power Issues and Choices.* Cambridge, Mass.: Ballinger.

Nuclear News. 1981. "Standardization Efforts to Date Have Been Few and Limited." 24(9)40.

Nuclear Projects, Inc. 1978. *Standardized Nuclear Unit Power Plan Systems—SNUPPS: Progress Report.* Rockville, Md.

Nuclear Regulatory Commission Special Inquiry Group. 1980. *Three Mile Island: A Report to the Commission and to the Public*, Vol. 2, Part 1. Washington, D.C.: GPO.

O'Connor, James. 1984. *Accumulation Crisis.* New York: Basil Blackwell.

——. 1973. *The Fiscal Crisis of the State.* New York: St. Martin's.

——. 1972. "Scientific and Ideological Elements in the Economic Theory of Government Policy." Pp. 367–97 in E. K. Hunt and Jesse Schwartz, eds., *A Critique of Economic Theory.* Baltimore: Penguin Books.

O'Donnell, E. P. 1977. Letter to Director, Office of Nuclear Reactor Regulation, U.S. Nuclear Regulatory Commission, September 8.

Offe, Claus. 1975a. "The Theory of the Capitalist State and the Problem of Policy Formation." Pp. 125–44 in Leon Lindberg, Robert Alford, Colin Crouch, and Claus Offe, eds., *Stress and Contradiction in Modern Capitalism.* Lexington, Mass.: Lexington Books.

——. 1975b. "Introduction to Part II." Pp. 245–59 in Leon Lindberg, Robert Alford, Colin Crouch, Claus Offe, eds., *Stress and Contradiction in Modern Capitalism.* Lexington, Mass.: Lexington Books.

——. 1974. "Structural Problems of the Capitalist State." Pp. 35–57 in Klaus von Beyme, ed., *German Political Studies*, Vol. 1. Beverly Hills, Calif.: Sage.

Offe, Claus, and Volker Ronge. 1975. "Theses on the Theory of the State." *New German Critique* 6:139–47.

Okrent, David. 1981. *Nuclear Reactor Safety: On the History of the Regulatory Process.* Madison: University of Wisconsin Press.

Olson, McKinley. 1976. *Unacceptable Risk: The Nuclear Power Controversy.* New York: Bantam Books.

Ouchi, William. 1977. Review of *Markets and Hierarchies: Analysis and Antitrust Implications,* by Oliver E. Williamson. *Administrative Science Quarterly* 22(3)540–44.

Owen, W. H. 1974. "Duplicate Plant Option." *Transactions of the American Nuclear Society* 18:237–38.

Pelzer, Norbert, and Werner Bischof. 1977. "Comparative Review of Public Participation in Nuclear Licensing Procedures in Certain European Countries." *Nuclear Law Bulletin* 19(May)53–72.

Perrow, Charles. 1984. *Normal Accidents: Living With High Risk Technologies.* New York: Basic Books.

Perry, Robert, A. J. Alexander, W. Allen, P. deLeon, A. Gandara, W. E. Mooz, E. Rolph, S. Siegel, K. A. Solomon. 1977. *Development and Commercialization of the Light Water Reactor, 1946–1976.* Santa Monica, Calif.: Rand Corporation.

Perry, Wane D. 1979. "Deferral of Nuclear Fuel Reprocessing and Plutonium Breeder Commercialization." *Resources and Energy* 2(4)341–72.

Phillips, Stephen. 1986. "Nuclear Plant Write-off and Rate Rise Allowed." *New York Times* March 8:21.

Piore, Michael J., and Charles F. Sabel. 1984. *The Second Industrial Divide.* New York: Basic Books.

Poulantzas, Nicos. 1978. *State, Power, Socialism.* London: New Left Books.

——. 1976. "The Capitalist State: A Reply to Miliband and Laclau." *New Left Review* 95:63–83.

——. 1973a. *Political Power and Social Classes.* London: New Left Books.

——. 1973b. "The Problems of the Capitalist State." Pp. 238–53 in Robin Blackburn, ed., *Ideology in Social Science.* New York: Vintage.

Premfors, Rune. 1983. "Government Commissions in Sweden." *American Behavioral Scientist* 26(5)623–42.

President's Commission on the Accident at Three Mile Island. 1979. *Report of the President's Commission on the Accident at Three Mile Island, The Need for Change: The Legacy of TMI.* Washington, D.C.: GPO.

Pressman, Jeffrey, and Aaron Wildavsky. 1979. *Implementation.* Berkeley: University of California Press.

Primack, Joel. 1974. "The Nuclear Safety Controversy." *Chemical Engineering Progress* 70(11)26–34.

Primack, Joel, and Frank von Hippel. 1974a. "Nuclear Reactor Safety: The Origins and Issues of a Vital Debate." *Bulletin of the Atomic Scientists* 30(8)5–12.

——. 1974b. *Advice and Dissent: Scientists in the Political Arena.* New York: Basic Books.

Pringle, Peter, and James Spigelman. 1983. *The Nuclear Barons*. New York: Holt, Rinehart, and Winston.

Quirk, Paul. 1980. "Food and Drug Administration." Pp. 191-235 in James Q. Wilson, ed., *The Politics of Regulation*. New York: Basic Books.

Raber, Martha. 1976. "EDF Continues Multiple Order Policy in Nuclear Programme." *Energy International* 13(6)22–23.

Ragnarson, Per. 1980. "Before and After: The Swedish Referendum on Nuclear Power." *Political Life in Sweden*, no. 5. New York: Swedish Information Service.

Rankin, William, Barbara Melber, Thomas Overcase, and Stanley Nealey. 1981. *Nuclear Power and the Public: An Update of Collected Survey Research on Nuclear Power*. PNL-4048. Report prepared for the U.S. Department of Energy. Seattle, Wash.: Battelle Human Affairs Research Center.

Rankin, William, Stanley Nealey, and Barbara Melber. 1984. "Overview of National Attitudes toward Nuclear Energy: A Longitudinal Analysis." Pp. 41–68 in William Freudenburg and Eugene Rosa, eds., *Public Reactions to Nuclear Power: Are There Critical Masses?* Boulder, Colo.: Westview.

Reactor Safety Research Review Group. 1981. *Report of the Reactor Safety Research Review Group to the President's Nuclear Safety Oversight Committee*. Washington, D.C.: GPO.

Reagan, Michael, and John Sanzone. 1981. *The New Federalism*. New York: Oxford University Press.

Rein, Martin, and Francine Rabinovitz. 1977. "Implementation: A Theoretical Perspective." Working Paper No. 43. Cambridge: Joint Center for Urban Studies of MIT and Harvard University.

Reinhold, Robert. 1986. "Texans Fight for Their Land and Way of Life." *New York Times* June 29(Section 4)5.

Reinsch, H. O. 1978. "Energy—The Challenges and the Realities." *Proceedings of the American Power Conference* 40:13–22.

Resnikoff, Marvin. 1975. "Expensive Enrichment." *Environment* 17(5)28–35.

Richardson, Jeremy, ed. 1982. *Policy Styles in Western Europe*. London: George Allen and Unwin.

Rippon, Simon. 1978. "La Hague: French Face Bright Prospects for Commercial Oxide Fuel Reprocessing." *Nuclear News* 21(14)58–62.

Rittenhouse, P. L. 1971. "Fuel-Rod Failure and Its Effects in Light Water Reactor Accidents." *Nuclear Safety* 12(5)487–95.

Rochlin, Gene, Margery Held, Barbara Kaplan, Lewis Kruger. 1978. "West Valley: Remnant of the AEC." *Bulletin of the Atomic Scientists* 34(1)17–26.

Rolph, Elizabeth. 1979. *Nuclear Power and the Public Safety*. Lexington, Mass.: D. C. Heath.

———. 1977. *Regulation of Nuclear Power: The Case of the Light Water Reactor*. Santa Monica, Calif.: Rand Corporation.

Rose, Richard, and Guy Peters. 1978. *Can Government Go Bankrupt?* New York: Basic Books.

Roweis, Shoukry. 1981. "Urban Planning in Early and Late Capitalist Societies: Outline of a Theoretical Perspective." Pp. 159–77 in Michael Dear and Allen Scott, *Urbanization and Urban Planning in Capitalist Society.* New York: Methuen.

Rüdig, Wolfgang. 1986. "Nuclear Power: An International Comparison of Public Protest in the USA, Britain, France and West Germany." Pp. 364–417 in Roger Williams and Stephen Mills, ed., *Public Acceptance of New Technologies.* London: Croom Helm.

Ruin, Olof. 1982. "Sweden in the 1970s: Policy-making Becomes More Difficult." Pp. 141–67 in Jeremy Richardson, ed., *Policy Styles in Western Europe.* London: George Allen and Unwin.

Rycroft, Robert, and Robert Brenner. 1981. *Nuclear Energy Facility Siting in the United States: Implications of International Experience.* Research Monograph No. 46. Princeton: Center for International Studies, Woodrow Wilson School of Public and International Affairs.

Sahr, Robert. 1985. *The Politics of Energy Policy Change in Sweden.* Ann Arbor: University of Michigan Press.

Saiter, Susan. 1983. "Shipments of Nuclear Waste Are Increasing Dramatically." *New York Times* February 21:1.

Saldarini, J. C. 1979. "Standardization and Final Design Evolution—An Architect/Engineer's Perspective." *Transactions of the American Nuclear Society* 32:605–6.

Saumon, Dominique, and Louis Puiseux. 1977. "Actors and Decisions in French Energy Policy." Pp. 119–72 in Leon Lindberg, ed., *The Energy Syndrome.* Lexington, Mass.: Lexington Books.

Sawhill, John. 1977. "Paralysis on the Potomac." *Saturday Review* 4(8)19–20.

Scheinman, Lawrence. 1965. *Atomic Energy Policy in France under the Fourth Republic.* Princeton: Princeton University Press.

Schmitter, Philippe C. 1984. "Neo-corporatism and the State." EUI Working Paper No. 106. Department of Political and Social Sciences, European University Institute, Florence, Italy.

Schubert, A. E. 1976. "Plutonium Recycle—The Impact of Indecision." *Proceedings of the American Power Conference* 38:116–21.

Seidman, David. 1977. "Protection or Overprotection in Drug Regulation? The Politics of Policy Analysis." *Regulation* 1(July/August)22–37.

Shanaman, Susan. 1982. "Halting Limerick II: The Reasons and Impacts." *Public Utilities Fortnightly* 110(1)48–49.

Shaw, Milton. 1968. "The United States Fast Breeder Reactor Program." *Proceedings of the American Power Conference* 30:173–88.

Sherwood, Glen. 1979. "The Role of Nuclear Island GESSAR in Plant Licensing." *Transactions of the American Nuclear Society* 32:604–5.

Shonfield, Andrew. 1965. *Modern Capitalism.* New York: Oxford University Press.

Skocpol, Theda. 1985. "Bringing the State Back In: Strategies of Analysis in Current Research." Pp. 1–43 in Peter Evans, Dietrich Rueschemeyer, and Theda Skocpol, eds., *Bringing the State Back In.* New York: Cambridge University Press.

Skowronek, Stephen. 1982. *Building a New American State: The Expansion of National Administrative Capacities, 1877–1920.* New York: Cambridge University Press.

Smartt, Lucien. 1976. "The Electric Utility Executives' Forum." *Public Utilities Fortnightly* 97(12)60–111.

Smith, C. Wesley, and William Bigge. 1970. "Commercial Light Water Fuel Recovery." *Proceedings of the American Power Conference* 32:286–94.

Smock, Robert. 1979. "Waste Disposal Problem Looms over Nuclear Power's Future." *Electric Light and Power* 57(4)54–55.

S. M. Stoller Corporation. 1980. *Study of Factors Governing U.S. Utility Nuclear Power Decisions.* DOE/ET/34009-T1. Report prepared for the U.S. Department of Energy. New York: S. M. Stoller Corporation.

———. 1975. *An Independent Assessment of Foreseeable Problems in the Nuclear Fuel Cycle.* ERDA-73. Report prepared for the U.S. Atomic Energy Commission / Energy Research and Development Administration under contract AT (49-1)-3695. New York: S. M. Stoller Corporation.

Solo, Robert. 1982. *The Positive State.* Cincinnati: South-Western.

———. 1967. *Economic Organizations and Social Systems.* New York: Bobbs-Merrill.

Steinhart, John. 1978. "The Impact of Technical Advice on the Choice for Nuclear Power." Pp. 239–48 in Lon Ruedisili and Morris Firebaugh, eds., *Perspectives on Energy.* New York: Oxford University Press.

Stich, Robert. 1971. "Financing Problems Facing Electric Utilities." *Public Utilities Fortnightly* 87(1)21–28.

Streeck, Wolfgang. 1984. "Neo-corporatist Industrial Relations and the Economic Crisis in West Germany." Pp. 291–314 in John Goldthorpe, ed., *Order and Conflict in Contemporary Capitalism: Studies in the Political Economy of Western European Nations.* New York: Oxford University Press.

Streeck, Wolfgang, and Philippe C. Schmitter. 1985a. "Community, Market, State—and Associations? The Prospective Contribution of Interest Governance to Social Order." Pp. 1–29 in Wolfgang Streeck and Philippe C. Schmitter, eds., *Private Interest Government: Beyond Market and State.* Beverly Hills, Calif.: Sage.

———. 1985b. *Private Interest Government: Beyond Market and State.* Beverly Hills, Calif.: Sage.

Strinati, Dominic. 1979. "Capitalism, the State, and Industrial Relations." Pp. 191–236 in Colin Crouch, ed., *State and Economy in Contemporary Capitalism.* New York: St. Martin's Press.

Swedish Institute. 1973. *Adult Education in Sweden.* Stockholm.

Sweezy, Paul. 1942. *The Theory of Capitalist Development.* New York: Monthly Review Press.

Szalay, Robert A. 1984. "A Nuclear Industry View of the Regulatory Climate." Pp. 295–306 in William Freudenburg and Eugene Rosa, eds., *Public Reactions to Nuclear Power: Are There Critical Masses?* Boulder, Colo.: Westview Press.

Szasz, Andrew. 1984. "Industrial Resistance to Occupational Safety and Health Legislation: 1971–1981." *Social Problems* 32(2)103–16.

———. 1982. "The Dynamics of Social Regulation: A Study of the Formation and Evolution of the Occupational Safety and Health Administration." Unpublished Ph.D. dissertation, University of Wisconsin, Madison.

Szelenyi, Ivan. 1981. "The Relative Autonomy of the State or State Mode of Production." Pp. 565–91 in Michael Dear and Allen Scott, eds., *Urbanization and Urban Planning in Capitalist Society.* New York: Methuen.

———. 1980. "Prospects and Limits of Power of Intellectuals under Market Capitalism." Unpublished paper, Department of Sociology, University of Wisconsin, Madison.

Tanguy, P. 1980. "French Emphasis on Research to Confirm Margins." *Nuclear Engineering International* 25(306)47–50.

Tannenbaum, Jeffrey. 1976. "White Elephant? Big Plant to Recycle Nuclear Fuel Is Hit by Delays Cost Rises." *Wall Street Journal* February 17:1.

Thurow, Lester. 1984. "Building a World Class Economy." *Society* 22(1)16–29.

———. 1980. *The Zero-Sum Society: Distribution and the Possibilities for Economic Change.* New York: Basic Books.

Touraine, Alaine, Zsuzsa Hegedus, Francois Dubet, and Michel Wieviorka. 1983. *Antinuclear Protest: The Opposition to Nuclear Energy in France.* Cambridge: Cambridge University Press.

Trezise, Philip, and Yukio Suzuki. 1976. "Politics, Government, and Economic Growth in Japan." Pp. 753–811 in Hugh Patrick and Henry Rosovsky, eds., *Asia's New Giant: How the Japanese Economy Works.* Washington, D.C.: Brookings Institution.

Tufte, Edward. 1978. *Political Control of the Economy.* Princeton: Princeton University Press.

U.S. Atomic Energy Commission. 1975. *Financial Statements: Final Report as of January 18, 1975.* Washington, D.C.: GPO.

———. 1974a. *Annual Report to Congress, 1973,* Vol. 2. Washington, D.C.: GPO.

———. 1974b. *Draft Environmental Statement, Management of Commercial High-Level and Transuranium Contaminated Radioactive Wastes.* WASH 1539. Washington, D.C.: GPO.

———. 1974c. *Programatic Information for the Licensing of Standardized Nuclear Power Plants.* Washington, D.C.: GPO.

———. 1974d. *Power Plant Capital Costs: Current Trends and Sensitivity to Economic Parameters.* WASH-1345. Washington, D.C.: GPO.

———. 1973a. *1972 Annual Report to Congress,* Vol. 1. Washington, D.C.: GPO.

———. 1973b. *Statistical Data of the Uranium Industry.* GJO-100(73). Grand Junction, Colo.: GPO.

———. 1973c. *The Nuclear Industry, 1973.* WASH-1174-73. Washington, D.C.: GPO.

———. 1972. "Commission Policy Statement on Standardization of Nuclear Power Plants." April 27. Washington, D.C.

———. 1970a. *Water Reactor Safety Program Plan.* WASH-1146. Washington, D.C.

——. 1970b. *Annual Report to Congress, 1969.* Washington, D.C.: GPO.

——. 1967. *Civilian Nuclear Power—The 1967 Supplement to the 1962 Report to the President.* Washington, D.C.: GPO.

——. 1966–74. *Financial Reports, 1966–1974.* Washington, D.C.: GPO.

——. 1962a. *Civilian Nuclear Power: A Report to the President.* Washington, D.C.: GPO.

——. 1962b. *Civilian Nuclear Power—Appendices to a Report to the President.* Washington, D.C.: GPO.

U.S. Congressional Budget Office. 1982. *Promoting Efficiency in the Electric Utility Sector,* Washington, D.C.: GPO.

——. 1979. *Delays in Nuclear Reactor Licensing and Construction: the Possibilities for Reform.* Washington, D.C.: GPO.

U.S. Department of Commerce. 1981. *Statistical Abstract of the United States, 1981.* Washington, D.C.: GPO.

U.S. Department of Energy. 1983a. *Nuclear Power Plant Cancellations: Causes, Costs, and Consequences.* DOE/EIA-0392. Washington, D.C.: GPO.

——. 1983b. *Delays and Cancellations of Coal-fired Generating Capacity.* DOE/EIA-0406. Washington D.C.: GPO.

——. 1983c. *Commercial Nuclear Power: Prospects for the United States and the World.* DOE/EIA-0438. Washington, D.C.: GPO.

——. 1981. *Federal Support for Nuclear Power: Reactor Design and the Fuel Cycle.* Energy Policy Study, Vol. 13. DOE/EIA-0201/13. Washington, D.C.: GPO.

——. 1978. *Study of Factors Inhibiting Effective Use of Domestic Nuclear Power.* TID-28694. Washington, D.C.: GPO.

U.S. Department of the Interior, Bureau of Mines. 1975. *Mineral Facts and Problems.* Bulletin 667. Washington, D.C.: GPO.

U.S. Federal Energy Administration. 1974. *Project Independence Blueprint, Final Task Force Report: Nuclear Energy.* Washington, D.C.: GPO.

U.S. General Accounting Office. 1986. *Nuclear Waste: Quarterly Report on DOE's Nuclear Waste Program as of March 31, 1986.* GAO/RCED-86-154FS. Washington, D.C.: GPO.

——. 1985a. *Department of Energy's Initial Efforts to Implement the Nuclear Waste Policy Act of 1982.* GAO/RCED-85-27. Washington, D.C.

——. 1985b. *The Nuclear Waste Policy Act: 1984 Implementation Status, Progress, and Problems.* GAO/RCED-85-100. Washington, D.C.

——. 1985c. *Nuclear Waste: Quarterly Report on DOE's Nuclear Waste Program as of September 30, 1985.* GAO/RCED-86-42. Washington, D.C.

——. 1981a. *Federal Energy Regulatory Commission Needs to Act on the Construction Work in Progress Issue.* EMD-81-123. Gaithersburg, Md.

——. 1981b. *Electric Power: Contemporary Issues and the Federal Role in Oversight and Regulation.* EMD-82-8. Gaithersburg, Md.

——. 1981c. *The Effects of Regulation on the Electric Utility Industry.* EMD-81-35. Gaithersburg, Md.

——. 1980a. *Electricity Planning—Today's Improvements Can Alter Tomorrow's Investment Decisions.* EMD-80-112. Gaithersburg, Md.

——. 1980b. *Construction Work in Progress Issue Needs Improved Regulatory Response for Utilities and Consumers.* EMD-80-75. Gaithersburg, Md.

——. 1980c. *Electric Power Plant Cancellations and Delays.* EMD-81-25. Gaithersburg, Md.

——. 1979. *Federal Facilities for Storing Spent Nuclear Fuel—Are They Needed?* EMD-79-82. Washington, D.C.: GPO.

——. 1978. *Nuclear Power Plant Licensing: Need For Additional Improvements.* EMD-78-29. Gaithersburg, Md.

——. 1977a. *Reducing Nuclear Power Plant Leadtimes: Many Obstacles Remain.* EMD-77-15. Washington, D.C.: GPO.

——. 1977b. *Nuclear Energy's Dilemma: Disposing of Hazardous Radioactive Waste Safely.* EMD-77-41. Washington, D.C.: GPO.

——. 1976a. *This Country's Most Expensive Light Water Reactor Safety Test Facility.* RED-76-68. Gaithersburg, Md.

——. 1976b. *Poor Management of a Nuclear Light Water Reactor Safety Project.* EMD-76-4. Gaithersburg, Md.

U.S. House of Representatives. 1982. *Least-Cost Energy Strategies: Hearings.* No. 97-86. Committee on Energy and Commerce, Subcommittee on Energy Conservation and Power. 97th Cong. 1st sess. Washington, D.C.: GPO.

——. 1981a. *Utility Financing: The Financial Condition of Utilities and Their Future in the 1980s.* Hearings. No. 97-36. Committee on Energy and Commerce, Subcommittee on Energy Conservation and Power. 97th Cong. 1st sess. Washington, D.C.: GPO.

——. 1981b. *Licensing Speedup, Safety Delay: NRC Oversight.* Committee print. No. 97-277. Committee on Government Operations. 97th Cong. 1st sess. Washington, D.C.: GPO.

——. 1980. *Nuclear Economics: Oversight Hearings.* Part 7. No. 96-8. Committee on Interior and Insular Affairs, Subcommittee on Energy and the Environment. 96th Cong. 1st sess. Washington, D.C.: GPO.

——. 1979. *Hearings on Spent Fuel Storage and Disposal.* No. 96-97. Committee on Interstate and Foreign Commerce, Subcommittee on Energy and Power. 96th Cong. 1st sess. Washington, D.C.: GPO.

——. 1978. *Hearings on the Nuclear Siting and Licensing Act of 1978.* Part 3. No. 95-18. Committee on Interior and Insular Affairs, Subcommittee on Energy and the Environment, 95th Cong. 2d sess. Washington, D.C.: GPO.

——. 1977a. *Hearings on Nuclear Power Costs.* Part 1. Committee on Government Operations, Subcommittee on Environment, Energy and Natural Resources. 95th Cong. 1st sess. Washington, D.C.: GPO.

——. 1977b. *Oversight Hearings on Nuclear Waste Management.* No. 95-15. Committee on Interior and Insular Affairs, Subcommittee on Energy and the Environment. 95th Cong. 1st sess. Washington, D.C.: GPO.

——. 1975. *Oversight Hearings on Nuclear Energy—Overview of the Major Issues.* No. 94-16. Committee on Interior and Insular Affairs, Subcommittee on Energy and the Environment. 94th Cong. 1st sess. Washington, D.C.: GPO.

U.S. Joint Committee on Atomic Energy. 1976. *Hearings on Radioactive Waste*

Management. Subcommittee on Environment and Safety. 94th Cong. 2d sess. Washington, D.C.: GPO.

——. 1974a. *Hearings on Development, Growth, and State of the Nuclear Industry.* 93d Cong. 2d sess. Washington, D.C.: GPO.

——. 1974b. *Hearings on Nuclear Reactor Safety,* Part 1, Phase I and IIa. 93d Cong. 1st sess. Washington, D.C.: GPO.

——. 1974c. *Hearings on Nuclear Reactor Safety,* Part 2: Vol. 1, Phase IIb and III. 93d Cong. 2d sess. Washington, D.C.: GPO.

——. 1968. *Nuclear Power Economics—1962 through 1967.* Joint Committee Print. Washington, D.C.: GPO.

——. 1967. *Hearings on Licensing and Regulation of Nuclear Reactors,* Part 1. 90th Cong. 1st sess. Washington, D.C.: GPO.

——. 1958. *Proposed Expanded Civilian Nuclear Power Program.* Joint Committee Print. 85th Cong. 2d sess. Washington, D.C.: GPO.

U.S. Nuclear Regulatory Commission. 1983. "Remarks by Victor Gilinsky, Commissioner, U.S. Nuclear Regulatory Commission, to the Seabrook Project staff of Public Service of New Hampshire and the Yankee Atomic Electric Company Portsmouth, New Hampshire: Facing the Realities of a Fragmented Nuclear Power Industry." October 12. Washington, D.C.

——. 1982a. *Information Report on State Legislation.* 8(1-6, 8, 10). Washington, D.C.

——. 1982b. *Summary Information Report.* Vol. 1, No. 1. NUREG-0871. Washington, D.C.: GPO.

——. 1982c. *Selected Review of Foreign Licensing Practices for Nuclear Power Plants.* NUREG/CR-2664. Washington, D.C.: GPO.

——. 1981a. *1980 Annual Report.* Washington, D.C.: GPO.

——. 1981b. *Information Report on State Legislation, Special Edition—State Laws: Radioactive Waste Disposal and Management.* Washington, D.C.

——. 1980a. *Program Summary Report 4(5).* NUREG-0380. Washington, D.C.: GPO.

——. 1980b. *1979 Annual Report.* NUREG-0690. Washington, D.C.: GPO.

——. 1978a. *1978 Review and Evaluation of the Nuclear Regulatory Commission Safety Research Program.* NUREG-0496. Advisory Committee on Reactor Safeguards. Washington, D.C.: GPO.

——. 1978b. *Review of the Commission Program for Standardization of Nuclear Power Plants and Recommendations to Improve Standardization Concepts.* Washington, D.C. GPO.

——. 1978c. *Annual Report, 1977.* Washington, D.C.: GPO.

——. 1977a. *Water Reactor Safety Research, Status Summary Report.* 4(5)1–43. NUREG-0135. Washington, D.C.

——. 1977b. *Annual Report, 1976.* Washington, D.C.: GPO.

——. 1977c. *Nuclear Power Plant Licensing: Opportunities for Improvement.* Washington, D.C.: GPO.

——. 1976. *Environmental Survey of the Reprocessing and Waste Management Portions of the Light Water Reactor Fuel Cycle: A Task Force Report.* NUREG-0116, supplement 1 to WASH-1248. Washington, D.C.: GPO.

U.S. Office of Technology Assessment. 1984. *Nuclear Power in an Age of Uncertainty.* OTA-E-216. Washington, D.C.: GPO.

———. 1981a. *Nuclear Powerplant Standardization: Light Water Reactors.* OTA-E-134. Washington, D.C.: GPO.

———. 1981b. *Nuclear Powerplant Standardization: Light Water Reactors,* Vol. 2, Appendices. Washington, D.C.: GPO.

U.S. Senate. 1981a. *Nuclear Power Development in France.* Committee print. Committee on Governmental Affairs. 97th Cong. 1st sess. Washington, D.C.: GPO.

———. 1981b. *Hearings on the National Nuclear Waste Policy Act of 1981.* No. 97-H32. Committee on Environment and Public Works, Subcommittee on Nuclear Regulation. 97th Cong. 1st sess. Washington, D.C.: GPO.

———. 1978a. *Hearings on Nuclear Waste Management.* No. 95-H58. Committee on Environment and Public Works, Subcommittee on Nuclear Regulation. 95th Cong. 2d sess. Washington, D.C.: GPO.

———. 1978b. *Hearings on Nuclear Siting and Licensing Act of 1978.* Committee on Environment and Public Works, Subcommittee on Nuclear Regulation. 95th Cong. 2d sess. Washington, D.C.: GPO.

———. 1977. *Study on Federal Regulation: Public Participation in Regulatory Agency Proceedings,* Vol. 3. Committee on Governmental Affairs. 95th Cong. 1st sess. Washington, D.C.: GPO.

———. 1974. *Financial Problems of the Electric Utilities: Hearings.* No. 93-50. Committee on Interior and Insular Affairs. 93d Cong. 2d sess. Washington, D.C.: GPO.

Useem, Michael. 1984. *The Inner Circle: Large Corporations and the Rise of Business Political Activity in the U.S. and U.K.* New York: Oxford University Press.

Utroska, Dan. 1982. "Nuclear Too Costly, Growing Evidence Demonstrates." *Electric Light and Power* 60(4)24, 98.

Van de Ven, Andrew H., and William Joyce, eds. 1981. *Perspectives on Organization Design and Behavior.* New York: John Wiley and Sons.

Vietor, Richard H. K. 1984. *Energy Policy in America since 1945: A Study of Business-Government Relations.* New York: Cambridge University Press.

Vogel, David. 1986. *National Styles of Regulation: Environmental Policy in Great Britain and the United States.* Ithaca: Cornell University Press.

———. 1978. "Why Businessmen Distrust Their State: The Political Consciousness of American Corporate Executives." *British Journal of Political Science* 8:45–78.

Wald, Matthew. 1986a. "Seabrook Feels the Chernobyl Syndrome." *New York Times* July 27(Section 4)5.

———. 1986b. "Delay on Seabrook Reactor Brings New Charges." *New York Times* June 9:10.

Walker, David. 1981. *Toward a Functioning Federalism.* Cambridge, Mass.: Winthrop.

Walker, William, and Måns Lönnroth. 1983. *Nuclear Power Struggles: Industrial Competition and Proliferation Control.* London: George Allen and Unwin.

Ward, John. 1977. "Nuclear Regulation: The Industry Point of View." *Proceedings of the American Power Conference* 39:120–26.

———. 1973. "Standardized Plants—Boon or Bane?" *Nuclear News* 16(10)51–56.

Wardell, William, and Louis Lasagna. 1975. *Regulation and Drug Development.* Washington, D.C.: American Enterprise Institute for Public Policy Research.

Warren, Bill. 1972. "Capitalist Planning and the State." *New Left Review* 73:3–29.

Wasserman, Harvey. 1979. *Energy War: Reports from the Front.* Westport, Conn.: Lawrence Hill.

Weaver, Lynn. 1980. "Future Prospects for Nuclear Energy." A presentation delivered at the National Society of Professional Engineers' Energy Seminar, Detroit.

Webb, Richard. 1976. *The Accident Hazards of Nuclear Power Plants.* Amherst: University of Massachusetts Press.

Weber, Max. 1978. *Economy and Society,* Vol. 1 and 2 (1921–22). Guenther Roth and Claus Wittich, eds. Berkeley: University of California Press.

Weidenbaum, Murray. 1984. "Budgetary Quandaries." *Society* 22(1)48–52.

Weinberg, Alvin. 1972. "Social Institutions and Nuclear Energy." *Science* 177(4043)27–34.

Weingast, Barry. 1980. "Congress, Regulation, and the Decline of Nuclear Power." *Public Policy* 28(2)231–55.

Weinraub, Bernard. 1983. "Attacks on Nuclear Agency Grow over Its Links to Plant Operators." *New York Times* October 16:1.

Weir, Margaret, and Theda Skocpol. 1985. "State Structures and the Possibilities for 'Keynesian' Responses to the Great Depression in Sweden, Britain, and the United States." Pp. 107–63 in Peter Evans, Dietrich Rueschemeyer, and Theda Skocpol, eds., *Bringing the State Back In.* New York: Cambridge University Press.

Welborn, David. 1977. *Governance of Federal Regulatory Agencies.* Knoxville: University of Tennessee Press.

Westfield, Fred. 1965. "Regulation and Conspiracy." *American Economic Review* 55(3)424–43.

Whitney, Simon. 1934. *Trade Associations and Industrial Control.* New York: Central Book.

Whitt, J. Allen. 1982. *Urban Elites and Mass Transportation: The Dialectics of Power.* Princeton: Princeton University Press.

Williamson, Oliver E. 1975. *Markets and Hierarchies: Analysis and Antitrust Implications.* New York: Free Press.

Williamson, Oliver E., and William Ouchi. 1981. "The Markets and Hierarchies Program of Research: Origins, Implications, Prospects." Pp. 347–70 in Andrew H. Van de Ven and William Joyce, eds., *Perspectives on Organization Design and Behavior.* New York: John Wiley and Sons.

Willrich, Mason. 1975. "The Electric Utility and the Energy Crisis." *Public Utilities Fortnightly* 95(1)22–28.

Wolfe, Alan. 1977. *The Limits of Legitimacy: Political Contradictions of Contemporary Capitalism.* New York: The Free Press.

Wright, Erik Olin. 1979. "Capitalism's Futures: A Provisional Reconceptualization of Alternatives to Capitalist Society." Paper presented at the International Colloquium on the State and the Economy, University of Toronto.

——. 1978. "Historical Transformations of Capitalist Crisis Tendencies." Pp. 111–62 in *Class, Crisis, and the State.* London: New Left Books.

Zinberg, Dorothy. 1984. "Public Participation in Nuclear Waste Management: A Brief Historical Overview." Pp. 233–53 in William Freudenburg and Eugene Rosa, eds., *Public Reactions to Nuclear Power: Are There Critical Masses?* Boulder, Colo.: Westview.

——. 1982. "Public Participation: U.S. and European Perspectives." Pp. 160–87 in E. William Colglazier, ed., *The Politics of Nuclear Waste.* New York: Pergamon.

Zysman, John. 1983. *Governments, Markets, and Growth: Financial Systems and the Politics of Industrial Change.* Ithaca: Cornell University Press.

——. 1978. "The French State in the International Economy." Pp. 255–94 in Peter Katzenstein, ed., *Between Power and Plenty.* Madison: University of Wisconsin Press.

——. 1977. *Political Strategies for Industrial Order: State, Market, and Industry in France.* Berkeley: University of California Press.

Index

AEC. *See* Atomic Energy Commission
Aircraft manufacturing industry, institutional arrangements of, 186–189
Air pollution regulation, 89–90
Alford, Robert, 16
Allgemeine Elektrizitäts-Gesellschaft (AEG), 139, 153
Allied General Nuclear Services, 113, 114, 117–119
Alsthom-Atlantique, 138
American Nuclear Energy Council, 185
American Physical Society, 71
Anderson, Cleve, 114, 115
Antinuclear movement, 5, 7–8
  goals of, 64–65
  historical roots, 65
  obstructionist politics of, 85–88
  and policy process, 75, 78, 79, 80, 84–88
  political strategies, 64
  and safety crisis, 63, 64–65
  waste disposal concerns, 126
  See also France; Sweden; West Germany
Aquaflour reprocessing process, 113, 114
Architect-engineering firms:
  single firm for nuclear sector, proposal for, 185
  standardization, views on, 35, 40, 43, 45–46
ASEA-ATOM, 139, 147, 152, 153
Atlantic Richfield, 114
Atomic brotherhood, 6–7
Atomic Energy Act of 1954, 25, 48, 53, 69, 75, 111
Atomic Energy Commission (AEC):

abolition of, 70
Advisory Committee on Reactor Safeguards, 52, 53, 59, 79, 80–81
contradictory goals, 53, 60–61, 64, 69
fast breeder reactor, development of, 55
legitimation issues. *See* Legitimation
policy process, 24, 76, 77, 79, 81, 82–84
safety issues. *See* Safety crisis
standardization and, 32, 34, 37
waste disposal policies, 28, 110, 111–112, 115, 116, 117, 118, 120–122
Atomic Industrial Forum, 36, 41, 44, 45, 46, 125, 130, 133, 185
Atomic Safety and Licensing Boards, 75, 77, 82, 83
Aviation Consumer Action Project, 188

Babcock and Wilcox, 23, 33, 35
Babcock-Brown Boveri, 139, 154
Banks, 19
Baran, Paul, 11
Boeing Corporation, 186, 187
Britain, 17
Bryan, Richard, 128
Bupp, Irvin, 6–7, 10

California Energy Commission, 130
Cancellation of plants:
  decline for demand in electricity and, 106–108
  financial crisis as cause, 92, 103–104
  industry losses due to, 3–4
Capitalist systems, long-term planning in, 192–195

225

policy process, 136–137, 143–145; op-
    position, role of, 163–166
revised national energy plan, 165
standardization in, 153–156
state–civil society intersection, 147–149
state structure, 143–145
technical support by the state, 148

waste disposal, 174–176
Westinghouse, 23, 33, 34, 35, 43
Whitney, Eli, 31
Wildavsky, Aaron, 76

Zinberg, Dorothy, 132
Zysman, John, 93, 194

Library of Congress Cataloging-in-Publication Data

Campbell, John L., 1952–
   Collapse of an industry.

   (Cornell studies in political economy)
   Bibliography: p.
   Includes index.
   1. Nuclear industry—United States. 2. Nuclear
industry—Government policy—United States. 3. Nuclear
power plants—United States. 4. Nuclear power plants—
Government policy—United States. I. Title. II. Series.
HD9698.U52C35 1988   333.79′24′0973   87-47856
ISBN 0-8014-2111-X (alk. paper)
ISBN 0-8014-9500-8 (pbk. : alk. paper)